A2

ENGLISH LITERATURE

for AQA **B**

Tony Childs
Jackie Moore

Consultant: Peter Buckroyd

Heinemann

Heinemann Educational Publishers
Halley Court, Jordan Hill, Oxford OX2 8EJ
Part of Harcourt Education
Heinemann is the registered trademark of Harcourt Education Limited

© Tony Childs and Jackie Moore 2005

First edition published 2001
This edition published 2005

10 09 08 07 06 05
10 9 8 7 6 5 4 3 2 1

British Library Cataloguing in Publication Data is available from the British Library on request.

ISBN 0 435 13232 6

Typeset by TechType, Abingdon, Oxon
Printed and bound by Bath Press in the UK

Acknowledgements
The publishers gratefully acknowledge the following for permission to reproduce copyright material. Every
effort has been made to trace copyright holders, but in some cases has proved impossible. The publishers
would be happy to hear from any copyright holder that has not been acknowledged.

'Twelve Songs IX' from Collected Poems by W. H. Auden, published by Faber and Faber © 1936 by W. H.
Auden. Reprinted with permission of Faber and Faber Limited, and Curtis Brown Ltd, New York; 'Valentine'
from *Mean Time* by Carol Ann Duffy, published by Anvil Press Poetry, 1993. Copyright © Carol Ann Duffy.
Reprinted with permission of Anvil Press Poetry; Extracts from *Birdsong* by Sebastian Faulks, published by
Hutchinson. Reprinted by permission of The Random House Group Ltd; Extract from *To the Lighthouse* by
Virginia Woolf. Reprinted by permission of The Society of Authors as the Literary Representative of the
Estate of Virginia Woolf; Extract from *The Color Purple* by Alice Walker, published by Orion. Reprinted by
permission of David Higham Associates Limited; Extract from *Sacred Hunger* by Barry Unsworth, published
by Penguin Books. Copyright © Barry Unsworth 1992. Reprinted with permission of Penguin Books Ltd;
Extract from *Invisible Man* by Ralph Ellison, published by Random House inc, Reprinted by permission of
Pollinger Limited on behalf of the author; Extract from *Beloved* by Toni Morrison. Copyright © Toni
Morrison. Reprinted by permission of International Creative Management Inc, New York; Extract from *The
Great Gatsby* by F Scott Fitzgerald, published by Penguin. Reprinted by permission of David Higham
Associates Ltd; Extract from *The Death of a Salesman* by Arthur Miller. Copyright © 1949 by Arthur Miller.
Reprinted by permission of International Creative Management Inc, New York; Extract from *Nineteen Eighty-
Four* by George Orwell. Copyright © George Orwell 1949. Reprinted by permission of Bill Hamilton as the
Literary Executor of the Estate of the Late Sonia Brownell Orwell and Martin Secker & Warburg Limited c/o
A M Heath & Co Ltd; Extract from *Translations* by Brian Friel, published by Faber and Faber Ltd. Reprinted
by permission of Faber and Faber Ltd; Extract from *Wilt on High* by Tom Sharpe, published by Secker &
Warburg. Reprinted by permission of The Random House Group Ltd and Sheil Land Associates; Extract from
Captain Corelli's Mandolin by Louis de Bernieres, published by Vintage (May 1995). Reprinted by permission
of The Random House Group Ltd; Extract from *Catch 22* by Joseph Heller. Copyright © Joseph Heller 1955.
Reprinted by permission of A. M. Heath & Company Ltd, on behalf of Joseph Heller and Random House UK
Ltd; Extracts from *Christopher Marlowe: Edward the Second*, edited by Martin Wiggins, New Mermaids 2003.
Reprinted with permission of A & C Black; Extract from *Measure for Measure: William Shakespeare*, edited by
J W Lever. Reprinted with permission of Thomson Learning (EMEA) Ltd; Extract from *The Changeline:
Thomas Middleton*, edited by Trevor R. Griffiths, Nick Hern Books 2000. Used with permission; Extract from
The Rover by Aphra Benn published by Methuen; Extract from *The Way of the World: William Congreve*,
edited by Brian Gibbons, New mermaids. Reprinted with permission of A & C Black Publishers; Extract from
She Stoops to Conquer: Oliver Goldsmith, edited by Trevor Millum, Longman 1994. Reprinted with
permission; Extract from *The General Prologue to the Canterbury Tales*, edited by James Winny, published by
Cambridge University Press 1965. Reprinted with permission of Cambridge University Press; Extract from
The Steamie by Tony Roper. Copyright © 1990 by Tony Roper. Reprinted from *Scot-Free: New Scottish Plays* by
permission of the publishers. www.nickhernbooks.co.uk. All rights reserved; 'Hard Times and Utilitarianism'
by Katie Dynina. Copyright © Katie Dynina. Reprinted with the kind permission of the author; Extract
from *Hard Times* by Allen Samuels, published by Palgrave Macmillan. Reprinted with the kind permission of
the publishers; Extracts from *An Inspector Calls* by J. B. Priestley, Copyright © Estate of J. B. Priestley 1947,
by permission of PFD (www.pfd.co.uk) on behalf of the Estate of J. B. Priestley.

Contents

Introduction

How this book will help you

This book is designed to help students following AQA Specification B in Advanced English Literature through their course. Most students approaching this Specification will already have studied AQA Specification B in Advanced Subsidiary (AS) English Literature, and this book has been written with that in mind. It is important to recognise from the start, however, that A Level is different from AS Level in that two of the Assessment Objectives (AOs) change. This is dealt with fully below. The book is not specifically a guide to individual set texts – after all, each of you will choose different texts to work on. Rather, it is a guide to what you have to do with your texts in order to succeed.

This Introduction deals with the Assessment Objectives for Specification B. Please don't overlook this part and go straight to the modules, however tempting that may be – the Assessment Objectives underpin all the work in the course, and an understanding of them is the key to gaining good marks. Remember, the marking is based entirely on these Objectives. The final module, Exploring Texts, tests all the Objectives.

The rest of this book deals with each of the three assessment modules for the course. For each module, we take you through its design and content with practical advice and exercises. The work you will be asked to do has been tailored to the type of assessment involved in each module; this might be external assessment, open or closed book, or coursework. We also provide examples of the sorts of questions and tasks that will be used to test each module as part of the examination. Specification issues are also noted. For instance, candidates who have studied *Measure for Measure* in Unit 3 must not study it in Unit 5.

You will find a glossary for this book on page 213; you will also find the glossary in the previous book, *AS English Literature for AQA B*, helpful.

The key to success: understanding the Assessment

Objectives

The Assessment Objectives for the module require that you:

Assessment Objectives	
AO1	communicate clearly the knowledge, understanding and insight appropriate to literary study, using appropriate terminology and accurate and coherent written expression
AO2ii	respond with knowledge and understanding to literary texts of different types and periods, exploring and commenting on relationships and comparisons between literary texts
AO3	show detailed understanding of the ways in which writers' choices of form, structure and language shape meanings
AO4	articulate independent opinions and judgements, informed by different interpretations of literary texts by other readers
AO5ii	evaluate the significance of cultural, historical and other contextual influences on literary texts and study

What the Assessment Objectives mean

The Assessment Objectives were dealt with in the book accompanying the Advanced Subsidiary (AS) Specification, and you will have worked with them during your AS course. It's important to recognise, though, that at A Level, AO2 and AO5 change, and so make new demands on students. At AS, AO2i asks candidates to 'respond with knowledge and understanding to literary texts of different types and periods'. At A Level, this becomes: 'exploring and commenting on relationships and comparisons between literary texts'. As you can see, this is quite different, reintroducing a requirement to compare texts that you were probably used to in your GCSE English Literature course.

AO5i at AS asks candidates to show 'understanding of the contexts in which literary texts are written and understood'. At A Level this becomes: 'evaluate the significance of cultural, historical and other contextual influences on literary texts and study'. What you have to think about, therefore, is how various factors have shaped the writing of the texts you're studying – and how they affect your reading of them. This is the first step. The second is to think about which **contexts** are important in reading the text, and of these, which are the most important. For a full response, therefore, you may need to explore not only the contexts informing the text, but also your characteristics as a reader.

Here are some of the relevant types of context which you might look at (questions of context will be fully developed later).

- The context of period or era, including significant social, historical, political and cultural processes, which could include period-specific styles. This could concern the period when the work was written, or the period that is being written about. A knowledge of Mozart's life and work, of course, might affect your reading of Peter Shaffer's *Amadeus*, as the content centres around these. There is also a very strong theatrical context in this play, though, as can be seen from the heavy stage directions and unusual staging. An assessment of the significance of context here will depend on the importance of each of them to the reader – you.

- The context of the work in terms of the writer's biography or **milieu**. This could involve considering, for example, how a personal experience of war or racial prejudice had influenced a writer's works.

- The literary context, which includes looking at works in terms of the genre to which they belong; a play, for instance, could be seen in terms of the genre of **Revenge Tragedy**. This can also be a period-specific context, an example being the genre of **Restoration Comedy**, which you would consider when reading Congreve's *The Way of the World* – the extent to which his play fits into this genre, and ways in which it might go beyond it, would be an evaluation of significance.

- The language context, including relevant episodes in the use and development of literary language, the question of colloquial and dialect styles, and so on.

- The different contexts for a work established by its reception over time – works may well have different meanings and effects in different periods.

Breaking down the Assessment Objectives

As you can see, the Assessment Objectives define the literary skills that you have to show in the course. It is vital to understand that they are awarded a different number of marks in different modules, and even for different texts. For example, in Module 5, which is the Set Texts module, the 30 marks available are divided like this:

AO1	5 marks
AO3	5 marks
AO4	10 marks
AO5ii	10 marks

In this module, you have to choose a pre-1770 drama text and a pre-1900 poetry text. The marks are divided between the texts like this:

Poetry: AO3	5 marks	**AO4**	10 marks
Drama: AO1	5 marks	**AO5ii**	10 marks

So it is important to remember that the marks depend on the Assessment Objectives, and that the marks are different in the different modules, and sometimes in the different sections, too. That's why there are boxes at the beginning of each of the three modules to show you exactly which Assessment Objectives count in that module, and the percentage of the marks each one carries.

An exercise in the A2 Assessment Objectives

VALENTINE

Not a red rose or a satin heart.

I give you an onion.
It is a moon wrapped in brown paper.
It promises light
like the careful undressing of love.

Here.
It will blind you with tears
like a lover.
It will make your reflection
a wobbling photo of grief.

I am trying to be truthful.

Not a cute card or a kissogram.

I give you an onion.
Its fierce kiss will stay on your lips,
possessive and faithful
as we are,
for as long as we are.

Take it.
Its platinum loops shrink to a wedding-ring,
if you like.
Lethal.
Its scent will cling to your fingers,
cling to your knife.

CAROL ANN DUFFY

STOP ALL THE CLOCKS

Stop all the clocks, cut off the telephone,
Prevent the dog from barking with a juicy bone,
Silence the pianos and with muffled drum
Bring out the coffin, let the mourners come.

Let aeroplanes circle moaning overhead
Scribbling on the sky the message He Is Dead,
Put crêpe bows round the white necks of the public doves,
Let the traffic policemen wear black cotton gloves.

He was my North, my South, my East and West,
My working week and my Sunday rest,
My noon, my midnight, my talk, my song;
I thought that love would last forever: I was wrong.

The stars are not wanted now: put out every one;
Pack up the moon and dismantle the sun;
Pour away the ocean and sweep up the wood,
For nothing now can ever come to any good.

W. H. AUDEN

SONNET 18

Shall I compare thee to a summer's day?
Thou art more lovely and more temperate.
Rough winds do shake the darling buds of May,
And summer's lease hath all too short a date:
Sometime too hot the eye of heaven shines,
And often is his gold complexion dimm'd;
And every fair from fair some time declines,
By chance, or nature's changing course, untrimm'd;
But thy eternal summer shall not fade
Nor lose possession of that fair thou ow'st;
Nor shall Death brag thou wand'rest in his shade,
When in eternal lines to time thou grow'st;
    So long as men can breathe or eyes can see,
    So long lives this, and this gives life to thee.

WILLIAM SHAKESPEARE

Although you may have come across these poems before, the aim here is to look at them in the context of the A Level Assessment Objectives. In other words you now need to look at them in a different way.

Assessment Objective AO2ii

AO2ii respond with knowledge and understanding to literary texts of different types and periods, exploring and commenting on relationships and comparisons between literary texts

Beginning to compare these poems is easy – all three are concerned with love and time. All three are personal poems written in the first person: 'Stop all the clocks' mourns the death of a loved one, while the other two make declarations of love, though not in a straightforward way. 'Valentine' in particular concerns itself with the realities of love ('I am trying to be truthful'), in other words with love's difficulties and dangers.

To compare the poems in a more detailed way, it is a good idea to use AO3 as a framework, comparing how the three poets use *form*, *structure* and *language* to shape meanings. Work your way through the poems using the following suggestions.

Form

There are three different forms illustrated by these poems – but simply identifying the forms is not enough; you need to compare how form expresses meaning in each case.

(1) The four separate verses of 'Stop all the clocks' suggest that each verse deals with a separate aspect of the subject. Is this in fact the case? How do punctuation and rhyme give a sense of finality?

(2) *Sonnet 18* is unpunctuated by verse divisions. Is it one continuous argument? If there are changes, how are they indicated by the form? Think about rhyme as well as page layout.

(3) 'Valentine' does not follow a set pattern of verse, or of rhyme, though there are repetitions and echoes. Can you find any of these? How does the author use the form to suggest unconnected but related thoughts about love, and about this particular relationship?

Now review your conclusions, and think about the relationships and comparisons between these texts.

Structure

In all three poems form is closely related to structure.

(1) You have already worked out the subjects of each of the verses in 'Stop all the clocks'. Is there a logical structure? How does the poem build to the last verse, and to the last line in particular?

(2) How does the first line of *Sonnet 18* set the agenda for the whole poem? Where does the view of time alter, and which word at the beginning of a line marks the shift? The final change is to introduce the idea of the life of the poem, not just the person. Where does this begin?

(3) 'Valentine' looks different from the others on the page, not only because of the lack of verse pattern, but also because of the varying line lengths. Look at the effects of some of the very short lines, and the three single lines. Why do you think the poem begins in the way it does, and then ends in the way it does?

Now review your conclusions, and think about the relationships and comparisons between these texts.

Language

There's a lot to say about the ways in which language is used to express meanings in these three poems. Here are a few questions to get you started.

(1) Look at all three poems for sentence forms. Where can you find commands, or questions? Why has the poet used a particular form?

(2) Two of these poems make use of repetitions, and one doesn't. What are the effects of the repetitions where they are used, and what does the lack of repetition in the other one tell you about that poem?

(3) Each of the three poems is characterised by a particular use of language: look at the verbs in 'Stop all the clocks'; the word-play in *Sonnet 18*; and the unorthodox sentences in 'Valentine'.

(4) Imagery is a central feature of all three poems.

- Look at the imagery in the last two verses of 'Stop all the clocks'. What is the effect of all of them taken together? How does each image contribute to the whole? Notice particularly the line about the moon and the sun, bearing in mind the other two poems.

- Both the other poems dwell on a single image. In 'Valentine', what gifts does the speaker *reject*, and why? Why does she find an onion appropriate, and what view of love does this reveal? Look at the further comparisons that stem from this central idea.

- *Sonnet 18* works on one image, introduced in the first line. As in 'Valentine', the conventional love comparison is here rejected. Look at the ways in which Shakespeare uses the idea to praise the object of the poem, developing more imagery along the way.

Now review your conclusions, and think about the relationships and comparisons between these texts.

Assessment Objective 5ii

AO5ii evaluate the significance of cultural, historical and other contextual influences on literary texts and study

At A Level it is not enough simply to recognise the contexts of each text studied. You also have to evaluate their significance for your reading of the text, particularly when you start to think about forming an interpretation. The thoughts and questions that follow should help you to see what this might mean, and to see how the Assessment Objectives are inter-related.

'Stop all the clocks' is an interesting poem to start with when thinking about contexts. You might already have two contexts for your reading of the text – as part of GCSE English Literature study you may have studied it in the context of other poems, or in the context of the film *Four Weddings and a Funeral*. If you have heard it read in this film, this context may well be significant in your response. In the film, the reading of this poem at a funeral is a very emotional moment, designed to move the audience, who may well also associate it with homosexual love. The first two verses of the poem were first published, however, in the prose/verse drama *The Ascent of F6*, by W. H. Auden and Christopher Isherwood. When you study the rest of the poem in this original version, you might well come to a very different interpretation of the verses.

ACTIVITY

Re-read the first two verses of 'Stop all the clocks' (page viii), then read the following three verses, which completed the piece in *The Ascent of F6*.

Hold up your umbrellas to keep off the rain
From Doctor Williams while he opens a vein;
Life, he pronounces, it is finally extinct.
Sergeant, arrest that man who said he winked!

Shawcross will say a few words sad and kind
To the weeping crowds about the Master-Mind,
While Lamp with a powerful microscope
Searches their faces for a sign of hope.

And Gunn, of course, will drive the motor-hearse:
None could drive it better, most would drive it worse.
He'll open up the throttle to its fullest power

And drive him to the grave at ninety miles an hour.

The poem may well look more like a satirical parody of love poetry now. How has the writer worked to create this tone? Think about:

* the effects of particular words
* the effects of particular rhymes
* the actions of the characters, and how they are described.

Clearly these two contexts – the film and the play – give rise to interpretations that are quite opposed to each other. Does this mean that the satirical reading of the poem is the 'right' one? No. If it did, it would mean that anybody's response to the poem based on the film alone would somehow be invalid. AO5i, the building block for AO5ii, concerns both the contexts in which literary texts are *written* and the contexts in which they are *understood* – but these need not be the same. Here, the poem is written in one context, and understood in another by the film's audience. Two meanings, or interpretations, are generated, and neither is invalid. Nor does it make any difference that the writer did not intend, or indeed know about, the film context. Once the text is written, the writer is merely one interpreter of its meaning.

In the other two poems – 'Valentine' and *Sonnet 18* – *gender* is an important context. Unlike 'Stop all the clocks', neither identifies the gender of the person addressed. Some research might reveal significant contexts here. If you assume that the speaker in the poem – the persona – is meant to be the poet (although that might not be the case), what might the sexual preferences of the writer tell you? When you have researched this, you might think about these issues:

- Does this information make any difference to your reading of the poems? In other words, are the contexts significant? Is there any indication in the poems that these contexts were significant to the writing – and if so, how significant were they?

- If you respond to the poems differently when you know about these contexts, why is that? Is it to do with the poems, or with you? This may lead you to evaluate yourself as a reader – to decide what it is that is most important to you.

- What evidence are you using in coming to a view about the poems? Context is a form of evidence in itself, as are the details of form, language and structure. The tone of 'Stop all the clocks' can perhaps be read either way, depending on how you view the evidence – but what evidence of context can you find in the other two poems?

You could, of course, investigate other contexts, and if you were studying these texts as part of your A Level course you would have to choose which to pursue – to decide which contexts might prove to be significant in the writing and the understanding of the texts. You might want to look at the features of the poems that place them in their historic and social contexts. With *Sonnet 18*, for example, you could look at the literary context of the sonnet form in this period, and at how Shakespeare uses it, or at how ambiguity appears in other Shakespeare sonnets. If you were tackling this as an A Level task, you would also need to evaluate the significance of these contexts to ask: which of these contexts are central to my understanding of the texts, and why?

You will have noticed that as you investigated and thought about contexts, more relationships and comparisons between the three texts occurred to you, taking you back to AO2ii. This is the real point. The A Level course, like the AS course, divides the subject into Assessment Objectives to test your knowledge of the ways that English Literature works, but these areas are very closely inter-related, and sometimes overlap. In the final module in the course, Exploring Texts, all the

Assessment Objectives are tested, to see what you have learned about the study of English Literature during the whole A Level course. In working through these three poems, you have already done exactly that – explored texts using each of the Assessment Objectives.

The Assessment Objectives for this module require that you:

ASSESSMENT OBJECTIVES

AO1   communicate clearly the knowledge, understanding and insight appropriate to literary study, using appropriate terminology and accurate and coherent written expression
(5% of the final A2 mark; 2½% of the final A Level mark)

AO2ii   respond with knowledge and understanding to literary texts of different types and periods, exploring and commenting on relationships and comparisons between literary texts
(10% of the final A2 mark; 5% of the final A Level mark)

AO3   show detailed understanding of the ways in which writers' choices of form, structure and language shape meanings
(5% of the final A2 mark; 2½% of the final A Level mark)

AO4   articulate independent opinions and judgements, informed by different interpretations of literary texts by other readers
(5% of the final A2 mark; 2½% of the final A Level mark)

AO5ii   evaluate the significance of cultural, historical and other contextual influences on literary texts and study
(5% of the final A2 mark; 2½% of the final A Level mark)

Content

This module meets the requirements for a prose text. Though this text may be taken from any period, there are some restrictions:

- The second text must be *substantial*, but it can be from any genre.

- The two texts must both be written originally in English.

- The two texts must **either** be of different *types* **or** of different *periods*.

Type

Type does not mean that the two texts must be of different genres (though you may use different genres if you like). It means that they must employ at least partially different approaches. For example, you would be allowed to compare a novel concerned with racial issues such as Toni Morrison's *Beloved*, which is written with flashbacks, with Alice Walker's *The Color Purple*, which is written in letter-form.

or

Period

The two texts must be of different periods (a 'period' consists of about 30 years). For example, you would be able to compare an early detective novel, such as Raymond Chandler's *The Big Sleep* (1939), with a novel in the same genre but from a different period, such as Michael Dibdin's *The Long Finish* (1998).

The most important factor in choosing the two texts lies in similarity and difference – the two texts need to be sufficiently different but sufficiently alike for comparison to be interesting and fruitful. If the texts are very similar, there's not much to contrast, and if they're very different, there's not much to compare.

This is also the module dealing with coursework, and it will be assessed in the same way as the examination modules, by moving up the ladder of the marking scheme.

Aim

The aim of this module is to provide you with the opportunity to compare two texts in order to focus on the ways in which they relate to each other. It involves all the Assessment Objectives listed, but gives a special emphasis to AO2ii, as you might expect. This means that whichever texts you use for this module, and however you tackle it, you must keep the requirement to explore comparisons at the centre of your work.

The next section, therefore, will deal with the ways in which you can start exploring comparisons, and then look at coursework issues (page 30).

Ways of looking at texts for comparison

It's important to identify at least two or three ways in which comparisons can be made, so that the individual texts are effectively illuminated by the comparison. That's one of the central points of AO2ii: by looking at a text in the light of another, you come to understand more about it. A good way to think about similarities and differences between texts is to focus on the other Assessment Objectives: after all, they are the basis of your course in English Literature.

The rest of this Section looks at these different ways of comparing texts:

AO3   Form
         Structure
         Language
         Meanings

AO4   Critical perspectives

AO5ii Historical contexts
Social contexts
Socio-cultural contexts
Socio-economic contexts
Language contexts
Generic and literary contexts

Obviously, you will not be writing about all these different ways in your essay; you will need to choose the ones that are most appropriate to the texts you are comparing. There may in fact be other contexts, not treated here, that are particularly relevant to your chosen texts. What is important is that you write something about each of the targeted Assessment Objectives, and this means that you will have to plan your essay so as to ensure that you are covering AO3, AO4 and AO5ii. Coverage of AO1 will be dealt with by the end of this module, and because you are comparing texts all the time in your essay, you will always be addressing AO2ii.

The ideas and related activities that follow are intended to offer you a wide range of possibilities for comparison.

Assessment Objective 3

AO3 show detailed understanding of the ways in which writers' choices of form, structure and language shape meanings

Form

Form is an interesting starting point for a comparison, as you can think about the ways that different forms can be used to explore the same subjects or ideas. You could, for instance, look at comparisons between the poetry of Wilfred Owen and the novel *Birdsong* by Sebastian Faulks. The following activities begin with comparing form, but move on to other issues – you should seek to do the same with your texts. The first text is Owen's 'Cramped in that funnelled hole'.

Cramped in that funnelled hole, they watched the dawn
Open a jagged rim around; a yawn
Of death's jaws, which had all but swallowed them
Stuck in the bottom of his throat of phlegm.

They were in one of many mouths of Hell
Not seen of seers in visions; only felt
As teeth of traps; when bones and the dead are smelt
Under the mud where long ago they fell
Mixed with the sour sharp odour of the shell.

In the following extract from *Birdsong*, Stephen, the main character of the novel, has taken refuge in a shellhole during an attack.

Stephen dropped his face into the earth and let it fill his mouth. He closed his eyes because he had seen enough. You are going to hell. Azaire's parting words filled his head. They were drilled in by the shattering noise around them.

Byrne somehow got the boy back into the shellhole. Stephen wished he hadn't. He was clearly going to die.

Harrington's sergeant was shouting for another charge and a dozen men responded. Stephen watched them reach the first line of fire before he realized that Byrne was with them. He was trying to force a way through the wire when he was caught off the ground, suspended, his boots shaking as his body was filled with bullets.

Stephen lay in the shellhole with the boy and the man who had died in the morning. For three hours until the sun began to weaken he watched the boy begging for water. He tried to close his ears to the plea. On one corpse there was still a bottle, but a bullet hole had let most of it leak away. What was left was a reddish brown, contaminated by earth and blood. Stephen poured it into the boy's beseeching mouth.

ACTIVITY 1

Compare the two extracts above, using these questions to help you.

- The *forms* are clearly different. The extract from the novel is exactly that, an extract. How do you know it is not complete in itself? What information might you expect to have been given before this point in the novel?

- The poem is a fragment – it was found after Owen's death, and thought to be incomplete. Can it stand by itself, though? How is it different from the prose in this respect, and why? Do you need to know anything else? These questions might lead you to think about the writer's intentions.

- Owen creates some effects with form not open to Faulks. Look at the effects of the end of the second line in each stanza, where the end of a line naturally creates a gap. You might look at the effects of rhyme, too – again not found in the prose.

- The ideas and situations – part of the *context* of the writing here – are clearly comparable. Sort them out. Think about the physical positions of the characters, their feelings and attitudes, the times of day, the sounds (or lack of them).

- The *language* used by each writer is revealing. In the poem, Owen uses from the beginning the idea that the shellhole is like a mouth. Find where the idea begins and trace it through, noticing how he uses it to comment on the men's situation.

- Although the prose is not as packed with imagery – a difference resulting from form, perhaps – Faulks does use language to create emotive effects. Look at the first and last lines of the extract with this in mind.

- Both writers use the senses extensively to involve the reader. Look for the ways they use sight, hearing, touch, smell or taste.

- What do you think is the attitude of each of the writers to the war? Notice that they both use the same key word to describe the nature of the experience.

If you had actually chosen this Owen/*Birdsong* pairing, the prose extract here might have led you to other poems by Owen, such as 'Anthem for Doomed Youth', 'Inspection', 'At a Calvary near the Ancre', or (as in Pair 2 below) 'Strange Meeting'.

Here are two more pairs of extracts from the same authors.

Pair 1

The opening four lines of 'Dulce et Decorum Est' by Wilfred Owen:

Bent double, like old beggars under sacks,
Knock-kneed, coughing like hags, we cursed through sludge,
Till on the haunting flares we turned our backs
And towards our distant rest began to trudge.

And from *Birdsong* by Sebastian Faulks:

It was dark at last. The night poured down in waves from the ridge about them and the guns at last fell silent.

The earth began to move. To their right a man who had lain still since the first attack, eased himself upright, then fell again when his damaged leg would not take his weight. Other single men moved, and began to come up like worms from their shellholes, limping, crawling, dragging themselves out. Within minutes the hillside was seething with the movement of the wounded as they attempted to get themselves back to their line.

'Christ,' said Weir, 'I had no idea there were so many men out there.'

It was like a resurrection in the cemetery twelve miles long. Bent, agonized shapes loomed in multitudes on the churned earth, limping and dragging back to reclaim their life. It was as though the land were disgorging a generation of crippled sleepers, each one distinct but related to its twisted brothers as they teemed up from the reluctant earth.

Pair 2

The first fourteen and last five lines of Owen's 'Strange Meeting':

It seemed that out of battle I escaped
Down some profound dull tunnel, long since scooped
Through granites which titanic wars had groined.

Yet also there encumbered sleepers groaned,
Too fast in thought or death to be bestirred.
Then, as I probed them, one sprang up, and stared
With piteous recognition in fixed eyes,
Lifting distressful hands, as if to bless.
And by his smile, I knew that sullen hall, –
By his dead smile I knew we stood in Hell.

With a thousand pains that vision's face was grained;
Yet no blood reached there from the upper ground,
And no guns thumped, or down the flues made moan.
'Strange friend,' I said, 'here is no cause to mourn.'

...

'I am the enemy you killed, my friend.
I knew you in this dark: for so you frowned
Yesterday through me as you jabbed and killed.
I parried; but my hands were loath and cold.
Let us sleep now...'

The next extract from *Birdsong* comes from the end of a chapter, and almost at the end of the account of the First World War in the novel. Stephen is pulled from a blown-up tunnel by a German soldier, who has also been trapped underground.

He looked up and saw the legs of his rescuer. They were clothed in the German *feldgrau*, the colour of his darkest dream.

He staggered to his feet and his hand went to pull out his revolver, but there was nothing there, only the torn, drenched rags of his trousers.

He looked into the face of the man who stood in front of him and his fists went up from his sides like those of a farm boy about to fight.

At some deep level, far below anything his exhausted mind could reach, the conflicts of his soul dragged through him like waves grating on the packed shingle of a beach. The sound of his life calling to him on a distant road; the faces of the men who had been slaughtered, the closed eyes of Michael Weir in his coffin; his scalding hatred of the enemy, of Max and all the men who had brought him to this moment; the flesh and love of Isabelle, and the eyes of her sister.

Far beyond thought, the resolution came to him and he found his arms, still raised, beginning to spread and open.

Levi looked at this wild-eyed figure, half-demented, his brother's killer. For no reason he could tell, he found that he had opened his own arms in turn, and the two men fell upon each other's shoulders, weeping at the bitter strangeness of their human lives.

ACTIVITY 2

Pair 1

- Consider what the use of direct speech in the prose adds to the effect.

- Compare the imagery used in the two pieces, this time noticing the intensity of the imagery in the prose.

- Look for words in the two pieces which are the same, or very similar. Why do both writers make these choices, do you think?

- Compare the situations depicted and the writers' attitudes to them.

Pair 2

- There's a lot to say about the effects of the different forms here. In the poem, look at the effects of the **half-rhymes**, and at the last line. The prose is also a closure – how does it read like an ending? Putting the two together, you can compare the different effects of form.

- Both language and situations are similar here. Look at them together. The similarities should reveal something about the attitudes and intentions of the writers.

- What futures are suggested in these endings?

You've done a lot of work on this pair of texts. If you look at the section on the strategic planning of your coursework (page 34), you'll see how this sort of analysis can be used in a complete piece of coursework.

Structure

Structure can be a key factor in making comparisons between texts. For instance, three novels that all deal with war, but differ significantly in structure, are Joseph Heller's *Catch-22* (1961), Martin Amis's *Time's Arrow* (1991), and Sebastian Faulks's *Birdsong* (1993). Although the central subject of each novel is war, there are significant differences in the way the writers use structures to present it. In *Catch-22* the emphasis moves from character to character and the narrative is shot through with flashbacks. *Time's Arrow* is in a sense chronological, for it tells the story of the Holocaust, but backwards, each chapter starting at a point before the previous one. *Birdsong* is chronological through the war episodes, but there are also significant leaps in time, a much later narrative being interwoven with the war episodes.

If you were to compare *Catch-22* with either of the other texts, you would be comparing texts of a different period, though of course they are of different types as well. A key element here would be the effects of the choice of structure: how, to echo the words of the Assessment Objective (AO3), the writers had shaped meanings from their choices. The contexts could also be compared, as well as the writers' attitudes, which might be conveyed by language as well as by structure. To enable you to address AO4, you might also like to think about which approach you found the more effective and interesting, and you could look at some critics' views of the texts, including reviews.

Language

Language can form key points for comparison between texts. There are texts, for instance, where dialect is a significant factor. Irving Welsh's novel *Trainspotting* could be compared with Peter Roper's play *The Steamie* (also set in Glasgow), or with a D. H. Lawrence novel in which dialect is used.

Changes in language over time could be looked at, if two texts from very different time periods are studied. Nathaniel Hawthorne's novel *The Scarlet Letter* (1850), for instance, which deals with the consequences of adultery, could be compared with A. S. Byatt's *Possession* (1990), which within itself has contrasting forms, with language shaped to reflect language changes over time.

Below is an activity centred on similarities and differences in the use of language. The two writers are depicting significant moments in the lines of their central characters.

ACTIVITY 3

In these two depictions of a meal, the writers use a range of techniques to convey pleasure. Compare the passages, using the questions below to help you.

In this extract from *A Christmas Carol* by Charles Dickens, the Cratchit family are enjoying their Christmas meal:

Such a bustle ensued that you might have thought a goose the rarest of all birds; a feathered phenomenon, to which a black swan was a matter of course; and in truth it was something very like it in that house. Mrs Cratchit made the gravy (ready beforehand in a little saucepan) hissing hot; Master Peter mashed the potatoes with incredible vigour; Miss Belinda sweetened up the apple-sauce; Martha dusted the hot plates; Bob took Tiny Tim beside him in a tiny corner at the table; the two young Cratchits set chairs for everybody, not forgetting themselves, and mounting guard upon their posts, crammed spoons into their mouths, lest they should shriek for goose before their turn came to be helped. At last the dishes were set on, and grace was said. It was succeeded by a breathless pause, as Mrs Cratchit, looking slowly all along the carving knife, prepared to plunge it in the breast; but when she did, and when the long expected gush of stuffing issued forth, one murmur of delight arose all round the board, and even Tiny Tim, excited by the two young Cratchits, beat on the table with the handle of his knife, and feebly cried Hurrah!

There never was such a goose. Bob said he didn't believe there ever was such a goose cooked. Its tenderness and flavour, size and cheapness, were the themes of universal admiration. Eked out by the apple-sauce and mashed potatoes, it was a sufficient dinner for the whole family; indeed, as Mrs Cratchit said with great delight (surveying one small atom of bone upon the dish), they hadn't ate it all at last! Yet everyone had had enough and the youngest Cratchits in particular, were steeped in sage and onion to the eyebrows!

In the following extract, from *To the Lighthouse* by Virginia Woolf, Mrs Ramsay is serving a meal to her guests, and feels that the 'coherence' she had wanted has happened at last.

Everything seemed possible. Everything seemed right. Just now (but this cannot last, she thought, dissociating herself from the moment while they were all talking about boots) just now she had reached security; she hovered like a hawk suspended; like a flag floated in an element of joy which filled every nerve of her body fully and sweetly, not noisily, solemnly rather, for it arose, she thought, looking at them eating there, from husband and children and friends; all of which rising in this profound stillness (she was helping William Bankes to one very small piece more and peered into the depths of the earthenware pot) seemed now for no special reason to stay there like a smoke, like a fume rising upwards, holding them safe together. Nothing need be said; nothing could be said. There it was, all around them. It partook, she felt, carefully helping Mr Bankes to a specially tender piece, of eternity; as she had already felt about something different once before that afternoon; there is a coherence in things, a stability; something, she meant, is immune from change, and shines out (she glanced at the window with its ripple of reflected lights) in the fact of the flowing, the fleeting, the spectral, like a ruby; so that again to-night she had the feeling she had had once to-day already, of peace, of rest. Of such moments, she thought, the thing is made that remains for ever after. This would remain.

'Yes,' she assured William Bankes, 'there is plenty for everybody.'

- Both writers suggest that the characters experience something unusual. How does each writer use viewpoint and narrative technique to get this idea across?

- Compare the physical effects of pleasure on the characters in both extracts.

- Look for movement and stillness in each piece, and how they are conveyed. You should look particularly at the repetition of words, at syntax, and at sentence length.

- Look for suggestions of:

  – religion
  – closeness or intimacy
  – the importance of family
  – humour.

- To sum up the differences between the two extracts: How are the tones of the extracts different? What could you conclude about the writers' intentions?

Language is a key feature in both novels. If you were comparing them, you could look at the ways each conveys childhood through sentence *forms*, differences in *structure*, and invented *language*.

Meanings

The central meanings of texts could obviously form the basis for a comparison, but if you are choosing texts for coursework you would do best to choose texts where the relationships and comparisons can develop into different areas. A 'rites of passage' novel like James Joyce's *A Portrait of the Artist as a Young Man* could be compared, for example, with J. D. Salinger's *The Catcher in the Rye*. Both depict a boy growing up, but the language and settings are very different. Alternatively, a play could be chosen for comparison with a rites of passage novel – Neil Simon's play *Brighton Beach Memoirs*, for instance, or his *Broadway Bound*. In this case, differences of form in dealing with a similar subject could be analysed as well, as with Activities 1 and 2 based on Wilfred Owen's poetry and Sebastian Faulks's novel *Birdsong*.

Assessment Objective 4

AO4 articulate independent opinions and judgements, informed by different interpretations of literary texts by other readers

So far, you have looked primarily at AO2ii, so it might now be helpful to take a closer look at the complex AO4 and AO5ii. This will help you to make a more informed choice about which precise area of these Objectives you would like to target in your coursework. Below is a more detailed look at AO4, and on page 15 you will find AO5ii broken down in the same way.

This Objective is targeted in coursework, and in the poetry section of Module 5. In the **Specification**, five areas are outlined for this Objective. It states that 'Candidates will be expected to show awareness of the following' (note, you will not be expected to write about all of them):

Area 1

That we, as readers, are influenced by our own experiences, actual or imagined, and that our cultural background has an effect on our interpretation: thus the interpretation of literary texts, or the determination of their significance, can depend on the interpretative stance taken by the reader.

Unpicking this area   Because we are the products of different personal experiences and different social and cultural backgrounds, we all look at a text in an individual way: we each form an independent, and to some extent unique, view of a text.

Coursework   This is something that you will do automatically as you form judgements on each text you study. You must always make your own judgement on a text clear. If you are working on the same text or texts as other people in a group, the ways in which their responses differ from yours may well reflect their differences as individuals.

Area 2

That there might be significant differences in the way literary texts are understood in different periods, and by different individuals or social groups.

Unpicking this area   This means that people from different historical periods, or from different social groups – for example, African Americans, or those with religious beliefs – may see texts very differently. You will see that part of Area 2 overlaps with Area 4 below.

Coursework   This area can be addressed by looking at responses to a text over two different historical periods.

Area 3

That texts do not reflect an external and objective reality; instead, they embody attitudes and values.

Unpicking this area   The key words here are 'attitudes' and 'values'. Whenever you study a text, you inevitably concern yourself with determining the 'attitudes and values' embodied in that text. You should also discuss what it is about the text that gives it a universal value: in other words, why a text can appeal to readers in different periods.

Coursework   In this module you will always be expected to look at the 'attitudes' and 'values' behind texts in order to discuss the elements that make a text 'important'.

Area 4

That there are different ways of looking at texts, based on particular approaches or theories (for example, those of **feminists**, critics influenced by **Marxism** or **structuralism**, and so on). Discussing these theories will require some understanding of critical concepts and terminology.

Unpicking this area   This area, which overlaps with Area 2 above, is a very easy area to target. You should not be too alarmed by the need to understand such theories. You are not expected to study critical texts in detail; you simply have to have a broad grasp of the principles behind certain key theories.

Coursework   An example of a feminist reading of a text will be discussed below using the novels *Jane Eyre* and *The Color Purple* 'Critical perspectives'.

Area 5

That literary texts are frequently open-ended, dialectical or controversial in method; thus ambiguity and uncertainty are central to the reading of texts, and examination tasks will therefore expect candidates to take part in genuine critical enquiry rather than simply to respond to tasks assuming the teacher/examiner already knows the 'right' answer.

Unpicking this area   This simply means that you must engage with the texts thoroughly, both in your coursework and in your study of texts for Module 5. You must be confident enough to form an independent opinion about the texts you are studying, and be able to offer a considered opinion about that text.

Coursework   While working through this module you will already have formed your own opinions about the texts, and of course will continue to do so. In order to write a successful response in terms of this Assessment Objective, however, it is necessary to consider other interpretations in arriving at your judgement. These might come from critical stances, as above, individual critics, readings or performances, other people within your group, or just different possible readings.

Critical perspectives

Thinking about critical perspectives can form a fruitful starting point for comparisons. One of the ways of illuminating texts such as *The Color Purple* by Alice Walker and *Jane Eyre* by Charlotte Brontë is to see them from a feminist perspective.

ACTIVITY 4

Read these two extracts, and then consider them in the light of the critical perspectives that follow.

In this extract from *Jane Eyre*, the housekeeper, Mrs Fairfax, is questioning Jane, a mere governess, about her relationship with their employer, Mr Rochester.

'I am sorry to grieve you,' pursued the widow; 'but you are so young, and so little acquainted with men, I wished to put you on your guard. It is an old saying that "all is not gold that glitters"; and in this case I do fear there will be something found to be different to what either you or I expect.'

'Why! – am I a monster?' I said: 'is it impossible that Mr Rochester should have a sincere affection for me?'

'No: you are very well; and much improved of late; and Mr Rochester, I daresay, is fond of you. I have always noticed that you were a sort of pet of his. There are times when, for your sake, I have been a little uneasy at his marked preference, and have wished to put you on your guard: but I did not like to suggest even the possibility of wrong. I knew such an idea would shock, perhaps offend you; and you were so discreet, and so thoroughly modest and sensible, I hoped you might be trusted to protect yourself. Last night I cannot tell you what I suffered when I sought all over the house, and could find you nowhere, nor the master either; and then, at twelve o'clock, saw you come in with him.'

'Well, never mind that now', I interrupted impatiently: 'it is enough that all was right.'

'I hope all will be right in the end,' she said: 'but, believe me, you cannot be too careful. Try and keep Mr Rochester at a distance: distrust yourself as well as him. Gentlemen in his station are not accustomed to marry their governesses.'

In this letter from Alice Walker's *The Color Purple*, Celie is describing the preparations for the funeral of Sofia's mother.

Harpo say, Whoever heard of women pallbearers. That all I'm trying to say.

Well, say Sofia, you said it. Now you can hush.

I know she your mother, say Harpo. But still.

You gon help us or not? say Sofia.

What it gon look like? say Harpo. Three big stout women pallbearers look like they ought to be home frying chicken.

Three of our brothers be with us, on the other side, say Sofia. I guess they look like field hands.

But peoples use to men doing this sort of thing. Women weaker, he say. People think they weaker, say they weaker, anyhow. Women spose to take it easy. Cry if you want to. Not try to take over.

Try to take over, say Sofia. The woman dead. I can cry and take it easy and lift the coffin too. And whether you help us or not with the food and the chairs and the get-together afterward, that's exactly what I plan to do.

These two extracts are taken from novels of two different periods: *Jane Eyre* was published in England in the middle of the nineteenth century, *The Color Purple* was published in the United States in the 1980s.

You could look at these extracts from several different critical perspectives. Here are five to consider:

- a social perspective
- a feminist perspective
- a cultural perspective
- the perspective of period
- your own critical perspective.

A social perspective:

- What is there in the extracts that suggests how society may be organised in terms of a social *hierarchy*?
- What is there in the extracts that suggests how society may be organised in terms of social *structure*?

A feminist perspective:

- What do you make of the situation and role of women in society in each extract and text?
- Are there any similarities?
- Are there any differences?

A cultural perspective:

- What do you learn from the culture and cultural attitudes embedded in these extracts and texts?
- Is there a difference in the cultures?
- What do you learn of customs at work and at leisure?

The perspective of period:

- What sense do you have of the historical periods in which these extracts are set?
- How is this indicated?
- Do either or both texts have a value for readers outside the specific period in which they are set?

Your own critical perspective:

When setting out your own critical perspective you must make clear:

- which of these readings interests you
- which you consider to be the most useful way into the book for you, and why.

Offering your own critical perspective, 'your own interpretation', is essential to achieving AO4, which states that students ought to be able to 'articulate independent opinions and judgements, informed by different interpretations of literary texts by other readers'.

For this reason, it's always necessary to make your own interpretation abundantly clear.

A feminist comparison of these two texts might include:

- the treatment of sexuality
- the ways in which feminist issues are reflected in the type of narrative used in each text – letters in *The Color Purple*, and the autobiographical mode in *Jane Eyre*
- the power struggles between male and female in the two narratives, which have very different outcomes.

The position of women in society could also be an important element in looking at less overtly feminist texts. For example, this point of view could be used to compare Nathaniel Hawthorne's *The Scarlet Letter* and Margaret Atwood's *The Handmaid's Tale.*

Comparing the presentation of power and social class in texts – the Marxist perspective, in other words – could also be a good starting point. The novel *Hard Times* by Charles Dickens and J. B. Priestley's play *An Inspector Calls* offer similar perspectives on society, though they differ in social and historical contexts, and have different forms. *King Lear* is also open to a Marxist interpretation, and comparing it with Thomas Hardy's novel *Far From the Madding Crowd* would raise issues of family and power, gender and power, and nature and humankind. A **psychoanalytical** reading of the nature of obsession in *Enduring Love* by Ian McEwan and in either *Hamlet* or *Othello* would provide some illuminating relationships and comparisons.

To return to the wording of this Assessment Objective, it is 'articulate independent opinions and judgements, informed by different interpretations of literary texts by other readers'. In order to score here, therefore, you have to consider different interpretations of the texts you have chosen. The assessment criteria in this strand for the top three mark bands run as follows:

16–20: clear consideration of different interpretations of text

21–25: clear consideration of different interpretations of text, with evaluation of their strengths and weaknesses

26–30: perceptive consideration of different interpretations of text, with sharp evaluation of their strengths and weaknesses.

Assessment Objective 5ii

> AO5ii   evaluate the significance of cultural, historical and other contextual influences on literary texts and study

This Assessment Objective is targeted in coursework, and in the drama section of Module 5. In the Specification there are seven areas outlined for this objective (set out below).

This is a crucial objective for you to grasp as it marks the difference between AS and A2 Level of study. At AS Level, you had simply to show an awareness that certain contexts existed for or within the texts; but at A2 Level you must discuss the relationship between the text and selected areas of context.

You have looked at relationships between context and text throughout this module, and you will also be able to evaluate the significance of the context when *Pride and Prejudice* and *Wilt on High* are discussed as **satires** (page 27–9). In other words, you will see how each text operates within the framework of satire as a genre.

The seven areas outlined for this Objective in the Specification are:

Area 1

The context of period or era, including social, historical, political and cultural processes.

Unpicking this area   This is probably the most accessible and useful form of context to analyse, as it involves so many different areas.

Coursework   You will look at this area over and over again in this module, for example in discussing *Catch-22* and *Captain Corelli's Mandolin* (page 39–42), where you will look at the context of war – a social, historical, and political context.

Area 2

The contexts of the writer's biography and/or milieu.

Unpicking this area   It would not be wise to concern yourself too much with an author's life, as this might take you away from the study of the text – and it is the text that matters.

Coursework   You might of course refer to an author's life as *one* element in your response to a text; for example, knowing that Heller was a bombardier in the Second World War might help to explain the vividness of his portrayal of some of the horrors of war. But to make such biographical considerations into something more than a brief issue would be to diminish the importance of the text. A good guide is to refer to biography where it might have affected the ways in which a writer thinks or feels, but remember that it is merely a *part* of what that writer has offered in the text.

Area 3

The context of the work in terms of other works, including other works by the same author.

Unpicking this area   You inevitably look at works by other authors when you compare texts.

Coursework   Throughout this module you will compare works by two different authors. Because of the period requirement, you will not often look at works by the same author, unless he or she has written in different literary forms; for example, you might look at the plays and novels of D. H. Lawrence, or at the poetry and novels of Thomas Hardy.

Area 4

The different contexts for a work established by its reception over time, including the recognition that works have different meanings and effects upon readers in different periods.

Unpicking this area   This looks very much like Area 2 of AO4 (see page 11).

Coursework   You have already considered this issue under Area 2 of AO4 above.

Area 5

The context of a passage in terms of the work from which it is taken, a part-to-whole context.

Unpicking this area   This simply refers to how an extract relates to the work from which it is taken.

Coursework   You inevitably discuss this area when you look at how different parts of a text come together to create the meaning of the whole text.

Area 6

The literary context, including issues of genre and period-specific styles.

Unpicking this area   This involves, for example, looking at a text in terms of genre to see how far it complies with traditional forms, and where – and why – changes are made.

Coursework   Genre will be considered in the context of satire (page 27); the context of period-specific styles overlaps with language context (Area 7, below).

Area 7

The language context, including relevant and significant episodes in the use and development of literary language. This would include matters of style, such as the use of colloquial, dialect, or demotic language.

Unpicking this area   You have already paid some attention to language use on page 8 of this module.

Coursework   This may well form one of the areas which you choose to use for comparison.

Having set out the seven areas in this Specification, below are the various contexts relating to AO5ii.

Historical contexts

Many texts have historical contexts that are significant for the reader. In pairing texts, you may want to compare historical contexts, or the ways in which the writers use such contexts. For instance, Mary Shelley in *Frankenstein* and Barry Unsworth in *Sacred Hunger* both write about eighteenth-century society, but use the contexts in different ways. (You could also use Daniel Defoe's *Moll Flanders* here.)

A C T I V I T Y   5

Read the extracts below, and then attempt the questions.

In this extract from *Sacred Hunger*, Paris is recalling his confinement in Norwich Jail.

In prison I was subject also to defect of heat, he thought, remembering the stone floor, the bare walls. At this interval of time Norwich Jail had assumed the shape of a pit in his mind, with descending levels of damnation. At the lowest level were those who had no money at all and small means of obtaining any. He had been one week here, on the orders of the outraged cleric who owned the prison, as punishment for printing seditious views concerning God's creation. Here men and women fought with rats in damp cellars for scraps of food thrown down to them through a trap-door, and huddled together for warmth upon heaps of filthy rags and bundles of rotten straw. Lunatics stumbled about here, women gave birth, people died of fever or starvation.

These were people yielding no profit. Higher in the scale were those who could pay for food and a private room and it was here that Paris, until redeemed by his uncle, had found lodging. Two shillings a week had provided him also with writing materials and given him access to the prisoners' common-room, where there were newspapers, and a fire in the coldest weather; but it had not been enough to free him from the stench of the place, nor the brutalities of some of his fellow-inmates – thieves and pimps mingled with debtors here. Higher yet, serenely above all this and freed from unpleasant associations, were the rich prisoners, who lived as the bishop's guests and entertained on a lavish scale.

Norwich Jail had given Paris his notion of hell, and its workings afforded an example of docility to law every bit as absolute as the motions of the blood postulated by Harvey. Money regulated every smallest detail of the place, from the paupers in the cellars to the profligate feasters above. All rents went to the bishop, who had spent a thousand pounds to acquire the prison and was laudably set on making his investment as profitable as possible, this being a time when the individual pursuit of wealth was regarded as inherently virtuous, on the grounds that it increased the wealth and well-being of the community. Indeed, this process of enrichment was generally referred to as 'wealth-creation' by the theorists of the day. The spread of benefits was not apparent in the prison itself, owing to the special circumstances there and particularly to the very high death-rate.

The keepers at their lower level sought to emulate the governor, pursuing wealth diligently through the sale of spirits, the purveying of harlots and the extortionate charges to visitors.

In the next extract, Frankenstein describes his surroundings, and his feelings, as he lies in prison.

But I was doomed to live; and in two months, found myself as awaking from a dream, in a prison, stretched on a wretched bed, surrounded by gaolers, turnkeys, bolts, and all the miserable apparatus of a dungeon. It was morning, I remember, when I thus awoke to understanding: I had forgotten the particulars of what had happened, and only felt as if some great misfortune had suddenly overwhelmed me; but when I looked around, and saw the barred windows, the squalidness of the room in which I was, all flashed across my memory, and I groaned bitterly.

This sound disturbed an old woman who was sleeping in a chair beside me. She was a hired nurse, the wife of one of the turnkeys, and her countenance expressed all those bad qualities which often characterise that class. The lines of her face were hard and rude, like that of persons accustomed to see without sympathising in sights of misery. Her tone expressed her entire indifference; she addressed me in English, and her voice struck me as one that I had heard during my sufferings: –

'Are you better now, sir?' said she.

I replied in the same language, with a feeble voice, 'I believe I am; but if it all be true, if indeed I did not dream, I am sorry that I am still alive to feel this misery and horror.'

'For that matter,' replied the old woman, 'if you mean about the gentleman you murdered, I believe that it were better for you if you were dead, for I fancy it will go hard for you! However, that's none of my business; I am sent to nurse you and get you well; I do my duty with a safe conscience; it were well if everybody did the same.'

I turned with loathing from the woman who could utter so unfeeling a speech to a person just saved, on the very edge of death; but I felt languid, and unable to reflect on all that had passed. The whole series of my life appeared to me as a dream; I sometimes doubted if indeed it were all true, for it never presented itself to my mind with the force of reality.

As the images that floated before me became more distinct, I grew feverish; a darkness pressed around me: no one was near me who soothed me with the gentle voice of love; no dear hand supported me. The physician came and prescribed medicines, and the old woman prepared them for me; but utter carelessness was visible.

- List the similarities in the physical conditions of the institutions described.

- What principles govern the two institutions?

- What are the attitudes to money and women in the two institutions? What seems important about them to each writer?

- Look for the references that relate to hell or hellishness in each extract.

- What are the attitudes of Paris and Frankenstein to the conditions they see? How are they similar, and how are they different? How are their attitudes conveyed?

If you were looking at these texts as a pair, you would naturally look at (a) the wider picture each text offers of the period in which the action takes place, and (b) the way each text uses different methods to tell its story. Language would also be a point of comparison, as one text represents the eighteenth century through twentieth-century eyes, and the other from the viewpoint of the nineteenth century.

Social contexts

Many writers comment through their writing on the social context within which a story is set. Dickens is an obvious example: his descriptions of Coketown in *Hard Times* or of London in *Bleak House* could be compared with William Blake's treatment of urban life in poetry such as *Songs of Innocence and of Experience*. Or you might use George Orwell's *Down and Out in Paris and London*. Such an approach could be developed into issues of form and language.

Many writers also comment on their own society by setting their texts in other societies. As we have seen, Brian Friel's play *Translations*, for instance, is set in Ireland in 1833; but for the audience at its first performance in Derry in Northern Ireland in 1980, the issues of change in society brought about by the presence of British soldiers would have been very relevant to their own lives.

Socio-cultural contexts

Social context is often intertwined with the cultural context. Consider the following extracts from two books that deal with racism.

ACTIVITY 6

In the first extract, from Ralph Ellison's *Invisible Man*, the narrator describes the events after a boxing match put on for the entertainment of white men.

Then the M.C. called to us, 'Come on up here boys and get your money.'

We ran forward to where the men laughed and talked in their chairs, waiting. Everyone seemed friendly now.

'There it is on the rug,' the man said. I saw the rug covered with coins of all dimensions and a few crumpled bills. But what excited me, scattered here and there, were the gold pieces.

'Boys, it's all yours,' the man said. 'You get all you grab.'

'That's right, Sambo,' a blond man said, winking at me confidentially.

I trembled with excitement, forgetting my pain. I would get the gold and the bills, I thought. I would use both hands. I would throw my body against the boys nearest me to block them from the gold.

'Get down around the rug now,' the man commanded, 'and don't anyone touch it until I give the signal.'

'This ought to be good,' I heard.

As told, we got around the square rug on our knees. Slowly the man raised his freckled hand as we followed it upward with our eyes.

I heard, 'These niggers look like they're about to pray!'

Then, 'Ready,' the man said. 'Go!'

I lunged for a yellow coin lying on the blue design of the carpet, touching it and sending a surprised shriek to join those fishing around me. I tried to remove my hand but could not let go. A hot, violent force tore through my body, shaking me like a wet rat. The rug was electrified. The hair bristled up on my head as I shook myself free. My muscles jumped, my nerves jangled, writhed. But I saw this was not stopping the other boys. Laughing in fear and embarrassment, some were holding back and scooping up the coins knocked off by the painful contortions of the others. The men roared above us as we struggled.

'Pick it up, goddammit, pick it up!' someone called like a bass-voiced parrot. 'Go on, get it!'

In this extract from Toni Morrison's *Beloved*, the white men are approaching the house and shed were Sethe is hidden with her baby:

When the four horsemen came – schoolteacher, one nephew, one slave catcher and a sheriff – the house on Bluestone Road was so quiet they thought they were too late. Three of them dismounted, one stayed in the saddle, his rifle ready, his eyes trained away from the house to the left and to the right, because likely as not the fugitive would make a dash for it. Although sometimes, you could never tell, you'd find them folded up tight somewhere: beneath floorboards, in a pantry – once a chimney. Even then care was taken, because the quietest ones, the ones you pulled from a press, a hayloft, or, that once, from a chimney, would go along nicely for two or three seconds. Caught red-handed, so to speak, they would seem to recognize the futility of outsmarting a whiteman and the hopelessness of outrunning a rifle. Smile even, like a child caught dead with his hand in the jelly jar, and when you reached for the rope to tie him, well, even then you couldn't tell. The very nigger with his head hanging and a little jelly-jar smile on his face could all of a sudden roar, like a bull or some such, and commence to do disbelievable things. Grab the rifle at its mouth; throw himself at the one holding it – anything. So you had to keep back a pace, leave the tying to another. Otherwise you ended up killing what you were paid to bring back alive. Unlike a snake or bear, a dead nigger could not be skinned for profit and was not worth his own dead weight in coin.

- Who are the victims in these extracts?

- What are the attitudes shown towards them?

- How are these attitudes conveyed? You might consider viewpoint, narrative structure, and the distinctive use of language.

- Can you see the differences in language use that arise from the period difference? (*Invisible Man* was published in 1951, *Beloved* in 1987.)

- What are the similarities and differences in the writers' attitudes?

There are many socio-cultural areas that might yield interesting and illuminating comparisons. The novel *Trainspotting* by Irving Welsh and the play *Shopping and F***ing* by Mark Ravenshill, for instance, both deal with drug culture, and there would be comparisons of language and structure to be made. The novel *The French Lieutenant's Woman* by John Fowles and the play *Mrs Warren's Profession* by George Bernard Shaw both centre on issues of love, marriage and prostitution, but embody very different cultural assumptions about them. As well as exhibiting differences in form, the play is a chronological narrative and the novel is a non-chronological narrative, a difference that offers further room for exploration.

Socio-economic contexts

A particular socio-economic theme that forms a context for many American texts is the 'American Dream' – the idea that working to acquire money and material goods will bring success, and with it happiness of every kind. Two texts that reflect on this are the novel *The Great Gatsby* by F. Scott Fitzgerald and the play *Death of a Salesman* by Arthur Miller.

ACTIVITY 7

Read the extracts below, and then answer the questions that follow.

In this extract from *The Great Gatsby*, the narrator, Nick, is describing the parties at the house of his new neighbour, the millionaire Jay Gatsby.

At least once a fortnight a corps of caterers came down with several hundred feet of canvas and enough coloured lights to make a Christmas tree of Gatsby's enormous garden. On buffet tables, garnished with glistening hors-d'oeuvre, spiced baked hams crowded against salads of harlequin designs and pastry pigs and turkeys bewitched to a dark gold. In the main hall a bar with a real brass rail was set up, and stocked with gins and liquors and with cordials so long forgotten that most of his female guests were too young to know one from another.

By seven o'clock the orchestra has arrived, no thin five-piece affair, but a whole pitful of oboes and trombones and saxophones and viols and cornets and piccolos, and low and high drums. The last swimmers have come in from the beach now and are dressing upstairs; the cars from New York are parked five deep in the drive, and already the halls and salons and verandas are gaudy with primary colours, and hair bobbed in strange new ways, and shawls beyond the dreams of Castile. The bar is in full swing, and floating rounds of cocktails permeate the garden outside, until the air is alive with chatter and laughter, and casual innuendo and introductions forgotten on the spot, and enthusiastic meetings between women who never knew each other's names.

The lights grow brighter as the earth lurches away from the sun, and now the orchestra is playing yellow cocktail music, and the opera of voices pitches a key higher. Laughter is easier minute by minute, spilled with prodigality, tipped out at a cheerful word. The groups change more swiftly, swell with new arrivals, dissolve and form in the same breath; already there are wanderers, confident girls who weave here and there among the stouter and more stable, become for a sharp, joyous moment the centre of a group, and then, excited with triumph, glide on through the sea-change of faces and voices and color under the constantly changing light.

Suddenly one of these gypsies, in trembling opal, seizes a cocktail out of the air, dumps it down for courage and, moving her hands like Frisco, dances out alone on the canvas platform. A momentary hush; the orchestra leader varies his rhythm obligingly for her, and there is a burst of chatter as the erroneous news goes around that she is Gilda Gray's understudy from the Follies. The party has begun.

In this extract from *Death of a Salesman*, Willy Loman is contemplating killing himself so that his family can collect the insurance money. Willy, a salesman, is ill, and has been fired from his job. He feels guilty about his lack of success, the trouble his wife has had to endure, and the contempt that his son Biff feels for him. In this scene he is 'talking' to his Uncle Ben, who was a successful entrepreneur; the conversation takes place in Willy's imagination.

WILLY: What a proposition, ts, ts. Terrific, terrific. 'Cause she's suffered, Ben, the woman has suffered. You understand me? A man can't go out the way he came in, Ben, a man has got to add up to something. You can't, you can't – [BEN *moves towards him as though to interrupt.*] You gotta consider, now. Don't answer so quick. Remember, it's a guaranteed twenty-thousand-dollar proposition. Now look, Ben, I want you to go through the ins and outs of this thing with me. I've got nobody to talk to, Ben, and the woman has suffered, you hear me?

BEN: [*standing still, considering*]: What's the proposition?

WILLY: It's twenty thousand dollars on the barrelhead. Guaranteed, gilt-edged, you understand?

BEN: You don't want to make a fool of yourself. They might not honour the policy.

WILLY: How can they dare refuse? Didn't I work like a coolie to meet every premium on the nose? And now they don't pay off! Impossible!

BEN: It's called a cowardly thing, William.

WILLY: Why? Does it take more guts to stand here the rest of my life ringing up a zero?

BEN: [*yielding*]: That's a point, William. [*He moves, thinking, turns.*] And twenty thousand – that *is* something one can feel with the hand, it is there.

WILLY: [*now assured, with rising power*]: Oh Ben, that's the whole beauty of it! I see it like a diamond, shining in the dark, hard and rough, that I can pick up and touch in my hand. Not like – like an appointment! This would not be another dammed-fool appointment, Ben, and it changes all the aspects. Because he thinks I'm nothing, see, and so he spites me. But the funeral – [*Straightening up*] Ben, that funeral will be massive! They'll come from Maine, Massachusetts, Vermont, New Hampshire! All the old-timers with the strange licence plates – that boy will be thunderstruck, Ben, because he never realized – I am known! Rhode Island, New York, New Jersey – I am known, Ben, and he'll see it with his eyes once and for all. He'll see what I am, Ben! He's in for a shock, that boy!

BEN: [*coming down to the edge of the garden*]: He'll call you a coward.

WILLY: [*suddenly fearful*]: No, that would be terrible.

BEN: Yes. And a damned fool.

WILLY: No, no, he mustn't, I won't have that! [*He is broken and desperate.*]

BEN: He'll hate you, William.

- Look for the words and phrases in the first extract that suggest:

  - abundance and excess

  - that things are dream-like or unreal

  - that things are transitory

  - that things are false

  - that though an effect has been aimed for, it hasn't quite succeeded.

- In the second extract, look for evidence in Willy's language of his desire to succeed. What else seems to drive him?

- Willy is planning to kill himself, but he describes it as though it were a business deal. Find evidence of this.

- Find evidence of Willy's sense of his own failure.

- Willy has always deluded himself about his own achievements. Can you find evidence of this here?

Both texts end in the death and failure of the central figures. Taking all the evidence you've found, show how both passages present the American Dream.

Language contexts

Of course all literary texts have a language context, but in some the language is a particularly important feature. Brian Friel's play *Translations* and George Orwell's novel *1984* both deal with the power of language to affect society and the individual.

ACTIVITY 8

Read these two extracts, and then respond to the questions that follow.

In this extract, from Orwell's *1984*, the central character, Winston Smith, is listening to a colleague in the Ministry of Truth telling him about the advantages of Newspeak. Newspeak is the language of Big Brother, who is the figurehead of the future totalitarian state in which the novel is set.

'Do you know that Newspeak is the only language in the world whose vocabulary gets smaller every year?'

Winston did know that, of course. He smiled, sympathetically he hoped, not trusting himself to speak. Syme bit off another fragment of the dark-coloured bread, chewed it briefly, and went on:

'Don't you see that the whole aim of Newspeak is to narrow the range of thought? In the end we shall make thoughtcrime literally impossible, because there will be no words in which to express it. Every concept that can ever be needed will be expressed by exactly *one* word, with its meaning rigidly defined and all its subsidiary meanings rubbed out and forgotten. Already, in the Eleventh Edition, we're not far from that point. But the process will still be continuing long after you and I are dead. Every year fewer and fewer words, and the range of consciousness always a little smaller. Even now, of course, there's no reason or excuse for committing thoughtcrime. It's merely a question of self-discipline, reality-control. But in the end there won't be any need even for that. The Revolution will be complete when the language is perfect. Newspeak is Ingsoc and Ingsoc is Newspeak,' he added with a sort of mystical satisfaction. 'Has it ever occurred to you, Winston, that by the year 2050, at the very latest, not a single human being will be alive who could understand such a conversation as we have having now?'

'Except –' began Winston doubtfully, and then stopped.

It had been on the tip of his tongue to say 'Except the proles,' but he checked himself, not feeling fully certain that this remark was not in some way unorthodox.

In this extract from *Translations*, Lancey, an English soldier, is warning the villagers of Ballybeg what will happen if his fellow officer, who has gone missing, is not found. In the play, set in the west of Ireland in 1833, Owen has been translating the officers' words into Irish, and has been helping to give English names to Irish places. Sarah, who is mute when we first meet her, learns to speak during the course of the play.

LANCEY: If that doesn't bear results, commencing forty-eight hours from now we will embark on a series of evictions and levelling of every abode in the following selected areas –

OWEN: You're not – !

LANCEY: Do your job. Translate.

OWEN: If they still haven't found him in two days' time they'll begin evicting and levelling every house starting with these townlands.
[LANCEY *reads from his list.*]

LANCEY: Swinefort.

OWEN: Lis na Muc.

LANCEY: Burnfoot.

OWEN: Bun na hAbhann.

LANCEY: Dromduff.

OWEN: Druim Dubh.

LANCEY: Whiteplains.

OWEN: Machaire Ban.

LANCEY: Kings Head.

OWEN: Cnoc na Ri.

LANCEY: If by then the lieutenant hasn't been found, we will proceed until a complete clearance is made of this entire section.

OWEN: If Yolland hasn't been got by then, they will ravish the whole parish.

LANCEY: I trust they know exactly what they've got to do.
[*Pointing to* BRIDGET.] I know you. I know where you live.
[*Pointing to* SARAH.] Who are you? Name!
[SARAH's *mouth opens and shuts, opens and shuts. Her face becomes contorted.*]
What's your name?
[*Again* SARAH *tries frantically.*]

OWEN: Go on, Sarah. You can tell him.
[*But* SARAH *cannot. And she knows she cannot. She closes her mouth. Her head goes down.*]

OWEN: Her name is Sarah Johnny Sally.

LANCEY: Where does she live?

OWEN: Bun na hAbhann.

LANCEY: Where?

OWEN: Burnfoot.

- How are language, and change to language, used to oppress people in each extract? Be as detailed and exact as you can.

- *1984* is about a society in the future, and *Translations* about a society in the past. What does each extract seem to be suggesting about the society in which it is set?

- In each extract one character does not speak – Winston starts to do so but stops. What might their silences suggest to the reader of *1984* and the audience of *Translations*? Look at the stage directions, and think how the play works differently from the novel.

If you were comparing these two works, you could go on to look at the importance of language in the complete texts. These two extracts would be good starting points.

Invented language is a feature of some texts, and could be an important element in comparing, say, *1984* and *A Clockwork Orange* by Anthony Burgess.

Generic and literary contexts

It might be a worthwhile exercise to compare two texts within the same genre, but from different periods.

Satire is a useful genre to look at: styles and attitudes may have changed, but it is interesting to see how much satirical focus is universal. You might find that although conventions have changed, intentions and reactions remain remarkably similar.

ACTIVITY 9

Below are the openings from two satirical novels, Jane Austen's *Pride and Prejudice*, and Tom Sharpe's *Wilt on High*.

From *Pride and Prejudice*:

It is a truth universally acknowledged, that a single man in possession of a good fortune, must be in want of a wife.

However little known the feelings or views of such a man may be on his first entering a neighbourhood, this truth is so well fixed in the minds of the surrounding families, that he is considered as the rightful property of some one or other of their daughters.

'My dear Mr Bennet,' said his lady to him one day, 'have you heard that Netherfield Park is let at last?'

Mr Bennet replied that he had not.

'But it is,' returned she; 'for Mrs Long has just been here, and she told me all about it.

Mr Bennet made no answer.

'Do not you want to know who has taken it?' cried his wife impatiently.

'*You* want to tell me, and I have no objection to hearing it.'

This was invitation enough.

'Why, my dear, you must know, Mrs Long says that Netherfield is taken by a young man of large fortune from the north of England; that he came down on Monday in a chaise and four to see the place, and was so much delighted with it, that he agreed with Mr Morris immediately; that he is to take possession before Michaelmas, and some of his servants are to be in the house by the end of next week.'

'What is his name?'

'Bingley.'

'Is he married or single?'

'Oh! single to be sure! A single man of large fortune; four or five thousand a year. What a fine thing for our girls!'

'How so? How can it affect them?'

'My dear Mr Bennet,' replied his wife, 'how can you be so tiresome! You must know that I am thinking of his marrying one of them.'

'Is that his design in settling here?'

'Design! Nonsense, how can you talk so! But it is very likely that he *may* fall in love with one of them, and therefore you must visit him as soon as he comes.'

'I see no occasion for that. You and the girls may go, or you may send them by themselves, which perhaps will be still better, for as you are as handsome as any of them, Mr Bingley might like you the best of the party.'

From Tom Sharpe's *Wilt on High*:

'Days of wine and roses,' said Wilt to himself. It was an inconsequential remark but sitting on the Finance and General Purposes Committee at the Tech needed some relief and for the fifth year running Dr Mayfield had risen to his feet and announced, 'We must put the Fenland College of Arts and Technology on the map.'

'I should have thought it was there already,' said Dr Board, resorting as usual to the literal to preserve his sanity. 'In fact to the best of my knowledge it's been there since 1895 when —'

'You know perfectly well what I mean,' interrupted Dr Mayfield. 'The fact of the matter is that the College has reached the point of no return.'

'From what?' asked Dr Board.

Dr Mayfield turned to the Principal. 'The point I am trying to make –' he began, but Dr Board hadn't finished. 'Is apparently that we are either an aircraft halfway to its destination or a cartographical feature. Or possibly both.'

The Principal sighed and thought about early retirement. 'Dr Board,' he said, 'we are here to discuss ways and means of maintaining our present course structure and staffing levels in the face of the Local Education Authority and Central Government pressure to reduce the College to an adjunct of the Department of Unemployment.'

Dr Board raised an eyebrow. 'Really? I thought we were here to teach. Of course, I may be mistaken but when I first entered the profession, that's what I was led to believe. Now I learn that we're here to maintain course structures, whatever they may be, and staffing levels. In plain English, jobs for the boys.'

'And girls,' said the Head of Catering, who hadn't been listening too carefully. Dr Board eyed her critically.

'And doubtless one or two creatures of indeterminate gender,' he murmured, 'Now, if Dr Mayfield –'

- What social 'institution' does each author satirise?

- How does each writer achieve her/his satirical effects?

- What are the similarities and differences in their methods? You might consider viewpoint, narrative structure, and use of language.

- Can you see the differences in language because of the periods in which they were written? (*Pride and Prejudice* was published in 1813, *Wilt on High* in 1984.)

- Which text appeals to you more, and why?

One clear literary context occurs when one text refers to another. This is the case, for instance, with *Jane Eyre* by Charlotte Brontë and *Wide Sargasso Sea* by Jean Rhys, with Rhys developing a character from the earlier novel; and with *Precious Bane* by Mary Webb and *Cold Comfort Farm* by Stella Gibbons – Gibbons's novel is a parody of the rural genre to which the earlier book belonged.

Literary forms and conventions can also form a context. In first-person narratives, for instance, the narrator might be 'reliable' or 'unreliable'. The 'unreliable' narrator in *The Remains of the Day* by Kazuo Ishiguro, for instance, could be examined through a comparison with the 'reliable' narrator in *David Copperfield* by Charles Dickens. On the other hand, comparing *The Remains of the Day* with a similar narrative of self-delusion, such as Dickens's *Great Expectations*, could also be fruitful.

Texts within particular literary genres can be compared. In detective fiction, *The Lady in the Lake* by Raymond Chandler could be compared with any of the Aurelio Zen novels by Michael Dibdin; or either of these could be compared with Ian McEwan's *Enduring Love*, which has strong elements of thriller writing, but used for different purposes. Another possibility is to use Gothic or horror texts from different periods.

Coursework

Preparation

For the coursework module, you will have to study and compare at least two texts, one of which must be a prose text, and produce an essay of between 2,000 and 3,000 words. You can write the pieces at school, at college or at home, and they will be marked by your teacher. The moderator from the Examination Board will then look at all the work from your centre, and decide on a final mark for each candidate's essay. In order to do well in your coursework, you need to think about the following:

- choosing a task
- reading the text
- planning your essay
- researching your essay
- writing your essay
- drafting and re-drafting your essay
- sticking to word and time limits.

Choosing a task

It's vital to choose a task that's appropriate – which means a task that addresses the Assessment Objectives. Coursework represents 15% of the whole A Level examination, and 30% of A2. It addresses AO1, AO3, AO4 and AO5ii equally, and places particular emphasis on AO2ii. This means that you must choose a task that is not simply about two texts – one of them a prose text – but a task that also makes you *compare* them. You then have to remember to focus on comparison throughout your essay.

These are some things to think about carefully when you are choosing a task:

- Does it allow me to compare the writers' choices of form, structure and language?

You don't have to treat all three aspects equally; depending on which texts you have chosen, you might have much more to say about one of them than you do about the others. But you do have to make sure that your comments are supported by detailed reference to the ways the texts are written.

- Does it allow me to discuss different interpretations of the texts?

One way of answering this question is to read some critical comments on the texts you have chosen. These might be from critical essays or books, or from articles on the Internet. But these different interpretations might also include those you can think about for yourself – for example, a feminist interpretation as opposed to a Marxist one. In any case, you will need to determine your position in relation to these interpretations in order to show that you have established your own interpretation of the text. In order to achieve top marks, you also need to evaluate the strengths and weaknesses of the different interpretations you have considered.

- Does it allow me to deal with different contexts in which the texts were written and can be understood?

If you were comparing a novel with a play or with poems, for example, you might want to think about the writers' choice of genre. Why is the form of a play or a novel particularly appropriate for what they have to say? But you might also want to consider several of the contexts outlined on pages 15–30. It's always useful to ask yourself the following questions: 'What have I gained by seeing the text in this way?' and 'How useful is it to think about the text in this way rather than in other ways?' By doing this you will be able to evaluate the significance of the particular context you are examining. In some texts it will be especially helpful to think in terms of historical or cultural context; in others, such as drama texts, it might be more useful to think in terms of performance issues and problems; in yet others, it might be useful to focus on what they are saying about language or social behaviour.

You will find in most cases that the context in which the text was written is very different from the context in which you are reading or hearing it. For instance, expectations about the behaviour of men and women might be quite different from those in the society in which you live. Remember that your own assumptions will affect the way in which you respond to a literary work. You might discover, having considered several contexts, that some are more useful than others. A knowledge of the Bible, for example, might be essential to a reading of Milton's *Paradise Lost*, but not very useful for *Hamlet*.

- Is it achievable in terms of length?

It's easy when you are preparing your coursework essay to get wrapped up in covering subject matter and to forget that you have more to do. Your task needs to be achievable, too. If you're setting out to write 2,500 words, then there's no point in embarking on a task that will take 10,000. As a general rule, the more precisely and sharply defined your task, the better, for it will help you to focus and thus keep to the word count – and you must keep within the word limit.

Reading the text

You'll probably read at least part of the texts in class, where you'll have the opportunity to discuss them with your teacher and with other students. But just as with your examination texts for Module 4, you'll need to read them again yourself. You need to demonstrate in your writing a 'knowledge and understanding' of the texts (AO2ii), and the more you read them the better your chances of finding and exploring relationships and comparisons between them. This will enable you to draw on a wide range of evidence when you write your final essay.

Planning your essay

Now you need to plan your essay. There are three general points to consider here:

- Your plan needs to be helpful to you in writing your essay – so that in working through it you produce a logical sequence of ideas which develop an argument and lead to a clear conclusion.

- You need to check your plan against the Assessment Objectives – is it clear how and where you are going to meet them?

- Because you don't want to have to change your plan much once you start writing, it's worth thinking about the length of your essay again at this stage. By the time your plan is fleshed out with argument and evidence, does it look as though the word count will be about right? Too many words? Too few to create a solid argument? If it doesn't look right, change your plan now.

Because AO2ii is the dominant Assessment Objective here, there should be a comparative framework built into your plan. This section has encouraged you to think about the two texts together throughout your preparation, so this should be relatively easy. Broadly, there are two appropriate ways of planning to compare:

(1) Plan the ideas you're going to use for each text alongside the other, and then write the essay in this way, holding the two together throughout. Of course, not every paragraph will be comparative, but the framework will be, and occasionally comparison will be integrated with detail.

(2) Write about the first text, and then the second, comparing back as you go through the second. This is quite acceptable, but you must be careful that you don't write so much about the first text that the treatment of the second becomes slight, especially as in the second half some of your writing will be about the first text. You still need to plan carefully what you're going to compare before you start – there's no point in writing a mass of material about one text if you're not going to use it in comparison with the other.

Approaches to planning are considered in more detail on page 34, under 'Strategies for planning your coursework'.

Researching your essay

Research may well involve reading articles or essays about your texts. These can be found in books or journals or on the Internet, but the most important source of information is still the primary source – the texts themselves. For instance, if you decided to write about the ways in which the American Dream is presented in *The Great Gatsby* and *Death of a Salesman*, you'd begin with a selective re-reading of the texts, looking for ideas and passages which might be useful to you. You might then want to research the writers, or the concept of the American

Dream, to see if you can add to the ideas you already have, to find some new angles to develop, or to provide additional evidence.

As you will also need to think about different interpretations, this will require thinking and research too, which might include the views of critics and reviewers. When you have read secondary sources as part of your research, you must mention them in the bibliography at the end of your essay (see 'Writing your essay', below).

Writing your essay

A significant proportion of the marks available for this module are simply for writing, and in your coursework you have the chance to score well for it – far more easily than in timed examinations. Five of the 30 marks are for the ability to 'communicate clearly the knowledge, understanding and insight appropriate to literary study, using appropriate terminology and accurate and coherent written expression' (AO1). As long as you give yourself plenty of time to write, you can take more care over the accuracy and clarity of your writing than you can in an examination – and you can take the time to check, revise and improve it when you've finished the first draft. These are specific marks for this, as you can see; it would be silly not to take the trouble to collect them.

AO2ii is the dominant Assessment Objective here – after all, the module is called Comparing Texts and the second part of this Objective asks you to explore and comment on 'relationships and comparisons between literary texts'. You also have to meet the first part of the Objective, though, and show your ability to 'respond with knowledge and understanding to literary texts'. Your understanding will be shown by the quality of your argument; but knowledge has to underpin everything you write, both in examinations and in your coursework. In coursework you have the leisure to practise what you had to do under time pressure in the examinations – provide support from the text for what you say. There are appropriate ways of showing knowledge, too. You can show it by referring to details or echoes of the text, or by quoting extracts. Short quotations (which are usually the most effective) can be included in the body of your writing, while longer quotations can be written on separate lines, so that they are easier to read. If you're quoting lines of verse, remember to show the line divisions.

If you're quoting from a secondary source, such as a critical essay, you should give details of your source in footnotes or endnotes, numbering each quotation and providing a guide to the numbers at the foot of the page or at the end of your essay. Here is an example:

'Blake's engravings also form a content, in that he seemed to want to make the experiences conveyed by the poems as concrete as possible. Perhaps he was suggesting that experience should be considered in physical as well as abstract terms.' [1]

The note at the bottom of the page or at the end of the essay would be:

[1] *T. Childs and J. Moore, A2 English Literature for AQA A (2001), p. 74*

If you use the words of other writers such as critics in your own writing, you must acknowledge them. You have to sign a declaration that the coursework is your own work, and if you 'lift' from other writers without acknowledging them – which is plagiarism – you might lose all your marks for the module.

Drafting and re-drafting your essay

When you have completed a first draft of your coursework essay, your teacher may allow you to re-draft it – as long as there is enough time left to do so. Your teacher is allowed to give only general advice as to how you might improve the essay, not to correct it or rewrite it – it must be your work, after all. Of course, you should heed any advice that you get – but you should aim for your first draft to be as good as you can make it. It's a lot easier to make minor changes than major ones.

Sticking to word and time limits

The word limit for A2 coursework is between 2,000 and 3,000 words. If you exceed it, you run the risk of being penalised – it's as simple as that. If your first draft comes to 3,500 words, you can probably trim it fairly easily, and you may want your teacher's guidance on which parts to prune. If it is 5,000 words, though, you're in trouble – cutting sentences here and there, and tightening expression, won't cut it by 50%. Too long an essay suggests that you made a mistake much earlier – in selecting the task, at the planning stage, or perhaps when you were part way through.

Your teacher will give you coursework deadlines, and it is important to stick to them – not just to please your teacher, but to improve your chances of success. You will only be able to cut/re-draft/re-think if you've got the time to do so.

Strategies for planning your coursework

The first part of this module offered you a range of methods for comparing texts, and therefore a range of possible combinations of texts. When you've chosen and read your texts, though, and chosen or negotiated a task with your teacher (who has to get the agreement of the coursework moderator), it's then up to you to start planning. Below are several strategies you could adopt. They are listed according to complexity. The teachers and moderators who assess your work do not favour one method over another, but they do mark to the Assessment Criteria. The criteria for the two top bands for the comparative element of AO2ii for this unit are:

- detailed and evaluative discussion of comparisons/contrasts

- detailed and perceptive consideration of issues raised through comparison and contrast of texts.

Methods 1 and 2 below are based on the study of *Birdsong* by Sebastian Faulks and the war poetry of Wilfred Owen, but the principles will apply to any choice of texts.

The basic questions you need to consider are:

- How do you respond to the ways in which war is presented in both *Birdsong* and Wilfred Owen's poetry?

- How might other readers respond differently to these texts?

Method 1

The simplest plan is to deal with one text first, then the other, and finally draw together the comparisons and contrasts. If you choose this method, you will need to make sure that the two sections are clearly parallel to each other. For instance, a plan might look like this:

Birdsong	Owen
Nature of war	Nature of war
Presentation through: • characters • novel • description • dialogue • echoes of earlier incidents in the narrative • developing narrative	Presentation through: • vignettes • poems • description • dialogue • images • concise impact
Aspects of war	Aspects of war
Responses at time written	Responses at time written
Interpretations	Interpretations
Evaluation of significance of contexts	Evaluation of significance of contexts
Your own response	Your own response

Method 2

A similar method is to begin writing about one text but then to compare and contrast elements in the second as you write. In other words, the difference from Method 1 is that instead of working down the first column and then down the second column, you work across the columns. You would have to make sure that you have a detailed plan, so that you don't use material on one text for which you can't find a parallel in the other text.

Method 3

The final method involves looking at the two texts alongside each other, but then organising your response to them according to a specific theme, focus or critical perspective. This method may make it easier for you to ensure that your responses will remain relevant and that you provide the reader with the required 'evaluative discussion of comparisons/contrasts'.

You could decide, for example, that the focus of your essay was going to be on different contexts and interpretations. You would then be able to address AO3 – which is concerned with how writers' choices of form, structure and language shape meanings – in order to gather your evidence.

You will already be familiar with the following material because you read it when you were working through the extracts from *Jane Eyre* and *The Color Purple* (pages 12–13). However, you were probably not thinking at that point that you could use this material as the basis for a plan.

Looking at texts from a different critical perspective will usually give rise to differing interpretations, because in order to make an interpretation we need to select material that suits a specific purpose. We then put the material together to see what we have found. This is therefore one way of linking contexts and interpretations, rather than by dealing with them separately, as was the case in Method 1 and Method 2.

Because you have to explain your own interpretation of the text in the light of different interpretations by other readers, this structure for your essay could be a helpful way of allowing you to link the material you have selected to use. The evidence for your writing about the different contexts and interpretations, as well as the evidence for your own interpretation, would then come from a close examination of the methods chosen by the writers to present their material: in other words, their choices of form, structure and language, and the ways in which these allow you to create meanings from the text. Because you are looking at different interpretations in terms of particular contexts, you can evaluate the significance of the different contexts when deciding what your own interpretation is and how it differs from other readers' interpretations.

As noted before, these two extracts are taken from novels from two different periods: *Jane Eyre* was published in England in 1847, while *The Color Purple* was published in the United States in 1982. You could look at these two extracts from several different critical perspectives. Here again are the five critical perspectives we looked at earlier (page 14):

- a social perspective
- a feminist perspective
- a cultural perspective
- the perspective of period
- your own critical perspective.

A social perspective:
- What is there in the extracts that suggests how society may be organised in terms of social *hierarchy*?
- What is there in the extracts that suggests how society may be organised in terms of social *structure*?

A feminist perspective:
- What do you make of the situation and role of women in society in each extract and text?

- Are there any similarities?
- Are there any differences?

A cultural perspective:

- What do you learn from the culture and cultural attitudes embedded in these extracts and texts?
- Is there a difference in the cultures?
- What do you learn of customs at work and at leisure?

The perspective of period:

- What sense do you have of the historical periods in which these extracts are set?
- How is it indicated?
- Do either or both extracts have a value for readers outside the specific period in which they are set?

Your own critical perspective:

When setting out your own critical perspective, you must make clear:

- which of these critical perspectives interests you
- which you consider to be the most useful way into the book for you, and why
- what other readers may have thought – critics, for instance.

One way of using these perspectives is to apply the same perspective to both texts. Alternatively, you could consider each text from a different perspective and then consider the appropriateness and significance of these perspectives for the study of the texts.

Preparing your final draft

In order to make sure that you are addressing AO1 as well as you can, you need to be able to read your essay critically when you think you have finished your draft. You need to ask yourself the following questions:

- Is my argument clear?
- Have I expressed myself clearly?
- Have I used literary terminology correctly and appropriately?
- Is my choice of words and syntax as interesting as it could be?
- Will my essay interest and persuade the reader?

Achieving high marks

When you've followed all the advice above about selecting texts and task, and about planning and writing your essay, you need to have an idea of how high a mark you're likely to achieve with it. Obviously your teacher will help you here, but it's worth knowing exactly what criteria teachers and moderators use to judge your essay. So far we have looked at all the assessment criteria; you now need to know how these will be used to measure the quality of your work.

The dominant Assessment Objective in this module is AO2ii: *candidates should be able to respond with knowledge and understanding to literary texts of different types and periods, exploring and commenting on relationships between literary texts.*

There are six mark bands. Here are the assessment criteria for three of the bands. (The bottom band in effect tells you what to *avoid*.)

Top band (26–30 marks):

AO1	use of appropriate critical vocabulary and technically fluent style/well-structured and coherent argument
AO2ii	secure, confident and well-informed understanding of text and task/excellent selection of supportive references
AO2ii	detailed and perceptive understanding of issues raised through comparison and contrast of texts
AO3	exploration and analysis of key aspects of form, structure and language with perceptive evaluation of how they shape meanings
AO4	perceptive consideration of different interpretations of texts with sharp evaluation of their strengths and weaknesses/confident personal judgements based on informed consideration of various interpretations with textual support
AO5ii	excellent understanding of a range of contextual factors with specific, detailed links between context/text/task

Middle band (16–20 marks):

AO1	use of accurate critical vocabulary and clear argument expressed accurately
AO2ii	clear focus on task with informed knowledge and understanding of texts/apt supportive references
AO2ii	detailed consideration of comparison and contrasts
AO3	commentary on how specific aspects of form/structure/language shape meanings
AO4	clear consideration of different interpretations of texts with clear evidence of personal response and textual support
AO5ii	examination of a range of contextual factors with specific, detailed links between context/texts/task

Bottom band (0–5 marks):

AO1	poor quality of writing hinders meaning/unclear line of argument
AO2ii	some simple narration of plot/events/characters
AO2ii	little sense of comparison between texts
AO3	very limited discussion of how language features shape meaning
AO4	little understanding of different interpretative approaches and little personal response
AO5ii	very limited awareness of significance of contextual factors

By becoming familiar with these criteria – in other words with what your teachers and moderators are looking for in your coursework – you will be able to monitor your own progress as you move through the various stages in the preparation of your coursework essay. Your teachers will be able to show you the whole of the mark scheme that is used for the assessment of your coursework.

Concluding exercise

Now that you have worked your way through Module 4, and have an understanding of both the Assessment Objectives and of methods you might use in comparing texts, here is a final exercise.

The following two extracts are from novels about war. Read them carefully, and then carry out Activity 10.

The first extract is from Joseph Heller's novel *Catch-22*, published in 1961.

Now Lieutenant Scheisskopf had confidence enough in his powers to spring his big surprise. Lieutenant Scheisskopf had discovered in his extensive research that the hands of marchers, instead of swinging freely, as was then the popular fashion, ought never to be moved more than three inches from the center of the thigh, which meant, in effect, that they were scarcely to be swung at all.

Lieutenant Scheisskopf's preparations were elaborate and clandestine. All the cadets in his squadron were sworn to secrecy and rehearsed in the dead of night on the auxiliary paradeground. They marched in darkness that was pitch and bumped into each other blindly, but they did not panic, and they were learning to march without swinging their hands. Lieutenant Scheisskopf's first thought had been to have a friend of his in the sheet metal shop sink pegs of nickel alloy into each man's thighbones and link them to the wrists by strands of copper wire with exactly three inches of play, but there wasn't time – there was never enough time – and good copper wire was hard to come by in wartime. He remembered also that the men, so hampered, would be unable to fall properly during the impressive fainting ceremony preceding the marching and that an inability to faint properly might affect the unit's rating as a whole.

And all week long he chortled with repressed delight at the officers' club. Speculation grew rampant among his closest friends.

'I wonder what that Shithead is up to,' Lieutenant Engle said.

Lieutenant Scheisskopf responded with a knowing smile to the queries of his colleagues. 'You'll find out Sunday,' he promised. 'You'll find out.'

Lieutenant Scheisskopf unveiled his epochal surprise that Sunday with all the aplomb of an experienced impresario. He said nothing while the other squadrons ambled past the reviewing stand crookedly in their customary manner. He gave no sign even when the first ranks of his own squadron hove into sight with their swingless marching and the first stricken gasps of alarm were hissing from his startled fellow officers. He held back even then until the bloated colonel with the big fat mustache whirled upon him savagely with a purpling face, and then he offered the explanation that made him immortal.

'Look, Colonel,' he announced. 'No hands.'

And to an audience stilled with awe, he distributed certified photostatic copies of the obscure regulation on which he had built his unforgettable triumph. This was Lieutenant Scheisskopf's finest hour. He won the parade, of course, hands down, obtaining permanent possession of the red pennant and ending the Sunday parades altogether, since good red pennants were as hard to come by in wartime as good copper wire. Lieutenant Scheisskopf was made First Lieutenant Scheisskopf on the spot and began his rapid rise through the ranks. There were few who did not hail him as a true military genius for his important discovery.

The next extract is from Louis de Bernières's novel *Captain Corelli's Mandolin*, published in 1994.

I will illustrate the pride of the populace by retailing what happened when we asked them to surrender. I had this story from Captain Corelli. He was prone to dramatic exaggeration in the telling of a story because everything about him was original, he was always larger than his circumstances, and he would say things for the sake of their value as amusement, with an ironic disregard for the truth. Generally he observed life with raised eyebrows, and he had none of that fragile self-pride that prevents a man from telling a joke against himself. There were some people who thought him a little mad, but I see him as a man who loved life so much that he did not care what kind of impression he made. He adored children, and I saw him kiss a little girl on the head and whirl her in his arms whilst his whole battery was standing at attention, awaiting his inspection, and he loved to make pretty women giggle by snapping his heels together and saluting them with a military precision so consummate that it came over as a mockery of everything soldierly. When saluting General Gandin the action was sloppy to the point of insolence, so you can see what kind of man he was.

I first came across him in the latrines of the encampment. His battery had a latrine known as 'La Scala' because he had a little opera club that shat together there at the same time every morning, sitting in a row on the wooden plank with their trousers about their ankles. He had two baritones, three tenors, a bass, and a counter-tenor who was much mocked on account of having to sing all the women's parts, and the idea was that each man should expel either a turd or a fart during the crescendos, when they could not be heard above the singing. In this way the indignity of communal defecation was minimised, and the whole encampment would begin the day humming a rousing tune that they heard wafting out of the heads. My first experience of La Scala was hearing the Anvil Chorus at 7.30 a.m., accompanied by a very prodigious and resolute timpani. Naturally I could not resist going to investigate, and I approached a canvas enclosure that had 'La Scala' painted on it in splashes of blanco. I noticed an appalling and very rank stench, but I went in, only to see a row of soldiers shitting at their perches, red in the face, singing at full heart, hammering at their steel helmets with spoons. I was both confused and amazed, especially when I saw that there was an officer sitting there amongst the men, insouciantly conducting the concert with the aid of a feather in his right hand. Generally one salutes an officer in uniform, especially when he is wearing a cap. My salute was a hurried and incomplete gesture that accompanied my departure – I did not know the regulation that governs the saluting of an officer in uniform who has his breeches at half-mast during a drill that consists of choral elimination in occupied territory.

Subsequently I was to join the opera society, 'volunteered' by the captain after he had heard me singing as I polished my boots, and had realised that I was another baritone. He handed me a piece of paper filched from General Gandin's own order pad, and on it was written:

TOP SECRET

By Order of HQ, Supergreccia, Bombadier Carlo Piero Guercio is to report for operatic duty at every and any whim of Captain Antonio Corelli of the 33rd Regiment of Artillery, Acqui Division.

Rules of engagement:

1)   All those called to regular musical fatigues shall be obliged to play a musical instrument (spoons, tin helmet, comb-and-paper, etc.).

2)   Anyone failing persistently to reach high notes shall be emasculated, his testicles to be donated to charitable causes.

3)   Anyone maintaining that Donizetti is better than Verdi shall be dressed as a woman, mocked openly before the battery and its guns, shall wear a cooking pot upon his head, and, in extreme cases, shall be required to sing 'Funiculi Funicula' and any other songs about railways that Captain Antonio Corelli shall from time to time see fit to determine.

4) All aficionados of Wagner shall be shot peremptorily, without trial, and without leave of appeal.

5) Drunkenness shall be mandatory only at those times when Captain Antonio Corelli is not buying the drinks.

Signed; General Vecchiarelli, Supreme Commander, Supergreccia, on behalf of His Majesty, King Victor Emmanuel.

ACTIVITY 10

Work through all the parts of this task. As you do so, remember to sequence your ideas carefully to produce a well-constructed argument; take care with the expression of your ideas and check your spelling; use technical terms where appropriate. (AO1)

- Compare and contrast the attitude of each author towards war. (AO2ii)

- Compare and contrast the ways in which each author presents certain aspects of war. (AO3)

- 'War is a noble subject.'
  Basing your answer on the two extracts, how far do you agree with this comment? (AO4)

- What do these extracts tell you about different aspects of war? What might you deduce from them about the nature and purposes of war in general? (AO5ii)

This concludes your study for Module 4.
You should now be able to choose which specific areas of AO4 and AO5ii you want to include in your coursework. This will enable you to look at the examination questions for Module 5, Set Texts, and recognise which area(s) is (are) being targeted. You should be able to offer a firm response.

Remember: in both your coursework and your examinations, you must be able to take on other readers' views of the texts, assess them, and respond to them, whether agreeing or disagreeing, but you must always go on to offer a judgement of your own.

MODULE (5) Set texts: Drama before 1770; Poetry before 1900

The Assessment Objectives for this module require that you:

ASSESSMENT OBJECTIVES

AO1   communicate clearly the knowledge, understanding and insight appropriate to literary study, using appropriate terminology and accurate and coherent written expression
(5% of the final A2 mark; 2½% of the final A Level mark)

AO3   show detailed understanding of the ways in which writers' choices of form, structure and language shape meanings
(5% of the final A2 mark; 2½% of the final A Level mark)

AO4   articulate independent opinions and judgements, informed by different interpretations of literary texts by other readers
(10% of the final A2 mark; 5% of the final A Level mark)

AO5ii evaluate the significance of cultural, historical and other contextual influences on literary texts and study
(10% of the final A2 mark; 5% of the final A Level mark)

In this module the Assessment Objectives are allocated as follows:

- Section A: Poetry Before 1900, targets AO3 and AO4, with the emphasis on AO4

- Section B: Drama before 1770, targets AO1 and AO5ii, with the emphasis on AO5ii

Introduction

Content

This module meets the Specification requirements for Drama and Poetry and for a pre-1770, and a pre-1900 text respectively. There is a list of Internet resources and a select bibliography on page 173.

The examination

The examination is split into Section A, Poetry, and Section B, Drama. You have to answer one question from each section. The marks are weighted equally, and are scaled to achieve the final mark. You are not allowed to take your texts into the examination.

Assessment

Your work will be assessed as you move through the bands of the marking scheme.

Links to work at Advanced Subsidiary Level

This module is designed to build upon the skills you acquired in your work on AS Level Module 2, Genre Study – Poetry and Drama. The Assessment Objectives for the Poetry section again draw on AO3, with the addition of the dominant AO4. The Assessment Objectives for the Drama section again test AO1 and also AO5ii, which is the more complex level for the fifth, and the dominant, Assessment Objective.

As you will be answering questions on two specific texts, you will be studying only two sections of this module closely. But you might find it helpful to look across at the actual questions set on the other texts too, to see a wide range of question types targeting the same Objectives.

Section A: Poetry before 1900

Assessment Objective 4

At A2 Level this is a more complex Assessment Objective than it is at Advanced Subsidiary Level. There are several ways of approaching AO4, as this Objective may be presented in different ways in the questions. You should remember that:

- texts are capable of multiple interpretations, depending upon the experiences and cultural or social background of the individual reader

- interpretations may change over time

- different social or cultural groups may interpret texts in different ways

- there are different ways of looking at texts, based on particular approaches or theories, for example feminist, Marxist, structuralist, etc.

- texts embody attitudes and values rather than present objective realities

- texts may be open-ended or controversial, and ambiguity and uncertainty are legitimate and reasonable responses.

In the examination you will be assessed both on your own interpretations of your chosen poetry text, and also on your responses to other readers' interpretations of the text.

This means that you should have a thorough knowledge and understanding of your poetry text, be flexible enough to take on board other readers' experiences of the text, and be confident enough to express and justify your own responses in both areas. In discussing how various interpretations are justified, by referring to the choices the writer has made, you will also fulfil AO3.

Exploring interpretations for Section A

For each poetry text you are offered six or seven critical perspectives to explore, looking at the ways in which the poet's uses of form, structure and language support this perspective. You can then develop these more fully in your own time.

The General Prologue – Geoffrey Chaucer

In *The General Prologue*, Chaucer introduces the characters who will tell the tales during the pilgrimage to Canterbury. He does so in ways that bring out their vices or their virtues, their dedication to matters material or spiritual. Using the dual narration of 'Chaucer the Pilgrim' and 'Chaucer the Poet' he also supplies a commentary to nudge the reader into certain responses to these characters.

Six critical perspectives are offered on *The General Prologue*:

- *The General Prologue* as a 'concise portrait of an entire nation'

- two methods of presenting character: by outward appearance; by 'inner characterisation'

- Chaucer's use of language

- four stages in the development of *The General Prologue*

- further aspects of the structure of *The General Prologue*

- Chaucer the Pilgrim and Chaucer the Poet.

The General Prologue as a 'concise portrait of an entire nation'

AO4

The claim that *The General Prologue* presents a 'concise portrait of an entire nation' was made by Neville Coghill. In considering this observation, you might ask yourself:

- whether you view *The General Prologue* simply as a series of portraits of individual characters, or

- whether the selection of characters offered may represent a whole nation; and if so, how this is achieved

- whether this portrait is 'concise' but fairly complete.

AO3

You might consider this assertion in various ways, beginning with a portrait of society divided into the 'three estates' of the **medieval** age. These three estates are:

- the military or knightly class

- the clergy and their associates

- the commons.

The Knight and the Squire are of the military or knightly class; the Nun (Prioress), the Monk, and the Parson are of the clergy; and the Doctor, the Franklin, and the Wife of Bath are members of the commons. Does it seem reasonable to suggest that Chaucer does construct a profile of the nation in this way?

ACTIVITY 1

- Do you think that Chaucer uses general terms such as 'the Pardoner' rather than personal names in order to suggest the whole social structure?

- What happens if you arrange the groupings differently, for example:

  - according to wealth, or

  - according to the degrees of their virtue or sinfulness?

Two methods of presenting character: by outward appearance; by 'inner characterisation'

AO4

'The most interesting thing about Chaucer's characters is their physical description.'

Here you are offered an opinion with which you may agree or disagree. You may either:

- agree, and discuss characters such as the Miller and the Cook, showing in what way their presentation is 'interesting', or

- disagree, and discuss the presentation of characters by other means, as in the case of the Parson.

AO3

Presentation by outward appearances

You might consider the presentation of the Miller, as he is described through his physical appearance:

> He was short-sholdred, brood, a thikke knarre;
> Ther was no dore that he nolde heve of harre,
> Or breke it at a renning with his heed.
> His berd as any sowe or fox was reed,

(lines 551–554)

ACTIVITY 2

- What features does Chaucer stress in these lines?

- Why do you think that Chaucer stresses these physical features?

- Why does Chaucer select specific details, use certain similes, and add other details? (This is probably the key question to ask yourself.)

- Why might Chaucer compare the Miller to these animals?

- Why does he add the details of breaking the door?

- Does the characterisation therefore move 'inward'?

You could look at Chaucer's portrait of the Cook to see a similar development.

Presentation by 'inner characterisation'

For this, you might consider the portrait of the Parson. Chaucer offers very little physical detail about the Parson, who is introduced immediately by the use of the word 'Poure'.

> He was a shepherde and noght a mercenarie.
> And though he hooly were and vertuous,
> He was to sinful men nat despitous,
>
> (lines 516–518)
>
> By good ensample, this was his bisynesse.
>
> (line 522)

ACTIVITY 3

- Why might Chaucer immediately stress that the Parson was poor?

- Why might there be no 'outer' description at all?

- Is there any doubt about the goodness of this man?

- Look carefully at the words 'mercenarie' and 'ensample': might Chaucer be making a dig at other characters such as the Knight and the Prioress?

- You should always bear in mind how much of these descriptions Chaucer the Pilgrim might offer, and which aspects might reveal Chaucer the Poet.

To take this a stage further, you could look at the description of the Prioress, and see how both types of description overlap and inter-relate.

Chaucer's use of language

AO4

'Chaucer's language is most interesting when he is being satirical.'

With this observation you are being offered an opinion with which you may agree or disagree. You may either:

- agree, and look at Chaucer's use of satire, or

- disagree, and suggest and illustrate other important aspects of Chaucer's style and method.

AO3

You might consider some of the ways in which Chaucer uses language. These include:

- his use of similes

- his use of 'loaded' words

- his use of **irony**.

Examples of these are discussed below, and you may continue with the work in your own time. Remember, these are just three of the possible areas of aspects of Chaucer's use of language; you may want to consider others.

Chaucer's use of similes

You have already considered Chaucer's use of similes (in Activity 2 above). Here are two further examples. The Summoner is described as being 'As hoot ... as a sparwe' (line 628), and the Squire 'as fressh as is the month of May' (line 92).

ACTIVITY 4

- What does Chaucer suggest through the use of these particular similes?

- Do they help to extend your response to these characters?

Similarly, the Wife of Bath's hat is described as being 'As brood as is a bokeler or a targe' (line 473); and the eyes of the Prioress are described as 'greye as glas' (line 152).

ACTIVITY 5

- Why should the Wife of Bath's hat be linked to the idea of war?

- Why should the eyes of the Prioress be described as though they were a lover's eyes? What might this suggest about your response to her?

Chaucer's use of 'loaded' words

As you read Chaucer, you will soon realise that he repeats certain 'loaded' words in his various portraits. For example, the word 'worthy' in the portrait of the knight, 'gay' in the case of the Yeoman, and 'semely' for the Prioress.

ACTIVITY 6

- What might the word 'gay' tell you about the Yeoman's character?

- Might the words 'worthy' and 'semely' be ironical? Is the Knight really 'worthy'? Should the Prioress be concerned with looking 'semely'?

Chaucer's use of irony

You have just seen how Chaucer sometimes introduces an ironic note into his descriptions. You might also look at some of the comments which Chaucer makes about the pilgrims, such as that directed at the Doctor:

For gold in phisik is a cordial,
Therefore he lovede gold in special.

(lines 445–446)

In modern terms, you might call this a 'snide' comment. Look through the portraits to see where and why these apparently harmless comments are made, often to 'undercut' the portrait offered. You will also see later how the placing of portraits side by side might create irony (see 'Further aspects of structure in *The General Prologue*', below).

Four stages in the development of The General Prologue

AO4

'The structure of *The General Prologue* seems clear when it begins by presenting characters of high social class. Then it becomes a jumble.'

Here you are offered an opinion that seems to suggest that there is no sustained structure in *The General Prologue* after the first few portraits. You may either:

- agree, and see the poem as simply a series of portraits, or

- disagree, perhaps tracing another type of structure in the poem, where the portraits of characters are just a part in the overall design.

AO3

There are four different stages discernible in the development of *The General Prologue*. The first is the introductory – idealised – account of the purposes of pilgrimage (lines 1–18); the second, the description of the pilgrims (lines 19–716); the third, the account of the evening at the Tabard, and the plan to tell the individual tales (lines 717–823); and finally, the drawing of lots to decide the sequence of tales (lines 822–860).

ACTIVITY 7

- Look carefully at the ways in which these parts inter-relate. For example, how does the opening account of the pilgrims' motives throw light on:

  - the individual portraits of the pilgrims
  - what the pilgrims do at the Tabard
  - the apparent necessity of entertainment?

- Are all these different elements compatible, or do they create ironies?

Further aspects of structure in The General Prologue

Chaucer's method of constructing this poem was discussed in 'Aspects of the poetry of Chaucer' in AS English Literature for AQA B, by Childs and Moore, page 69. It would be helpful to look again at that section. As a brief reminder, Chaucer did not work in the same way as modern authors. There is no linear development; rather, different elements are placed together in a specific way for specific purposes. The whole effect, like that of a medieval cathedral, is a juxtaposition of all the parts to make a whole that is **interlaced**.

One of the most important aspects of this approach is the placing of parts or portraits alongside each other. You have already glanced at this in Activity 7 above, and here is another example. The portrait of the worldly and material Merchant is followed by that of the unworldly and spiritual Clerk of Oxenford. Is there a purpose for this placement? Is it ironic? Does it help to enlarge your understanding of both characters?

But Chaucer goes further than just placing them side by side; there are other echoes. The Merchant is described in his conversations as obsessed with 'Sowninge alwey th'encrees of his winning' (line 277) and the Clerk immediately afterwards as 'Sowninge in moral vertu was his speche' (line 309).

ACTIVITY 8

- Why might Chaucer use the word 'sowinge' for both characters? Irony?

- Look carefully through the text to identify other examples.

Chaucer the Pilgrim and Chaucer the Poet

AO4

'There is no significant difference between Chaucer as Pilgrim and as Poet.'

AO3

In considering the relationship between Chaucer the Pilgrim and Chaucer the Poet, you must remember that the Pilgrim has only just met these characters. How much might you expect him to know about them? There will be physical description, perhaps accounts of conversations or attitudes. But you must be aware of the point at which the portraiture goes beyond what the Pilgrim can reasonably know. When there are assessments of character, when there are comments or asides, or when you come to consider any of the aspects of style or structure discussed above, you are working firmly in the area of Chaucer the Poet. You might also consider differences in tone: the naive, often over-enthusiastic descriptions offered by Chaucer the Pilgrim, in contrast to the irony or disapproving tone of Chaucer the Poet.

ACTIVITY 9

- Look carefully through one of the portraits to see how these two areas are interwoven, for example in the portrait of the Knight.

- You might consider the effects of the combination of poet and pilgrim as a source of humour or irony, or a means of adding depth to the characterisation.

Conclusion

This completes your study of six critical perspectives on *The General Prologue* (remember that this list is not exhaustive). Using this model framework, you can go on to explore other critical perspectives on your own, such as Neville Coghill's comment that in *The General Prologue* Chaucer presents a picture of medieval life 'as robust as it is representative'. You should always bear in mind, however, that straightforward character studies are not in themselves sufficient for this level of work. Your views on character must always be seen within the perspectives on Chaucer's methods and purposes outlined above.

Selected Poems – Gerard Manley Hopkins

In 1866 Gerard Manley Hopkins converted to Roman Catholicism and in 1868 he began studying for the priesthood at Stoneyhurst where he developed his distinctive theories of poetry. His central concern was for the appreciation and understanding of God through nature. Hopkins believed that in getting to the essence of a thing – Hopkins called this 'inscape' – in some way it was possible to know something of God himself. The 'inscape' was held together by a force which Hopkins called 'instress'; as this force came directly from God, He was ever-present in nature, and it was even possible to address God directly, as in 'Hurrahing for Harvest'. In this way, Gerard Manley Hopkins's two central experiences, the love of God and the love of nature, were interlinked and so his work as a poet and a priest were in harmony at this stage of his life.

Hopkins became a priest of the Jesuit order in 1877, living for just 12 years after this. However, the work as a priest was taxing; sometimes Hopkins felt great compassion for the poverty amidst which he worked, and expressed this in poems such as 'Felix Randal'. Unfortunately, this work also wore his spirit down, and his despair partly led to the 'Sonnets of desolation', such as 'Carrion Comfort'. Some critics believe that his internal conflict between the love of beauty expressed in his poetry, and the strict vows of poverty, chastity and obedience, importantly intellectual and spiritual obedience, created a breakdown, ending his poetry writing, and perhaps his life.

Critics believe that his poetry is powerful and complex, both emotionally and intellectually, and that there is great creativity as Hopkins strove to find language and forms which he felt allowed himself to express his ideas and feelings powerfully.

Six critical perspectives are to be considered:

- Hopkins's innovative techniques **scape**, inscape, instress, **underthought, sprung rhythm**: 'Binsey Poplars'

- Hopkins' philosophy of nature: 'That Nature is a Heraclitean Fire and of the comfort of the Resurrection'

- Sonnets of joy: 'The Windhover'

- A celebration of God in nature: 'God's Grandeur'

- Poems of compassion: 'Felix Randal'

- Sonnets of desolation: 'Carrion Comfort'

Hopkins' innovative techniques: 'Binsey Poplars'

AO4

'Hopkins felt the need to find a poetic language and form which was natural and echoed the rhythms of speech. How is this evident in his poetry?'

AO3

In this task you are invited to consider Hopkins's techniques, and since this is such a striking part of his poetic skill, it may be helpful to think about some of these before going into his poetry. For this exercise, the selected poem is 'Binsey Poplars'.

Scape is the surface appearance of things before inscape becomes evident.

Inscape is the most famous of Hopkins's invented terms. It refers to the distinctive and essential quality of a thing, its uniqueness, whether of a person, place, animal or object. This 'inscape' is created by God.

Instress is related to 'inscape', as it is the force which holds the unique object together, yet again, a force given by God, showing His presence on earth.

Underthought is the underlying idea within a poem, the deeper 'theme', indicated by language use, such as metaphors.

Sprung rhythm sounds very complicated; however, all you need to grasp is that Hopkins believed that his poetry should be *heard*. By reading poems aloud the sprung rhythm becomes evident, and the example Hopkins himself gave was the reading aloud of 'Harry Ploughman'.

How are these qualities represented in 'Binsey Poplars'?

The first three lines suggest the naturalness and good qualities of the aspens:

> My aspens dear, whose airy cages quelled,
> Quelled or quenched in leaves the leaping sun, …

Look at the image here: you may notice that, as in so much of Hopkins's poetry, it is a strongly visual image; the poplars are like bars holding the sun captive; trees and nature are in harmony.

Then comes the intrusive line which shows how sprung rhythm works:

> All **fe**lled, **fe**lled, are **all** **fe**lled:

(The stresses are in bold.) You will see that the rhythm works exactly as you would read the poem aloud.

Immediately, Hopkins changes the sequence of images:

> Of a fresh and following folded rank
>   Not spared, not one
>   That dandled a sandalled
>   Shadow that swam or sank
> On meadow and river and wind-wandering weed-winding bank.

What is going on in the poem now?

ACTIVITY 1

- Look at the **register** of the words 'felled', 'follower', 'rank'. What sort of people might be thought of here?

- Sandals as part of their uniform might suggest the age of the river. Could the straps of the sandals also represent the criss-crossed shadows thrown by the trees? Who else might have worn sandals? These questions may lead you into the history of the scene.

- Think about the phrases 'wind-wandering' and 'weed-winding': what sort of river course do you imagine? Does it contrast with the harshness and unnaturalness of chopping down beautiful trees? How do the sounds convey the meaning?

- Can you see the inscape of the trees now? Can you see that by blemishing the naturalness of the scene, by cutting down the trees, all that is left is a scape detached from nature and its own past? Look at the later line: 'After-comers cannot guess the beauty been.'

- Can you also see how these metaphors reveal the underthought of the poem?

To reveal the instress of the scene, Hopkins uses a religious **motif**; he echoes the voice of Jesus dying on the cross, calling out to his father: 'Father forgive them for they know not what they do' when he writes:

O if we but knew what we do
　　When we delve or hew—
Hack and rack the growing green!

ACTIVITY 2

- What might Hopkins imply by using this echo of the Bible?

- What is Hopkins's attitude towards the destroyers?

- How does the link with God, and nature, His creation, suggest the instress which gives the scene its strong significance?

You will have seen that these terms are accessible, and help to open up Hopkins's poetry, and to reveal how complex and how tightly woven it is. The sound of the poems read aloud matters, but also the fast sequences of visual images. You could work out a similar exercise using 'Spring and Fall', where the sequence of the destruction of beauty is carried out by nature herself. But why? What had man done to deserve this? You might begin by thinking about the relationship between autumn (or fall), the **Fall of Man,** and the natural cycle of human life.

Hopkins' philosophy of nature: 'That Nature is a Heraclitean Fire and of the comfort of the Resurrection'

AO4

'How might the philosophy of Heraclites affect Hopkins's ideas and his poetry?'

AO3

Here you are asked for a straightforward discussion of a particular poem. In this exercise the focus will rest on this poem only.

This topic follows naturally the study of technical aspects of Hopkins's poetry, because this philosophy underpins much of his work, and this exercise might make some of his ideas clearer and more accessible.

Heraclites was a Greek philosopher who believed that fire was the base and essential element of life. But there must always be change: fire moves downwards to become sea or water; water condenses and becomes earth; earth itself becomes liquid and finally becomes the element of fire which the Sun and the stars represent. In this way, change actually becomes the constant and the unchanging state of nature. How is this idea evident in the poem?

The poem may be seen to celebrate change:

> Delightfully the bright wind boisterous I ropes, wrestles, beats
> earth bare
> Of yestertempest's creases; in pool and rut peel parches
> Squandering ooze to squeezed I dough, crust, dust;

ACTIVITY 3

Can you see the sense of change, but also of vitality in these lines? You might think about the following:

- How does the sequence of verbs in the first line create effects? What effects can you think of?

- What sort of change is captured here?

- Is the tone of the poem lively and accepting, or troubled?

- Do you think that Hopkins sees what he describes as natural and healthy or not?

The ideas of fire and water are developed, as 'nature's bonfire burns on', but the bright fire becomes darkness and is drowned, as is the fame of man on earth, when 'death blots black out'. Perhaps Hopkins is suggesting here that when man is simply a part of natural forces, he counts for little. How does Hopkins suggest that man may defeat the flux and change of nature? The answer is by fire, but by a special sort of fire, revealed in line 15 onwards:

> Enough! the Resurrection,
> A heart's-clarion! Away grief's gasping, | joyless days, dejection.
> Across my foundering deck shone
> A beacon, an eternal beam.
> …
> This Jack, joke, poor potsherd, | patch, matchwood, immortal
>   diamond,
> Is immortal diamond.

In other words, whilst the process of constant change is acceptable and right for nature, man rises above this. How does Hopkins present this idea?

ACTIVITY 4

The idea of the gleam of fire is picked up in the eternal beam of light, the flaming beacon of God's love shown in the Resurrection. You might think about the following:

- How does the Resurrection bring about another change?

- Why might Hopkins use all the different terms to represent man in the long second-to-last line? What do they suggest about his status whilst he is on earth?

- Look at the final change for man: rock hardened by fire becomes carbonised, and forms diamonds. What happens to elements that change in nature?

- How might the fire of love, the fiery force of Christ's love for us and his death and resurrection turn humble man into a diamond? Why is it important that a diamond (even now) symbolises immortality?

- What is the importance of the last short line of the quotation above?

Here is a pretty clear statement of Hopkins's views on the state of nature and of man; nature must always change, and this must lead to decay. But man is different from the world he lives in because of the presence of Christ in our world. You could follow up both ideas in his poetry. All of the nature poems, such as 'Spring', reveal the constant changes in nature; and the late poems, such as 'Thou art indeed just, Lord' reveal how important Hopkins thought it was for man to be resurrected with God. However, remember the inscape of natural beings and objects is never lost. For another clear statement of belief, you could consider 'The May Magnificat'.

Sonnets of joy: 'The Windhover'

AO4

'Gerard Manley Hopkins thought that this was the best of his poems. How far do you agree?'

AO3

Here you are asked to express an opinion and support it by using the texts. You may feel that this is indeed the best of the poems. Or you may wish to disagree, and suggest another from your selection. However, for the next exercise, let's assume agreement, and set out to see why this poem is evidently so successful.

Once again, you need to look closely at the sequence of images; visually, they fade into each other rather as computerised images can be made to do. If you have not seen a kestrel, perhaps you could look at the sequence in the film *Kes* where Billy flies his falcon for his teacher. The first impression you have in the poem is of the bird soaring in the skies. But you need to pick out key words in the first two lines.

ACTIVITY 5

- To get at the heart of what the kestrel represents, his inscape, consider these words: minion, kingdom, and dauphin. How do they 'place' the falcon in the divine scheme of nature? If you remember that 'minion' means favourite, and that the 'dauphin' was the heir to the throne of the kingdom of France, what is the Windhover's relationship to God?

- Remember, the poem is not in praise of the kestrel; it is dedicated to Christ. So who then is the Lord the dauphin serves? In this way you will get to the inscape of the bird.

Initial visual and aural images show the falcon in flight as he swings through the air, his wings wimpling, or quivering to hold his course, as he celebrates the joy of flight, part of his inscape. You will find this series of images in the first eight lines.

However, there is a change in the visual imagery in the next three lines of the sestet:

Brute beauty and valour and act, oh, air, pride, plume, here
   Buckle! AND the fire that breaks from thee then, a billion
Times told lovelier, more dangerous, O my chevalier!

Note: a **chevalier** was a medieval knight.

Suddenly the first image of the bird is overlaid with another image. If you were to see a kestrel full-on, the beak and head are like the colour of armour, bluey-grey; the big beak and chubby cheeks make him look as though he is wearing armour. So what is now being presented in the poem?

ACTIVITY 6

Think of the change in register here, marked by the word 'Buckle'; what might this suggest to you? You might think about the following:

- The moment the wings of the bird fold as he swoops or dives.

- What other meanings are carried? Think about other contexts, the fastening of a buckle: is this a sense of things being brought together?

- How might it apply to a knight going into battle?

- Are you moving to the heart of the poem now? Who might the 'chevalier' of line 10 be?

- The 'fire' is the flash of the bird at speed and the 'fire' of battle. How might this refer to the power of God?

- What is the instress, or link, between nature and Christ — how the poem becomes a prayer?

The final lines switch to another visual image of farming: the initial blue-grey of the bird's feathers suggested armour, and now represents firstly a ploughed field, then the 'blue-bleak' embers of a fire. You might think about how fierce love is kindled from these embers; and also about the 'gall' given to Christ to drink at his crucifixion; what might the 'gash' and 'gold-vermilion' be?

In this exercise the visual aspect of the imagery has been explored; using this as a model, you could go on to consider other joyful poems, such as 'As Kingfishers Catch Fire', 'Hurrahing in Harvest', 'Pied Beauty', 'The Starlight Night' and 'Spring'. In the next section the focus will be on language choices and uses.

A celebration of God in nature: 'God's Grandeur'

AO4

'Hopkins said that the opening image in the poem was that of gold-foil, which when shaken looks like sheet lightning.' How does this comment affect your reading of the poem?'

AO3

To address another aspect of Hopkins's skill, the focus here will be on language choices and sequencing, looking at how the movement of the poem develops. In this poem, Hopkins praises the presence of God in the world. This presence blazes out like gold foil when it is shaken (as Hopkins explained himself), and makes the world alive as if by an electrical charge.

In the first line, four words are linked by the repetition of the letter 'd': world, charged, God and Grandeur. This spells out for you the theme of the poem, the manifestation of God's greatness in our universe. Why are the sounds hard? Could it be to reflect the sudden shock of an electrical charge? This is followed by a linked sequence of words with the 'f' of flame and foil, the 'sh' and the 'z' of ooze, with a return to hard sounds in 'Crushed'. What does this sequence suggest to you?

ACTIVITY 7

You might think about the following:

- How do the quiet sounds mimic the sense of the poem as with all its biblical connotations, olive oil is crushed and harvested?

- How might this quiet and smooth passage reflect peace in the world? How are the brightness of God and His richness represented here?

- What are the effects of the return to a harsh sound in 'Crushed'? Can you see how this word refers to the image of the oil, but also leads into the next harsher section of lines 4–8?

Using the model above, work out how the sequence of images and sound patterning, including the repetition of 'trod', develop the dark meaning of these lines.

The sestet of the sonnet, the last six lines, returns to the quiet mood of the opening. The key effects are achieved by the patterned use of words using the softly sounded letters 'b', 'w', 's'. You will be able to trace the patterning yourself, and see how meanings are developed. The end of the poem may link very clearly with the beginning. Consider the last two lines:

Because the **Holy Ghost** over the bent
  World broods with warm breast and with ah! bright wings.

First of all, think about the images of the first three lines of the poem: the brightness of God and the warmth and richness of crushed olive oil. You will then be able to see how these ideas are re-established in the poem, getting over the harshness of the earlier lines.

ACTIVITY 8

Finally, work out the sense of the last two lines, and ask yourself whether Hopkins aims at reassuring the reader that really all is well in the world. You might think about the following:

- The linking of world, warm and wings: what sort of feeling is conveyed?

- The linking of broods (like a broody hen hatching eggs?), breast, bright: what is the importance of 'breast'? How does this sequence confirm a sense of well-being?

- Why might Hopkins use the quiet exclamation 'ah!'?

Other poems in the 'Sonnets of joy' are expressed using similar techniques: you might begin by looking at 'Hurrahing in Harvest' which has very similar ideas and methods to this poem.

Poems of compassion: 'Felix Randal'

AO4

'How does Hopkins create the note of compassion in his poetry?'

AO3

Here you are asked to make an assessment of a poem particularly concerning tone and mood.

This is one of the poems written a couple of years after the triumphant sonnets. Hopkins is a priest, working in his parish with a sympathetic eye cast on his parishioners. This time the exercise will explore how Hopkins creates tone. The name Felix is Latin for 'happy' or 'fortunate': this will give you a clue to the tone of the poem. The surname 'Randal' may be chosen to suggest 'random' or 'ransom', as is used in the poem.

The poem is based on the story of a young man who dies early of TB; but the poem does not dwell on negatives. That does not seem to be Hopkins's purpose.

The first quatrain might be seen to suggest the lingering death of the young man. But the tone is not angry, or passionate; instead, the death seems to be rather quiet.

ACTIVITY 9

- How does Hopkins create the tone and mood of his choice? With your experience of the last exercise, you will be able to look at word patterning; there is much use of the letters 'w', 'b', 'p', and 's' – all quiet sounding.

- How does Hopkins convey the decay of the youth? Look at his coinage 'hardy-handsome' in line 2 (This hyphenated compound word is typical of Hopkins's use of language.)

- What picture does this convey to you of the physique of the healthy young man?

The second quatrain, among other things, might be seen to explain why the death was quiet, although the man had cursed at first:

> but [he] mended
> Being anointed and all; though a heavenlier heart began some
> Months earlier, since I had our sweet reprieve and ransom
> Tendered to him.

Here Hopkins is referring to the last Sacrament, **Extreme Unction**, given to those dying to ensure passage to heaven. How does Hopkins create the tone of assurance here?

ACTIVITY 10

You might explore:

- how the repetition of certain letters and sounds links the words 'mended', 'being' and 'anointed' to reassure the reader that death is not dreadful

- how the patterning of quiet 's' and 'r' sounds might explain why Hopkins is so certain of this fact, and may be trying to persuade readers of this.

With these models in mind, you will be able to work out the tone of the last stanza. Here you may well find something rather curious; although the last three lines reflect on the life and work of the young man, Hopkins maintains the quiet tone of the poem. How does he do this? Why do you think that he wants to maintain this sense of quiet?

You could then move on to consider another poem, 'Harry Ploughman', where Hopkins again maintains a quiet tone as he explores the 'inscape' and 'instress' of the life of this young man who serves God, and also represents the divine plan in nature as he works amidst nature. However, you could also look at a complete contrast to this poem, 'Tom's Garland'. This dark poem shows how man suffers at the hands of greedy and uncaring government. The garland has echoes of Christ's crown of thorns; man, divorced from his true life, loses his role and divine qualities, being linked instead to animals such as a dog and a wolf.

Sonnets of desolation: 'Carrion Comfort'

This dark poem suggests Hopkins's desolation of spirit and of mind. Loving the beauty he sees in nature as a revelation of God, nevertheless his life was surrounded by the misery of people, their unemployment, riots, and drunkenness. In addition to this, it has been suggested that Hopkins never got over a sense of guilt in writing poetry because of his vows as a Jesuit. All these appear to have combined to crush him, making him 'Time's eunuch', as he says in 'Thou Art Indeed Just Lord'. What might he mean by this? Think of the image of a eunuch unable to create a child; how might this refer to his poetry. This later poem appears to show resignation, but how easily do you think this image sits with the idea of acceptance?

AO4

'Hopkins said of "Carrion Comfort" that it was "written in blood". What do you think he meant by this?'

AO3

Here you are asked to think about Hopkins's own view of his poem. To do so, you will need to explore the ideas and presentation of the poem.

'Carrion Comfort' is representative of the late poems in its tone and ideas. In this exercise there will be a consideration of sound and punctuation. (The title is often presented in brackets because Hopkins left the poem untitled, and Robert Bridges, a friend, named it.)

The very title suggests unease with the hard 'c' sounds and the unpleasant images related to the word 'carrion'; carrion crows, for example, scavage on roads, devouring animals knocked down in traffic. The word 'feast' in the first line also supports this idea. You may think that the title signifies the ideas and the tone. This would appear to be a fair judgement.

The poem is autobiographical, written in the first person. You will immediately notice the layout of the poem: lots of question marks, heavy punctuation with semicolons, dashes, the use of italics. These will alert you to the fact that the poem will be choppy, energetic, and perhaps angry. Have a look at the first eight lines, the octet; how does Hopkins portray himself? He starts off by expressing his state of mind by begging – perhaps God:

> Not untwist – slack they may be – these last strands of man
> In me or, most weary, *cry I can no more*. I can;
> Can something, hope, wish day come, not choose not to be.

ACTIVITY 11

What sort of state of mind is expressed here, and how might the punctuation aid the meaning of the poem? You might ask yourself these questions:

- How might Hopkins display his state of mind by using the dashes of the first line above?

- What are the effects of the use of italics?

- What are the effects of the heavy use of commas in the third line above? How might this display his situation?

As you read on, the idea of the poem being written in blood becomes yet clearer. An image becomes clear, the 'lionlimb': what does this suggest? (In the Bible both the Devil and God are presented as a lion; there is uncertainty as early in the poem as this, as there is in the rest of the poem.) Then as ever, this image is swiftly merged into another: the 'bruised bones' lying 'heaped up': what image succeeds that of the lion? Is there any sense at all that Hopkins has won his great battle?

In the sestet, Hopkins tries to persuade maybe himself, or us, that he has done so. Does this work for you? The doubts creep in through the use of punctuation. Hopkins asserts that he kissed the rod, perhaps a reference to God's rule, and perhaps to the harsh rule of the Jesuits, but look at the last three lines:

Cheer whom though? The hero whose heaven-handling flung me,
    foot trod
Me? or me that fought him? O which one? is it each one? That
    night, that year
Of now done darkness I wretch lay wrestling with (my God!) my
    God.

What is going on here? Yes, it is clear that Hopkins is looking back, telling us that the struggle is resolved, the darkness 'done' and over with, but do you think that the force of the poem really conveys this?

ACTIVITY 12

Look at how significant the punctuation is:

- Look at the series of questions: is there any certainty here?

- Look at the choppy sentence structure, sometimes a three- or four-line sentence asking a question: does this convey calm or certainty?

- Is the man fighting this enemy brave or foolish?

- Do you sympathise with the man or the adversary/victor?

- Do you actually believe that Hopkins has really thrown away the despairing mood of the first eight lines?

For most readers, these late poems reveal the bleak despair of the poet/priest. You will be able to see similarities in the way punctuation supports meaning in 'No Worst There is None', and the sense of inevitably-defeated spirit is evident in the late dark poems such as: 'I Wake and feel the fell of Dark'; 'My own heart let more have Pity on'; 'Patience, Hard Thing!'; and even, as already noted, in 'Thou Art Indeed Just'.

It can be sad to read these poems of despair; to see a spirit die; to compare these with the early poems of joy and happiness in life. But that is what happened to Gerard Manley Hopkins, so perhaps you will carry with you in your head 'The Windhover', to counteract this final sadness.

Conclusion

This completes your work on the Selected Poems of Gerard Manley Hopkins. In exploring the poetry, you have looked at different aspects of the poems: technical terms and their meaning; Hopkins's philosophy of nature; patterning of merged images; language choices and sequencing; tone and mood; finally, language and punctuation. Each of these has been explored in a separate poem. Now it is time for you to return to your selection and, using the models above, relate *all* of these aspects to each poem, perhaps at first working through the grouping suggested in these exercises.

The Rape of the Lock – Alexander Pope

Alexander Pope wrote during the reign of Queen Anne when society became recognisably modern, as money and power were linked to social status. He was critical in some ways of the values of this society, but as he was also a respected member of this society he preserves a balance between affection and criticism in *The Rape of the Lock*.

Pope wrote this poem in response to an actual event which took place in the summer of 1711, when Robert, 7th Lord Petre cut off part of the elaborate coiffure of Arabella Fermor, a society beauty. To add insult to injury the baron then married someone else. This act caused great trouble between the two families, and Pope wrote *The Rape of the Lock* as a private poem to defuse the situation. However, the poem was published anonymously in two cantos in 1712, and caused some offence to people included in it, so Pope wrote the fuller version and it was published in 1714 to great acclaim.

This slight social incident was used by Pope as an opportunity to address larger social concerns. So, whilst the poem pleased people with its **wit** and humour there is some strong criticism of the polite social world where commonsense and good order had been replaced to some extent by concerns for artificiality, foolish conventions, and quibbles over trifles, and where some serious issues of **morality** needed to be addressed.

Six critical perspectives will be offered on this poem:

- Pope's use of the **mock-heroic** genre

- considerations of Belinda and of the ways in which she is presented

- explorations of the image of the 'frail china-jar'

- considerations of the role and significance of Clarissa

- criticisms of the society of the age

- considerations of aspects of Pope's style.

Pope's use of the mock-heroic genre
AO4

'How effectively does Pope use the mock-heroic genre in *The Rape of the Lock*?'

AO3

In this task you are being asked to consider Pope's use of this genre, and how this is suited to his purposes in this poem. To carry this task out several examples of Pope's use of the mock-heroic genre will be explored. These include:

- the worshipping of the Gods before battle (Belinda's toilet)

- the offer of a sacrifice to the Gods (the coffee ceremony)

- the battle or warfare (the card game and the war between the sexes).

What is the mock-heroic genre?

The mock-heroic genre is also known as the mock-epic genre. **Epic** poetry was written as long **narrative poems** to glorify the brave deeds of famous historical or legendary heroes. Pope borrows, for example, from Homer's *Iliad* (which he translated), an account of the battles around the siege of Troy in ancient Greek history. Pope's use of the mock-heroic style in *The Rape of the Lock* uses the conventions from epic poetry to create humour by relating these to much more apparently trivial matters. So he uses these borrowings to play about with scale. Imagine if you look through a telescope or binoculars through the correct end first; then all you see is magnified. But if you reverse this, then all you see is diminished in size. That is roughly how Pope's technique works in this poem. A few examples will make this clearer.

Belinda's toilet

In Canto I Pope presents us with a picture of Belinda at her dressing table, putting on her make-up (or armour) for the affairs (or battles) of the day. This is described as if it is a maiden going to offer prayers at the altar of a goddess before the battle begins:

> And now, unveil'd, the Toilet stands display'd,
> Each silver Vase in mystic order laid.
> First, rob'd in white, the nymph intent adores,
> With head uncover'd, the Cosmetic pow'rs.
> A heav'nly Image in the glass appears,
> To that she bends, to that her eye she rears; (lines 121–126)

Here you have an image of a white-clad virgin getting her precious vials ready to worship the Goddess; but the Goddess of what? Some critics say that she worships herself, but others believe that she is worshipping at the shrine of beauty. This recalls episodes from epics such as the *Iliad*, where the heroes worship at the shrine of the gods to preserve their lives and grant them success in battle. In this sense, the epic echo teases Belinda for her vanity, and makes her concerns look very small. However, Pope goes on to say that Belinda

> Sees by degrees a purer blush arise,
> And keener lightnings quicken in her eyes. (lines 143–144)

ACTIVITY 1

- What is happening here? You might consider:

    - whether she really is presented as being beautiful

    - and also an artist in her make-up skills

    - and whether the 'lightning' from her eyes might not be just as deadly to men as the 'lightning' from, a Trojan warrior's eyes.

- You might then think that on the other hand the mock-heroic style actually makes her affairs seem rather important, so increasing the scale and purposes of her preparations.

The coffee ceremony

This episode occurs after the card game in Canto III, and works in a similar way. The serving of tea becomes a ritual sacrificial offering:

> For lo! the board with cups and spoons is crown'd,
> The berries crackle, and the mill turns round;
> On shining Altars of *Japan* they raise
> The silver lamp; the fiery spirits blaze:
> From silver spouts the grateful liquors glide,
> While *China's* earth receives the smoaking tyde: (lines 105–110)

ACTIVITY 2

- Pope creates here a sense of ritual offerings to the Gods. Do you think it is appropriate or not? You might consider:

    - how Pope uses colour and texture here

    - his uses of sibilance and strong aural and visual effects

    - the references to Japan and China: how might these extend the sense of time and space from one small room in Hampton Court to the whole world?

- Might there then be something significant and ritualistic in this battle between a man and a woman?

The card game of ombre

Yet again, you will be able to see Pope playing about with perspectives here through his use of the mock-heroic tradition. The card game called ombre might be seen to represent the battle between the sexes, at this moment between the Baron and Belinda. Here, in the actual cards themselves, the grand heroic world of epic poetry is miniaturised into the colourful pack of playing cards. Pope describes the Kings 'in majesty revered' and Queens with 'their softer power',

> And particolour'd troops, a shining train,
> Draw forth to combat on the velvet plain.   (lines 43–44)

ACTIVITY 3

- When people play games they enact war situations, usually in a peaceful environment with clear rules; aggressiveness becomes competitiveness. How appropriate a borrowing do you think this is from the epic tradition?

- You might think about the 'velvet plain', originally literally the field of battle. But here, at a garden party and at a card table at Hampton Court, what other meanings might there be?

- How does the use of the mock-heroic tradition help Pope to get his point across with truth but also with humour?

You will be able to find many other examples of this technique as you become familiar with this text.

Considerations of Belinda and of the ways in which she is presented

AO4

'Some critics see Belinda as a bad-tempered flirt; others think that she is presented as an attractive and endearing young beauty. How do you respond to Belinda and the ways in which she is presented?'

AO3

Here you are offered contrasted views on Belinda; you should decide how you see Belinda, and argue your case. In this exercise the argument will support the second viewpoint. (Critics generally believe that this is Pope's own view.) To carry this out, four aspects of Belinda will be explored:

- Belinda as goddess

- Belinda as temptress

- Belinda as warrior

- Belinda as woman.

Belinda as Goddess

In Activity 1 you have seen Belinda worshipping at the shrine of beauty, almost a goddess herself as lightning flashes from her eyes. She is often presented in this way throughout the poem. Here is an example from when she goes down the Thames to Hampton Court at the beginning of Canto II:

> Bright as the sun, her eyes the gazers strike,
> And, like the sun, they shine on all alike.
> Yet graceful ease, and sweetness void of pride
> Might hide her faults, if *Belles* had faults to hide: (lines 13–16)

ACTIVITY 4

- How does Pope present Belinda here? What ideas does he offer? There are some very subtle comments here; you might think about:

  – how Pope conveys her goddesslike power

  – how he conveys her character and appearance.

- Are there any subtle suggestions of flaws, perhaps in the way that the sun shines, or in the idea of flaws?

- What is your impression of Belinda in this passage overall?

Belinda as temptress

Pope makes it quite clear that Belinda is a tease, at the beginning of Canto II:

> This Nymph, to the destruction of mankind,
> Nourish'd two Locks, which graceful hung behind
> In equal curls, and well conspir'd to deck
> With shining ringlets the smooth iv'ry neck:
> Love in these labyrinths his slaves detains,   (lines 19–23)

What is Pope implying here? Do you think that Belinda 'dresses to kill' and is aware of her charms? Well, so is the Baron, whom Belinda discovers she rather fancies. So she decides to play cards with them, in Canto III:

> *Belinda* now, whom thirst of fame invites,
> Burns to encounter two advent'rous Knights,
> At *Ombre* singly to decide their doom;
> And swells her breast with conquests yet to come.   (lines 25–28)

And so the card game starts.

ACTIVITY 5

What do you make of Belinda's attitude and intentions here? You might think about:

- her motives for playing

- her attitude towards the game

- how Pope uses the idea of an epic battle here.

Belinda as warrior

The trouble with the Baron is that he breaks the rules of polite society and offends Belinda when he takes her lock as a trophy. The Baron is not a rapist in the modern sense, although there are echoes of this: he is a raptor. He takes away her lock, but perhaps also takes away some of her heart, 'And wins (oh shameful chance!) the Queen of Hearts', Canto III. Belinda appears to win the card game:

An Ace of Hearts steps forth: The King unseen
Lurk'd in her hand, and mourn'd his captive Queen:
He springs to vengeance with an eager pace,
And falls like thunder on the prostrate Ace.   (lines 95–98)

Belinda has outsmarted him in the game. Because he was defeated, the Baron snips off her lock, and then Belinda changes, as you can see in Canto IV, as she descends into the cave of Spleen and has a tantrum. Is it because of the Baron's insult? Or perhaps do you think that as she secretly fell in love with him, she is peeved because he does not persist? What do you think?

Belinda as woman

Beneath Pope's delicate treatment of the card game, there is a deeper meaning. The Baron has flirted with Belinda. She begins to respond during the card game, but is scared when the Baron wins her heart and she faces temptation:

At this, the blood the virgin's cheek forsook,
A livid paleness spreads o'er all her look;
She sees, and trembles at th' approaching ill,
Just in the jaws of ruin, and *Codille*.   (lines 89–92)

ACTIVITY 6

Here the tone seems to become serious. You might consider:

- why Pope stresses the word 'virgin'

- why Belinda becomes so afraid

- what could lead to her ruin

- what it is the Baron is attempting to achieve (which is represented by the card game).

This leads on to another area of the poem. Pope makes fairly explicit sexual references throughout the poem, including stressing Belinda's hairs. For example, at the end of Canto III,

What wonder then, fair nymph! thy hairs shou'd feel
The conqu'ring force of unresisted steel?   (lines 177–178)

Then, at the end of Canto IV, Belinda wonders:

Oh hadst thou, cruel! been content to seize
Hairs less in sight, or any hairs but these!   (lines 175–176)

And more explicitly, in Canto II when Pope describes the petticoat's hoops which:

Form a strong line about the silver bound,
And guard the wide circumference around.   (lines 121–122)

ACTIVITY 7

- Work out all these sexual references, the hairs, the steel, the circumference and others which are delicately placed throughout the poem.

- Consider what is suggested by the word 'rape'.

- Think about how the direction of the poem has moved from an account of Belinda's day to thoughts about sexual morality and dangers posed to young women.

Many critics believe that these ideas are crystallised in one particular set of images, which will be considered in the next topic.

Explorations of the image of the 'frail china-jar'

AO4

'Several critics believe that the image of the frail china-jar is central to the meaning of the poem. How far do you agree with this judgement?'

AO3

As you get to know the poem you will form your own views on this, and in this section the significance of this image will be explored.

The image of the china vase is referred to explicitly three times in this poem. The first time is in Canto II, when Pope talks of the 'black omens' of Belinda's day:

> Or some frail *China* jar receive a flaw,
> Or stain her honour, or her new brocade,   (lines 106–107)

Then in Canto III Pope talks of the commotion when a dog or husband dies:

> Or when rich *China* vessels fall'n from high,
> In glitt'ring dust, and painted fragments lie!   (lines 159–160)

And in Canto IV Pope comments that 'The tott'ring China shook without a wind' (line 63).

ACTIVITY 8

Think of the context of these images: Belinda has flirted, and then fallen a little in love with the Baron; he has responded with force. Belinda is suddenly in real danger. What might the significance be? Think about:

- the frailty of fine china

- but also that whilst beautiful, it is just decorative if it is without a purpose, an empty vessel.

How might this relate to the virgin Belinda?

This central image is made more explicit by the role which Pope gives to Clarissa in the poem.

Considerations of the role and significance of Clarissa

AO4

'Clarissa has been described as a sour prude, but also as the voice of common sense. How do you respond to Clarissa and her role in this poem?'

AO3

Again, you are offered two views to ponder; you may choose one, or answer on both with a final judgement. Here the second view will be supported.

Pope translated Homer's *Iliad* and commented on the bravery and 'generosity' of Sarpedon, leader of one of the allies who had come to fight for Hector to try to repel the siege of Troy. In one famous speech, Volume III, Book XII, Sarpedon makes a speech showing true bravery and generosity in vowing to give his life to help his friend:

> Brave tho' we fall, and honour'd if we live,
> Or let us Glory gain, or Glory give!

Clarissa's speech in Canto V is an echo of Sarpedon's words as she too tries to defend Belinda in the moment of siege against her honour:

> Say why are Beauties prais'd and honour'd most,
> The wise man's passion, and the vain man's toast?
> Why deck'd with all that land and sea afford,
> Why Angels call'd, and Angel-like ador'd?
> [...]
> How vain are all these glories, all our pains,
> Unless good sense preserve what beauty gains: (lines 9–16)

Clarissa is responding to Belinda's tantrums seen in Canto IV; she is trying to present the view of common sense to put what she might see as Belinda's over-reactions into perspective.

ACTIVITY 9

• Think about what Clarissa has to say here: how does she argue her case?

Additionally, many critics believe that it is Clarissa who expresses the darker side of the poem, as she warns Belinda about real-life problems, and the errors of judgement she believes her friend might fall into. Initially, it was Clarissa who handed the Baron the 'two-edged weapon', the scissors to gain the lock. You might want to think about why Pope uses that particular phrase: what is 'two-edged'? Might it be the meaning? What could Clarissa be keen to cut through apart from the literal meaning of the lock of hair?

Clarissa continues in a sombre tone, presenting to Belinda the dangers of over-reacting to the Baron's assault:

> Oh! if to dance all night, and dress all day,
> Charm'd the small-pox, or chas'd old-age away;
> [...]
> But since, alas! frail beauty must decay,
> Curl'd or uncurl'd, since Locks will turn to grey;
> Since painted, or not painted, all shall fade,
> And she who scorns a man, must die a maid;   (lines 19–28)

ACTIVITY 10

Think about these words of Clarissa's which for the first time bring in the actual problems of eighteenth-century life as they might affect Belinda.

- Why does Pope give Clarissa such dark words?

- Which actual health problems are suggested?

- How is the vision of life presented here?

- What might be the true purpose of Belinda's beauty?

- Why might Pope use the word 'frail'?

These 'grave' words are not popular; look at Thalestris' reactions shortly before, where the concerns seem to be for 'reputation' and 'honour'. Clarissa's cool-headed common sense seems to defy the fun-loving life Belinda obviously enjoys. But it is Clarissa's words that seem to prepare for the ending of the poem:

> When those fair suns shall set, as set they must,
> And all those tresses shall be laid in dust;
> This Lock, the Muse shall consecrate to fame,
> And 'midst the stars inscribe *Belinda's* name.   (lines 147–150)

ACTIVITY 11

How do the closing couplets pick up Clarissa's ideas? You might think about:

- how Belinda might achieve some immortality

- whether this immortality might also extend to Pope in some way

- how you find these lines suitable as an ending to the poem.

Criticisms of the society of the age

AO4

'Critics agree that beneath the humorous surface Pope is critical of his contemporary society. How does Pope present such criticism?'

AO3

You are asked here for some straightforward responses to interpretations of the poem. Here are some of the ideas you might begin to consider.

Criticism of Belinda

Pope does not shy away from gently rebuking Belinda for some superficiality. Here are three examples.

In Canto I Pope lists her collection on her dressing table: 'Puffs, Powders, Patches, Bibles, Billet-doux' (line 138). When she dresses and goes out in Canto II he describes her jewellery: 'On her white breast a sparkling Cross she wore' (line 7). Later, in Canto IV in her tantrum over the Baron she angrily wishes that he had taken 'Hairs less in sight, or any hairs but these!' (line 176).

ACTIVITY 12

- How is Pope criticising Belinda here?

- What is wrong in her attitude to religion, or to morality?

- Might she be truly a little superficial in her ideas?

Of course, criticism extends to other areas of society; to royals and to politicians for example, who 'Dost sometimes counsel take – and sometimes Tea' (Canto III, line 8), and to the system of justice:

The hungry Judges soon the sentence sign,
And wretches hang that jury-men may dine; (lines 21–22)

The aristocrats are mocked for their false values also when they make the same commotion 'When husbands or when lap-dogs breathe their last.'

Beginning with these three examples, you will be able to assess how Pope criticises a society which shows moral disorder, confusion in values, and a muddle about what is trivial and what is significant.

Considerations of aspects of Pope's style

You will become aware as you get to know the poem of how brilliantly and with what great subtlety this poem is written. In assessing these aspects you will be achieving AO4 by responding to the idea that Pope is a great poet and AO3 as you explore the various aspects of style.

Here are a few aspects of style to start you off: the use of the heroic couplet; the creation of texture by the use of the **fixed epithet**; the use of **caesura**; the use of **zeugma**. In each case you will be offered some examples to explore.

The use of the heroic couplet

You need to look at the effects of the stresses and of the end-rhymes here, for example when Pope talks of the impermanence of human vanity or human achievement at the end of Canto III with the date/fate rhyme:

> What Time would spare, from steel receives its date,
> And monuments, like men, submit to fate!   (lines 171–172)

The use of the fixed epithet

In epic poetry there are certain conventional adjectives or adjectival phrases used to create effects, often of grandeur. Pope borrows from this device throughout *The Rape of the Lock*. For example, he builds up effects in Canto I by the use of the words related to gold and silver: the 'golden crowns' and the 'gilded chariots'; there are 'silver vases' on the dressing table. This usage continues throughout the poem. You will be able to extend your list, and work out how these usages create a sense of the beauty and richness of London society.

The use of caesura

This is one of Pope's key devices for implying criticism of his contemporary society. Here is an example from Canto II of how the caesura, a break or pause in the line, works. Pope talks of the dangers which might threaten young women, or perhaps all of society:

> Or stain her honour, or her new brocade,
> Forget her pray'rs, or miss a masquerade,
> Or lose her heart, or necklace, at a ball;   (lines 107–109)

ACTIVITY 13

If you think about these lines, you will find some serious comments on attitudes within society. How does Pope use the caesura to make his point?

You will be able to continue and develop this point through the poem as a whole.

The use of zeugma

This is an important device because Pope's poem works by yoking incongruities together, linking items and ideas that normally do not work together, for example (in Canto III) in the lines addressed to the Queen herself:

> Here thou, great ANNA! whom three realms obey,
> Dost sometimes counsel take – and sometimes Tea.   (lines 7–8)

Clearly Pope hints at moral disorder; by linking incongruous ideas together, Pope suggests impropriety in attitude as it seems that the act of governing is not always taken seriously. As you gain confidence in handling this text you will be able to open up and explore this aspect of Pope's style, perhaps considering how such a device is used to add great humour, but also great sympathy to the tone of the poem.

These are just a few examples to start you off exploring aspects of Pope's style.

ACTIVITY 14

Extend this study of Pope's style on your own. But remember, it is not enough to list and explain characteristics; you must always go on to show how these techniques help to develop the meaning of the poem, perhaps assessing how effective you think that they are.

Conclusion

This completes your study of six critical perspectives on *The Rape of the Lock* by Alexander Pope (remember that this list is not exhaustive). Using this model framework, you can go on to explore other critical perspectives on your own, perhaps beginning with Activity 14, considerations of the purposes and significance of Pope's use of epic '**machinery**', such as the sylphs, the gnomes and the epic battles. You might begin by reading what Pope himself has to say about these things in his introduction to the poem. You might think for example that the idea of the sylphs works on several levels: as the 'airy creatures' of epic myth; as physical manifestations of Belinda's moods; as psychological manifestations of her state of mind, as when she is flirting, or when she is angry and peevish, when Ariel disappears to be replaced as her guardian by Umbriel. Finally, remember the activities you have carried out are based on one set of interpretations of *The Rape of the Lock*. There are many more interpretations, and as you gain in confidence and understanding you will go on to develop ideas of your own in response to this funny, delicate, serious and surprisingly relevant work of art.

The Rime of the Ancient Mariner – Samuel Taylor Coleridge

Coleridge believed that imagination was the driving force behind poetry, and it is thought that he celebrates this in *The Rime of the Ancient Mariner*. A variety of influences lie behind the poem, notably Coleridge's familiarity with the seafaring men he met at Bristol and, through his knowledge of German literature, the story of the **Wandering Jew** and of ships guided by the dead. From his wide reading of travel books he would have learned of strange sea-creatures, of the glow of phosphorescence and lights at sea, of changeable tropical seas, and of the frozen seas of the North. All were combined in *The Rime of the Ancient Mariner* to create a strange and open-ended poem. Coleridge himself said that readers would have to **suspend disbelief** and accept the poem on its own terms.

Seven critical perspectives are offered on *The Rime of the Ancient Mariner*:

- the variety of voices used
- the narrative structure
- mankind and nature
- a religious reading
- a historical reading of I: the French Revolution
- a historical reading of II: the slave trade
- a literary reading: Coleridge's use of the **ballad** form.

The variety of voices in The Rime of the Ancient Mariner

AO4

'It has been suggested that in *The Rime of the Ancient Mariner* there is a mixture of voices in subtle disagreement.'

AO3

There seems to be a range of voices in, and related to, this poem; it is up to you to decide whether you think they disagree or not, and also what their function is. To respond to this critical comment you might consider the reactions of: the Pilot and the Pilot's boy; the Hermit; the Wedding-Guest; the Mariner; the narrator; the poet; and you as reader.

The Pilot and the Pilot's boy

Both of these personae are terrified at the appearance of the Mariner. The Pilot's boy goes crazy, saying 'The devil knows how to row', and the Pilot is 'a-fear'd' and 'fell down in a fit'.

The Hermit

The Hermit's response is very different. Not afraid, he urges them to 'Push on, push on!' to rescue the Mariner. He also fulfils the Mariner's hopes:

He'll shrieve my soul, he'll wash away
The Albatross's blood.

ACTIVITY 1

- What is the difference in attitudes of these three men?

- Do you think that the first two acted in fear and superstition?

- What difference is there in the Hermit's response?

- What might be the importance of the Hermit to the Mariner?

- What different perspectives might these three voices bring to the poem?

The Wedding-Guest

At first the Wedding-Guest is moody, having to listen to this 'loathsome tale'. He is missing the wedding celebrations and hears the 'loud bassoon' ruefully. However, his attitude changes, and he becomes afraid, saying 'I fear thy skinny hand'. He doesn't speak at the end of the poem, but we are told he has been 'stunned'.

ACTIVITY 2

- How does Coleridge use the Wedding-Guest at the start of the poem?

- What do you make of the changing responses of the Wedding-Guest?

- How might he affect your response to the Mariner?

- Might he represent the Church or society that the Mariner seems to reject?

The Mariner

The Mariner is described as 'ancient' – perhaps because he tells an old tale suggestive of myths and legend; perhaps because, as he relates his story, it becomes obvious that he himself lived through it all a long time ago. He has a 'glittering' eye which 'holds' his listener, just as he 'holds him with his skinny hand'. The Wedding-Guest seems to be hypnotised: 'He cannot choose but hear', for the Mariner exerts a strange and compelling power: 'The Mariner hath his will.' At times he seems to be old-fashioned, using the pre-Reformation Catholic prayer 'To Mary Queen'.

ACTIVITY 3

- How many times has the Mariner told his tale? Do you actually know?

- Why do you think the Wedding-Guest feels compelled to listen?

- In the poem, the Mariner tells of supernatural events, but how much of them does he interpret for you or understand himself?

- Do you think the Mariner is fully alive, or is he in a state of death-in-life?

The narrator

The narrator introduces the Mariner very briefly: 'It is an ancient Mariner'. Why do you think this introduction is so brief? And why do you think he uses the present tense? Might it suggest that the Mariner is *always* in this state of life? In the last verse of the poem, the narrator adds the conclusion:

A sadder and a wiser man
He rose the morrow morn.

ACTIVITY 4

- Why might the narrator describe the Mariner at the end of the poem in the same way as he had at the beginning?

- Why might the narrator be made to draw a final moral for the reader?

The poet

You are made aware of the poet's presence through his skilful use of the ballad metre and its variations, the selection and arrangement of episodes, and his ability to resolve the complexities in the poem. An example is the use of the Two Voices (Part One), which the Mariner hears even though he is in a 'trance'. Logically, these voices have to be included in order to explain the ship's movement to the reader. If you look at the gloss Coleridge wrote for the 1817 edition, you can also hear *his* voice as he tells you what to think: 'The ancient Mariner earnestly entreateth the Hermit to shrieve him: and the penance of life falls on him.' Why do you think that Coleridge added this and other glosses?

You as reader

You create another 'voice' in the context of the poem as you think about and discuss its possible meanings and interpretations, and so extend its significance.

ACTIVITY 5

What might be the combined effect of all these different voices?

The narrative structure of The Rime of the Ancient Mariner

AO4

'There is great clarity of design in this poem.'

In response to this claim about the design of *The Rime of the Ancient Mariner*, you may either:

- agree, and demonstrate a clear structure in the poem, or

- disagree, and demonstrate that there is no clear design in the poem. You may think that the poem is open-ended, or even confused.

AO3

One of the key structural devices in *The Rime of the Ancient Mariner* is the reference to the Albatross that ends the first six parts, and is also present in the seventh part. Here are the endings to each part:

- Part One: 'with my cross bow / I shot the Albatross'

- Part Two: 'Instead of the cross, the Albatross / About my neck was hung'

- Part Three: 'And every soul it pass'd me by. / Like the whiz of my Cross-bow'

- Part Four: 'The Albatross fell off, and sank / Like lead into the sea'

- Part Five: this ends with the debate about the Albatross and reference to penance.

- Part Six: 'He'll shrieve my soul, he'll wash away / The Albatross's blood'

- Part Seven: this echoes references to the Albatross made earlier. 'The Ship went down like lead' echoes the end of Part Four, which in turn echoes the words describing the bird as it 'Went down' at the beginning of Part Two, and also the account of the crew as they too 'dropp'd down'.

ACTIVITY 6

- Why might these references be made at the end of each part?

- How might these references help to reveal the structure of the poem?

- What do you think the Albatross might represent? (You might find it helpful to read other perspectives on the poem and then come back to this question.)

Mankind and nature in The Rime of the Ancient Mariner

AO4

Critics disagree over Coleridge's attitude to nature in this poem. Some suggest that in it nature may be seen to have restorative qualities and may offer support to mankind. Others think that nature is presented as **amoral** and indifferent to the well-being of mankind. For yet others, nature in this poem may be seen as only partly curative, at times supportive at other times terrifying.

AO3

One of the difficulties in seeing nature as kindly is that although the Mariner blessed the sea-snakes, this didn't satisfy the Polar Spirit. So perhaps whilst a Christian God was happy, the other, mythological figure, was not, and doomed the Mariner to penance:

> He loved the bird that loved the man
> Who shot him with his bow.

When the ship is becalmed, the water is terrifying:

> Water water, every where,
> […]
> Nor any drop to drink.

Elsewhere nature is shown as ugly:

> The very deep did rot: […]

ACTIVITY 7

- What qualities can you see in nature here?

- Might there be a suggestion of a need to co-operate with nature?

To assess Coleridge's attitude to nature you could consider his relationship with his friend William Wordsworth, the great poet of nature. Wordsworth believed that nature was kindly and revealed God's workings, as part of a Divine Universe, so that if people become part of nature they will find emotional, spiritual and physical completeness. Many critics think that the Hermit represents Wordsworth:

> He singeth loud his godly hymns
> That he maketh in the wood.

He seems at peace with nature. But the Hermit has his limitations, as he thinks that the Mariner's ship is 'skeletons of leaves'.

ACTIVITY 8

- What do you make of the Hermit?

- Is he able to help the Mariner?

- Is his knowledge limited to what he can perceive through nature?

- Might his sort of natural knowledge be the best sort? Better, perhaps than the formal religion of the Wedding-Guest at the Kirk?

- Do you think that overall Coleridge had an ambiguous attitude to nature?

A religious reading of The Rime of the Ancient Mariner
AO4

'*The Rime of the Ancient Mariner* is a parable of guilt and redemption.'

In response to this comment you could look at three areas:

- the poem as a parable (a story with a moral)

- mankind's guilt

- mankind's redemption.

You may agree with this comment, disagree, or agree with a part of it.

AO3

You could consider the poem in terms of three areas:

- the **sacramental** aspects of the poem

- the Old Testament

- the New Testament.

Remember, when you consider readings of the poem, you should always bear in mind that these are interpretations by other readers: the author did not necessarily intend them. These suggested readings are applied to specific parts or specific incidents in this poem, rather than to the poem as a whole. You may agree or disagree with them.

Sacramental aspects of the poem

The areas in the poem that can be termed sacramental are those which relate to religious practices and sacraments. These include the references to the cross, related to both the Albatross and the Hermit, who might be seen to administer the sacrament of Holy Confession. In order to receive Holy Confession, a person must feel contrite for his/her sins, confess them, and then perform a penance. The Hermit begins this process when he asks the Mariner, 'What manner of man art thou?' The Mariner tells the tale of his sins, and thus carries out his penance by telling his tale. The sacramental act of prayer is apparent:

> He prayeth well, who loveth well
> Both man and bird and beast.

ACTIVITY 9

- Do you think that the telling of the tale is the Mariner's atonement for his sins?

- What about the crew? What did they do, and what happened to them?

The Old Testament

If you recall the biblical story of Cain and Abel, you will remember that Cain killed his own brother, the first sacrifice. But strangely, the killing became part of the route that led to mankind's salvation (you could consider it as prefiguring Christ's death). What about the Mariner? Did he commit a 'murder'? But was he also a victim of the unkindly Polar Spirit? Was he punished for the whole crew, who thought at one point that it was right to kill the bird? Do you think that the Mariner could be a mixture of both Cain (who was condemned to wander the earth as punishment for his crime) and Abel?

The New Testament

This area is concerned with the biblical story of Christ's death on the cross in order to redeem mankind. When reading the poem, you can see a picture of the Mariner with the Albatross hung around his neck like a cross. The Mariner says that he suffers 'a woeful agony', and he repeats the word 'agony'. Perhaps he suffers to atone for the sins of the whole crew.

ACTIVITY 10

- Do you think that there are suggestions that the Mariner can be understood as both Cain and Abel?

- Do you think he might be seen as a Christ-like figure?

A historical reading of The Rime of the Ancient Mariner I: the French Revolution

AO4

'Referring to the French Revolution, Coleridge said that he felt guilt for believing that "mankind could improve itself by its own actions without grace".'

In this comment you are told of Coleridge's views on the French Revolution. He felt that without the Grace and help of God, mankind was helpless. You may agree that there is a reading of the poem which refers to the French Revolution, or disagree and offer an alternative reading.

AO3

Originally the French Revolution had many supporters because of its aim of overthrowing a corrupt monarchy in order to establish 'Liberty, Equality and Fraternity' for all. But the revolutionaries became as corrupt as the old monarchy, massacring many thousands of innocent people in a reign of terror. Some critics see this later stage represented in *The Rime of the Ancient Mariner*. To consider this perspective you might think about the questions in the next activity.

ACTIVITY 11

- When, where and why does the community on the ship seem to have broken down?

- Did the crew, and especially the Ancient Mariner, have any freedom?

- The nature of the justice you see in the poem: you might think about whether the crew deserve to die, and whether the Ancient Mariner's punishment is just or too harsh. Might the justice meted out to him seem random or arbitrary, given that the Spirits don't agree over his case?

- What degree of violence is evident in the events of the poem? You could list all the physical and mental violence that occurs to human and non-human beings.

A historical reading of The Rime of the Ancient Mariner II: the slave trade

AO4

'Coleridge felt that the slave trade implicated all of his countrymen in "a shameful commerce". This is what *The Rime of the Ancient Mariner* is about.'

In this comment you are told of Coleridge's response to the slave trade as carried on by Britain, as well as by other nations. He thought that this sort of trade was 'shameful'. You might agree that the poem refers to the slave trade, or disagree and offer an alternative reading.

AO3

To consider this aspect you might think about the questions in Activity 12 below.

ACTIVITY 12

- Is the spectral ship a slave ship, rotted with the diseased slaves it carried?

- Might the Mariner with the Albatross around his neck be seen to carry the chains of a slave?

- Might the Mariner, in his loss of home and freedom, his forced penance, and his physical and mental suffering, be like a slave?

A literary reading: Coleridge's use of the ballad form

AO4

'Coleridge uses a simple ballad form in *The Rime of the Ancient Mariner*.'

Here you are offered a comment about the sort of poem that Coleridge wrote. You are invited to agree or disagree about whether he used the ballad form, and whether his use of it was simple.

AO3

To respond to this perspective you might consider whether certain characteristics of the ballad form are evident in this poem. These are reviewed in Activity 13 below.

ACTIVITY 13

Which of the following characteristics of the ballad form do you find in *The Rime of the Ancient Mariner*:

- a vividly told story

- a tale of heroism and suffering

- certain **stock** characters (such as the Spirits)

- certain stock events (such as battles)

- the use of simple, brief dialogue

- the use of some sort of refrain

- a simple four-stressed rhythm (which may be complicated at times)

- as a ballad in the Romantic tradition, a stress upon the importance of the imagination?

Conclusion

This completes your study of seven critical perspectives on Coleridge's *The Rime of the Ancient Mariner* (remember that this list is not exhaustive). Using this model framework, you can go on to explore other critical perspectives on your own, perhaps looking at the **socialist** reading of the poem, based on the idea of the ship as a community.

Prescribed poems – Alfred Lord Tennyson

Tennyson published poetry for sixty-five years of his long life, and the prescribed poems cover a span of fifty-nine of those years. He was appointed Poet Laureate when he was forty-one, and was initially much loved by his readers, although his poetry became less popular in the later years of his life. Critics generally praise the musical and **lyrical** qualities of his poetry; they also point to an inner conflict in Tennyson's mind. This conflict may have been a reflection of the tensions inherent in the robust industrial world of Victorian England; in particular, he struggled with the poet's sense of isolation in such a society.

Seven critical perspectives are offered on the prescribed poems by Alfred Lord Tennyson:

- suppressed sexuality: 'Locksley Hall'

- landscape in Tennyson's poetry: 'Mariana'

- the relationship of the poet to society: 'The Lady of Shalott'

- social commentary: 'Godiva' and 'Locksley Hall'

- the conflict between freedom and duty: 'Ulysses'

- the use of the **dramatic monologue**: 'Tithonus'

- the significance of the sea: 'Break, Break, Break' and 'Crossing the Bar'.

Suppressed sexuality: 'Locksley Hall'

AO4

'Tennyson did not explicitly write about love or sexuality; but these subjects are an undercurrent in "Locksley Hall".'

Here you are offered a viewpoint on the poem. You are free to disagree by offering different readings of the poem, or you might agree and try to track the voice in the poem which may be seen to discuss these topics.

AO3

First you might trace the movements in the poem, and consider:

- the speaker's initial tone

- the reasons for this tone and the rejection of his love

- the speaker's reaction to rejection

- the way forward found

- the final image.

'Locksley Hall' is a multi-layered poem, each layer put down by a different voice, each promoting a different theme to present a jigsaw puzzle of a poem. Tennyson had been rejected by Rosa Baring of Harrington Hall, but while this experience may have sharpened his feelings, it would be unwise to identify Tennyson and the speaker too closely. As it is a complex poem to address, it might be helpful for you to follow the outline above.

The speaker's initial tone

The poem opens on a loud and assertive note, as the speaker seems to address his male friends:

Comrades, leave me here a little, while yet as 't is early morn:
Leave me here, and when you want me, sound upon the bugle-horn.

What do you make of this mood? It is rather contradictory, as he wants to be with his friends, yet wants to be left alone; he seems rather passive and isolated, as he leaves it up to them to call him. Why is he so thoughtful? Why is he seeking male company? Could it be because of a failed love affair?

The reasons for this tone and the rejection of his love

Very soon it is revealed that this is the case. The speaker has been rejected by his beloved 'Amy', the name meaning love. How does he explain the rejection? Amy is:

… Puppet to a father's threat, and servile to a shrewish tongue! …

ACTIVITY 1

- Why does the speaker think Amy has rejected the speaker?

- What are the attitudes of her parents?

- What might these suggest about Victorian society and morality?

The speaker's reaction to rejection

Obviously angered, the speaker implicitly compares the love he offered to that which the new husband will offer:

As the husband is, the wife is: thou art mated with a clown,
And the grossness of his nature will have weight to drag thee down.

The speaker then links the husband's love to that offered to a 'dog' or a 'horse'.

ACTIVITY 2

- In what terms does the speaker define her new 'love'?

- Does he see sexuality as natural and healthy, or gross and distorted here?

On the other hand, the speaker has clear, strong and sexual memories of his own love-making with Amy, and has a better solution to the present situation than her 'forced' marriage:

Better thou and I were lying, hidden from the heart's disgrace,
Roll'd in one another's arms, and silent in a last embrace.

ACTIVITY 3

- What alternative does the speaker offer here?

- How does he suggest sexual closeness?

- What are the links between sex and death here?

The way forward found

After much ranting and raving, the speaker finds a solution to his wretched state of mind. He suppresses his sexuality, or perhaps converts his sexual vigour into the energy of Victorian industry and enterprise:

I myself must mix with action, lest I wither by despair.

Here the speaker finds a solution in Victorian industrialism and commerce, a 'Vision of the world', of the vigour of industrialism, the 'ringing grooves of change'. It is a solution which you will come across often in Tennyson's poetry, for it is linked to a vision. But, curiously, it is a vision of the future in terms of the past, at times like Paradise, '… the heavy-fruited tree— / Summer isles of Eden'.

Typically, Tennyson does not offer a rational solution for the speaker, but offers an escape into a dream or visionary world away from problems. So the poem takes on a triumphant tone, but the ending is curious.

The final image

Surprisingly, the speaker has not yet finished with his attack upon Locksley Hall and the values represented there. He ends the poem with an image of oppositions as a thunderbolt destroys hall and inhabitants:

Let it fall on Locksley Hall, with rain or hail, or fire or snow;
For the mighty wind arises, roaring seaward, and I go.

Here it is helpful to look at Tennyson's technique as well as his ideas.

ACTIVITY 4

- Can you see the opposition in the scheme of spaces here?

- Can you sense the claustrophobia of the house, a feeling of being trapped, socially and emotionally?

- Do you recognise the contrasted freedom offered by the sea, supported by the mighty vigour of the wind, perhaps the wind of change in society?

- Look at the punctuation, and how the pace of both lines is controlled.

- How do the patterns of alliteration, such as 'r' and 's' , help the sense?

But remember, a study of 'Locksley Hall' should cover several areas, including the speaker's praise for Victorian achievement and his fears of democracy. You can also see more attitudes to sexuality in 'Godiva', for example.

Landscape in Tennyson's poetry: 'Mariana'

AO4

'In his poetry Tennyson presents landscape as a mood or state of mind.'

Here it is suggested that Tennyson uses landscape in his poetry to create a mood, but also a state of mind. You could respond in one of three ways:

- agree, demonstrating how Tennyson uses landscape for both purposes

- partly agree, showing how he uses landscape for only one of these purposes, or

- disagree, suggesting completely different uses for landscape (such as creating a vivid picture).

AO3

In this area you might consider how Tennyson uses landscape to present a situation in which there is no possibility of action. Some critics claim that the subject matter of 'Mariana' is inaction and isolation. Might Tennyson feel that this is the situation of the poet in the modern world?

In the first stanza of the poem, Tennyson emphasises sadness and decay. He first describes the house, concluding:

Weeded and worn the ancient thatch
Upon the lonely moated grange.

ACTIVITY 5

- What sort of a picture does Tennyson present here?

- How does he present a picture of decay?

- How is the isolation conveyed?

- How is this conveyed by sound effects? (Consider for example the use of soft consonants such as 'w', and internal half-rhymes, such as 'moated' and 'lonely'.)

Tennyson then moves from a description of the house to a description of the landscape around the house:

Hard by a poplar shook alway,
    All silver-green with gnarled bark:
    For leagues no other tree did mark
    The level waste, the rounding grey.

ACTIVITY 6

- How is the isolation conveyed here?

- Why do you think the colours are dark or drab?

- What might the shaking poplar represent?

- Consider his use of sound effects (such as the soft 's' and 'd' sounds, and the rhymes). How might such effects help to convey a mood?

You might think that in Mariana's refrain 'I am aweary, aweary' Tennyson emphasises her unhappiness and isolation. Why do you think the second line of the refrain changes in the last verse? In this presentation of an isolated, lonely individual who cannot help her situation, do you think that the poet could be using this female character from a different period to suggest certain conditions of his own mind? Do you think that he succeeds in presenting such conditions?

To discuss this issue, you might also refer to 'The Lady of Shalott' and 'St Agnes' Eve'; and to discuss his use of landscape, you might study 'To Virgil' and 'The Brook'.

The relationship of the poet to society: 'The Lady of Shalott'
AO4

'Tennyson makes melancholy the subject of his poetry.'

AO3

One of the questions often asked about 'The Lady of Shalott' is whether it is a mirror of Tennyson's own experience – his use of a mirror may certainly suggest as much. As in 'Mariana', you might also find evidence of a lack of harmony within the poet and in his relationship with nature and society. In 'The Lady of Shalott', Tennyson describes the island as follows:

> Four grey walls, and four grey towers,
> Overlook a space of flowers,
> And the silent isle imbowers
> The Lady of Shalott.

ACTIVITY 7

- Why are the words 'four' and 'grey' repeated?

- Why is there emphasis on space and silence?

- What might be the force of the word 'imbowers'?

Tennyson then describes the lonely and repetitive life of the Lady:

> But in her web she still delights
> To weave the mirror's magic sights,
> For often thro' the silent nights
> A funeral, with plumes and lights,

ACTIVITY 8

- Does she have any part in social life?

- What is the function of the mirror?

- Might there be a reference here to the role of women at the time?

Tennyson goes on to describe the effects of the 'meteor' that disturbs her life when Lancelot rides by:

> Thick-jewell'd shone the saddle leather,
> The helmet and the helmet-feather
> Burn'd like one burning flame together,

ACTIVITY 9

- How does Tennyson convey the masculine image of Lancelot here?

- How does he create vitality and texture?

- Why is there a double stress on 'burning'? Might it be sexual?

- Might the lady be destroyed for feeling such emotions?

To take the idea a little further, you could consider what Tennyson suggests about society, and how he presents the mirror. Society appears in the references to the funeral pageantry and lovers. But the Lady is apart from them. Might there be a suggestion that such things will not concern an isolated poet? Might her state of mind again be that of the poet in disguise? Tennyson writes:

The mirror crack'd from side to side:
'The curse is come upon me,' cried
    The Lady of Shalott.

ACTIVITY 10

- Might the mirror represent the poet's relationship with society?

- Might there be a suggestion that art mirrors life?

- Might there be a suggestion that though the poet observes society, he is not a part of it?

- Might the poem be seen as an expression of the poet's alienation from society?

You might also consider 'Mariana' and 'St Agnes' Eve' here.

The conflict between freedom and duty: 'Ulysses'

AO4

'Tennyson uses mythology to discuss contemporary matters, and matters concerning his inner feelings.'

In this comment two uses of mythology are suggested: Tennyson may wish to discuss matters concerning the society in which he lives, or matters that concern himself. Here you may:

- agree that myth is used for either or both of these purposes; or

- think of other purposes that would allow you to disagree in part with this opinion.

AO3

Perhaps Tennyson allows the character Ulysses to present his own ideas about loss of identity.

You can identify four stages in the poem. In the first few lines (1–5), Ulysses explains the situation that forced him to make the decision to travel; in the following lines (6–32), he justifies his need for travel and experience; in the third part (lines 33–43), he thinks about his son, Telemachus; and in the fourth and final part (line 44 to the end) he makes heroic claims about what he intends to achieve. Critics have suggested that this is an exploration of the role and trials of the poet in society.

Having justified his need to travel ('It little profits that an idle king'), and having rejected his wife, family and responsibilities, Ulysses describes how it is vile:

For some three suns to store and hoard myself,
And this gray spirit yearning in desire
To follow knowledge like a sinking star,
Beyond the utmost bound of human thought.

ACTIVITY 11

- What is the tone of the conclusion to this part of the poem?
- Is there any sense of spiritual fulfilment here?
- Might the 'fading margin' be death?
- Is it enough just to experience things? Or are the feelings important, too?

In the third part, the poem seems to change tone: here Ulysses thinks of his son, Telemachus, recalling his virtues and his rule 'by slow prudence':

Most blameless is he, centred in the sphere
Of common duties, decent not to fail
In offices of tenderness, [...]

ACTIVITY 12

- Is Ulysses wholly blameless in leaving these responsibilities behind?
- Are these social and religious virtues necessary to society?
- Is Ulysses therefore alienated, unable to move away from a heroic past to a more ordinary life in society?
- Again, might this be the situation of the poet?

The conclusion to the last part of the poem might seem ambiguous. Again, it could be that Tennyson sounds a note of heroic challenge as Ulysses urges his band 'to seek a newer world', to gain experience until death. Tennyson concludes the poem with a bold-sounding statement:

> One equal temper of heroic hearts,
> Made weak by time and fate, but strong in will
> To strive, to seek, to find and not to yield.

ACTIVITY 13

- Which do you think is important in the poem – the striving or the achievement?

- Might this refer to a sense of duty in the face of difficulties?

- Might it refer to the courage to carry on the ancient tradition of being a poet?

- Might it refer to the fact that the poet has to live in contemporary society, but finds it hard to do so?

You might also consider 'Tithonus', 'The Lotus-Eaters' or 'Locksley Hall' here.

The use of the dramatic monologue: 'Tithonus'

AO4

'Life involves maintaining oneself between contradictions that can't be solved by analysis.'

This critic offers the opinion that in life there are contradictions which we are forced to accept and live with. They cannot be resolved by analysing them. You are asked if this line of thought is evident in Tennyson's poetry. You may either:

- agree, showing that there are conflicts in the poetry which cannot be resolved, or

- disagree, showing that in certain poems contradictory situations or ideas are resolved.

AO3

You could consider here whether Tennyson uses the dramatic monologue to re-create certain types of personal experiences, but by using the persona of the speaker is able to distance himself from what that persona says. Again, you may feel that Tennyson explores a state of mind which reveals his own attitudes, feelings and thoughts.

As in 'Ulysses', Tennyson here uses classical mythology: in this case, the myth of Tithonus, who was granted immortality by the goddess Aurora, but not eternal youth. Tithonus looks around him as he ages, and wishes that he were part of the natural cycle and so able to die:

> The woods decay, the woods decay and fall,
> The vapours weep their burthen to the ground,
> Man comes and tills the field and lies beneath,
> And after many a summer dies the swan.
> Me only cruel immortality
> Consumes: I wither slowly in thine arms,
> Here at the quiet limit of the world,
> A white-hair'd shadow roaming like a dream.

ACTIVITY 14

- How does Tennyson present the natural cycle of life and death here?

- How does Tennyson present the unnaturalness of Tithonus's situation?

- What might be the effect of the word-order of line 4 of this extract?

- What might the 'quiet limits of the world' represent?

- Who might the 'white-hair'd shadow' be? Might this also represent the poet?

Tennyson presents the effects of ageing in Tithonus's responses and diminishing vigour. At first, the landscape is presented with great beauty as Tennyson describes the time when Tithonus felt his blood

> Glow with the glow that slowly crimson'd all
> Thy presence and thy portals, [...]

Then Tennyson shows how the aged Tithonus later feels:

> Coldly thy rosy shadows bathe me, cold
> Are all thy lights, and cold my wrinkled feet

ACTIVITY 15

Compare the language in the two brief extracts above: how is vitality conveyed in the first extract? You might look at:

- the use of colour

- the use of active verbs

- the sound patterns, in particular **assonance** (such as 'glow', 'slowly')

- the use of repetition.

Now look at the second brief extract:

ACTIVITY 16

- What has happened in this extract? How is it conveyed?

- What has happened to the colours?

- What is the effect of repetition here?

- What are the effects of the use of the hard consonant 'c'?

- Where do the stresses fall in the second line?

- Might Tennyson be reflecting on his own loss of poetic energy?

At the end of the poem Tithonus expresses a tragic outlook: he wishes to die, and not to be cut off from the rest of nature by his immortality:

Of happy men that have the power to die,
And grassy barrows of the happier dead.

You might also consider 'Ulysses', 'The Lady of Shalott', and the use of different voices in 'Locksley Hall' here.

ACTIVITY 17

- How does Tennyson present Tithonus and his state of mind now?

- How might the loss of energy and life be a goal worth achieving?

- Might this be the presentation of a nightmare for the poet: weak and not able to be what he was, but forced to continue writing?

Social commentary: 'Godiva' and 'Locksley Hall'

AO4

'Tennyson avoids the discussion of views related to the society of his age.'

Here you are asked to consider whether Tennyson ignores social matters in his poetry. You could either:

- disagree, and discuss poems which you think demonstrate his concern with society, or

- agree, and suggest that Tennyson has other reasons for writing his poetry.

AO3

Tennyson cleverly uses historical perspectives when he looks at a past episode from the perspective of his own age. You might consider four places in the poem 'Godiva' where Tennyson seems to be making social comments:

ACTIVITY 18

- Why does Tennyson use the setting of a Victorian railway station, but talk about the past? Might he be trying to avoid criticism himself for criticising certain aspects of his own age?

- Lines 1–23: might the taxes refer to aspects of policy in his own society?

- Lines 24–25: might the husband's patronising attitude to his young wife say something about the treatment of women in Victorian society?

- When Tennyson refers to the 'blind walls', and 'Chinks' and 'holes', might he be mocking Victorian prudishness or hypocrisy?

You might also consider 'Locksley Hall' here; think about the praise of industry and its leaders, for example stanzas 60/61ff; the fear of the social unrest of Chartism, stanzas 69ff, and the apparent approval of colonialism with the 'savage woman', stanzas 85ff.

The significance of the sea: 'Break, break, break' and 'Crossing the Bar'

AO4

'Imagery related to the sea was important in Tennyson's poetry.'

Here you are asked to consider Tennyson's use of sea imagery, and the effects created by this imagery in Tennyson's poetry.

AO3

'Break, break, break' and 'Crossing the Bar' offer two contrasting examples.

'Break, break, break', as the repetitive title suggests, is a bleak poem about heartbreak and loss, probably brought about by the loss of Tennyson's dear friend, Arthur Hallam. Again, Tennyson creates oppositions in his poem to achieve his effect. He describes 'the fisherman's boy' who 'shouts' with his sister and 'the sailor lad' who 'sings in his boat', but the poet cannot 'utter' his distress. Meanwhile, the sea has a pattern, as it will continue to 'break, break, break' on the shore, below the 'crag'.

ACTIVITY 19

- How does Tennyson use this contrast?

- Look at the poem and explore the use of the senses and of repetition.

- Is there any sense of hope here, or does the speaker feel that all life is pointless?

- Might the lack of the poet's voice suggest something about writing poetry?

In complete contrast to the image of the sea you have just looked at, Tennyson offers a totally different response in his poem 'Crossing the Bar'. He requested that this poem should always be placed last in a collection, and so it is here at the end of this section.

Tennyson's request seems to say a lot about his own feelings about this poem; perhaps he felt that he had achieved peace in his life and so was resigned about death.

The perfect form of the poem might suggest this harmony. You might consider here both the ideas, and also the language and form of the poem.

ACTIVITY 20

- Compare the tone and mood of this poem to those of poems you have looked at already: how is it different? How would you describe the mood?

- What might the image of crossing the bar suggest?

- Look at the use of language: quiet words, perfect rhymes – how does this help to present the meaning?

- Look also at the line lengths: why is the long line always checked by the shorter following line? Might this remind you of the movement of the waves?

Conclusion

This completes your study of seven critical perspectives on the prescribed poems by Tennyson (remember that this list is not exhaustive). Using this model framework, you can go on to explore other critical perspectives on your own, perhaps beginning with a consideration of the role of women in society as presented in 'St Agnes' Eve'.

Prescribed poems – Emily Dickinson

The American poet Emily Dickinson is something of a puzzle for biographers, as she never revealed the facts behind two key events in her life. The first of these is what she called in a letter 'the terror of September 1861'. Some critics have guessed that it might be linked to the illness of her brother between 1856 and 1860; others think that it may have been a failed love-affair, heterosexual or gay; and others suggest that she may have had a nervous breakdown. Whatever the cause, in many of the poems written after that date, which include those in this selection, there is a sense of terror at something unspecified.

The second notable event of her life was her withdrawal from society, which she admitted herself in a letter of 1866: 'I do not cross my father's ground to any House or Town.' Again there are uncertainties about the cause, possibly a breakdown, rejection in love, the death of a friend, the serious problems she had with her eyesight or perhaps boredom with society. This sense of isolation is evident in many of her poems.

Six critical perspectives are offered on the prescribed poems by Emily Dickinson:

- poems that may be interpreted as dramatic monologues

- poems written from the perspective of the dead or of death

- poems about nature

- poems that move from outward observation to inner contemplation

- poems with biographical concerns

- poems that present common experiences.

You will see that for the purpose of these activities, the prescribed poems have been divided into six groups. But remember that these groupings are not authoritative: you may choose to place the poems in totally different groupings, or place individual poems in several groups.

Poems that may be interpreted as dramatic monologues
AO4

What are Emily Dickinson's 'dramatic monologue' poems?

In this type of poem Emily Dickinson imagines a specific voice, and often a specific situation. Elizabeth Philips, for example, suggests that Emily Dickinson 'created not one, but many persona whose voices enlarge our visions of life – and of death'. In this category you could consider the poem 'Because I would not stop for Death', in which a 'gentleman' takes a younger person, presumably a lady, for a coach ride:

Because I could not stop for Death,
He kindly stopped for me;
The carriage held but just ourselves
And Immortality.

ACTIVITY 1

- What does Dickinson imagine here? Might it be both a voice and a situation?

- Is it an individual experience or one that is shared with the reader?

The poem continues with some narrative:

We passed the school where children played
Their lessons scarcely done;
…
We paused before a house that seemed
A swelling on the ground;

And then the conclusion of the poem is reached:

I first surmised the horses' heads
Were toward eternity.

ACTIVITY 2

- What sort of description of the early evening ride is offered?

- What might the house with the 'swelling ground' suggest?

- Why might the horses' heads turn towards eternity?

AO3

How Dickinson presents this dramatic monologue

Looking at the first quotation above, you might ask yourself:

ACTIVITY 3

- Might the poet be using the image of a young lady seduced by a lover?

- What is the tone at the beginning of the poem? Does it change?

Then you might look again at the second and third extracts above, asking yourself questions such as:

ACTIVITY 4

- How does Dickinson create the suggestion of human activities?

- How does she introduce the thoughts of death?

- How is the image of the journey used overall?

- How would you define the tone of the poem? Is there any change from the casual opening? Is it shocking? Or menacing? Or dramatic?

These characteristics seem to typify Emily Dickinson's style in these dramatic monologues. The reader is first drawn into the poem by a deceptively casual tone; there are then changes of tone, pace and language; and finally the poem moves from the outer human world to an inward contemplation of death.

You might also consider under this heading 'I dreaded that first Robin, so' and 'The only ghost I ever saw'.

Poems written from the perspective of the dead or of death
AO4

Emily Dickinson often wrote about death and about what happens after death.

Several critics – such as Yvor Winters, believe that she was wholly successful in conveying the sense of what is left behind at death.

To explore this type of poem, you might consider ''Twas just this time last year I died':

'Twas just this time last year I died.
   I know I heard the corn,
When I was carried by the farms, –
   It had the tassels on.

ACTIVITY 5

- Can you tell that this is written from the viewpoint of a child?

- What does the dead person recall about life? Is this a country person?

You can now read the whole poem. You will see that the first three verses describe country life, and then the focus changes to family life:

If father'd multiply the plates
    To make an even sum.

And if my stocking hung too high,
    Would it blur the Christmas glee,

ACTIVITY 6

- Are there other family members presented in the poem now?

- How might they be seen to react to the absence of the dead child?

At the end of the poem the perspective seems to be adjusted again, where the 'I' persona says that 'this sort' of memory is hurtful, so thinks about:

When just this time, some perfect year,
    Themselves could come to me.

ACTIVITY 7

- What sort of comfort does the child-persona find?

- Is there any sense that death is the end of everything?

- Alternatively, is some sort of life after death suggested?

AO3

How Dickinson presents these ideas

> ### ACTIVITY 8
>
> You might consider the way the world of nature is presented. What senses are used? Is it like a painting of a country scene?
>
> - What about family life? Is this presented through actions and feelings?
>
> - What might these reactions tell us about the family members?
>
> - Might the poem again move from concrete description to abstract ideas?

You might also consider under this heading 'Ample make this bed' and 'Though I get home how late, how late!'

Poems about nature

When Emily Dickinson wrote her poem 'A light exists in spring', she acknowledged her debt to Wordsworth in her efforts to achieve a clarity of vision in her account of nature, and in her attitude to it. The poem begins:

> A light exists in spring
> > Not present on the year
> At any other period.
> > When March is scarcely here
>
> A color stands abroad
> > On solitary hills

AO4

It would be useful when assessing Emily Dickinson's response to nature to bear in mind Robert Frost's comment about some of his own poems: 'it is realism with the dirt washed off.' You might look at this opening verse and think about what it is in nature that interests Dickinson.

In responding to Robert Frost's comment, you could consider how Emily Dickinson presents nature. Is it a 'prettified' sort of nature, or is there some realism, with the presentation of some of the more negative aspects of nature?

ACTIVITY 9

- Is Emily Dickinson specific about the time-frame of the poem?

- How much concrete detail is there? Is the scene fully described?

- Do you think that she is more concerned with depicting a mood?

The poem continues:

It waits upon the lawn;
    It shows the furthest tree
Upon the furthest slope we know;
    It almost speaks to me.

AO3

How Dickinson presents her response to nature

ACTIVITY 10

- How does Dickinson suggest distance here? Might it be through the use of single words?

- What is the tone of the poem?

- How does Dickinson create this tone? You could consider: the use of alliteration, of sibilance, and of 'quiet' consonants; and the use of a regular alternate rhyme scheme.

In the last five lines of the poem, the range of enquiry again broadens, as Dickinson introduces the question of our relationship to nature. Here she uses the word 'sacrament'. What might this suggest about her attitude?

Dickinson's descriptions of nature have been extended to include some philosophical themes, so to suggest that she writes about nature only may be very misleading. Perhaps it is more accurate to say that natural description is a platform for a deeper contemplation, as may be seen in the next group of poems.

Poems that move from outward observation to inner contemplation

Here you are asked about what Emily Dickinson prioritises in her poetry. Is it nature? Or is it human nature? It is up to you to decide which, offering evidence to support your choice.

AO4

Emily Dickinson wrote in a letter: 'Of all nature, human nature is the most interesting and quickening to me.' How do you interpret her response to nature?

You may perhaps conclude that in the course of her nature poems the interest in nature gives way to Dickinson's interest in human concerns. You may see this in the first and last verses of her poem 'There's a certain slant of light':

> There's a certain slant of light
> On winter afternoons,
> That oppresses, like the weight
> Of cathedral tunes.
>
> …
>
> When it comes, the landscape listens,
> Shadows hold their breath;
> When it goes, 'tis like the distance
> On the look of death.

AO3

How Dickinson represents her response to nature

ACTIVITY 11

- How might the words 'slant' and 'weight' suggest the poet's feeling?

- Might you conclude that the poet feels oppressed or isolated in the quiet world?

- Why might the shadows 'hold their breath'? What might they anticipate?

- Why might Dickinson use religious language?

- Is there any sense in this poem of a life after death?

You might also consider the religious imagery and the ideas of a life after death in the poems 'As imperceptibly as grief' and 'I started early, took my dog'. In this second poem you may see a sense of nature becoming menacing in a non-specific way.

Poems with biographical concerns

In some of her poems Emily Dickinson offers a brief account of important experiences in somebody's life. Is this sort of poem evident in the prescribed poems?

- If there are such poems, how do they work?

- If you think there are no such poems, how would you define the range of her poetry?

In such poems, men or women are given voices in a short biography. Examples include 'Safe in their alabaster chambers' and 'She rose to his requirement', which begins:

> She rose to his requirement, dropped
> The playthings of her life
> To take the honorable work
> Of woman and of wife.

ACTIVITY 12

- What do you make of the two opposite directions described in the first line?

- How important are the words 'rose' and 'dropped'?

- Might the word 'honorable' be ironic?

If you continue to study this poem, you will find the outline biography of a woman who keeps everything to herself ('it lay unmentioned'). But you might also find that the 'downward movement' of the poem continues. It is up to you to decide whether this movement is towards the inner heart of the woman, or downwards towards darkness and death. Are the pearl and the weed of equal value, of different values, or are they opposed? The poet seems to leave this open, but critics such as Vivian Pollack see her as a 'psychological realist'.

This open-endedness and reticence seem to be one of the poet's characteristics, as the critic William Shurr commented: 'The reader feels that some essential information is missing.' Why might Emily Dickinson withhold personal information?

Poems that present common experiences

Emily Dickinson is seen by many critics, including Elizabeth Philips, as offering a 'gratifying and haunting record of human experience'. Philips suggests three things: (1) that Emily Dickinson writes about human experience; (2) that she does so in a way which is pleasing; and (3) that she does so in a way that is so moving that the poetry is haunting. You have to ask yourself whether:

- she does in fact write about human experience, or about something else

- you agree or disagree that her poetry is pleasing

- you agree or disagree that her poetry is haunting.

As you saw in 'Because I could not stop for death', Dickinson's poems often require the reader to explore personal experiences. Similar poems include 'It can't be summer, – that got through', 'Victory comes late', and 'The last night that she lived', a poem in which she describes the experience of tending to the dying. Read through this poem and ask yourself:

ACTIVITY 13

- How might the poet make the use of a little imagery effective?

- Might this both relieve and intensify emotions? If so, how?

- Are the 'we' figures seen as united in experience and in grief?

Conclusion

This completes your study of six critical perspectives on the prescribed poems by Emily Dickinson. Using this model framework, you can go on to explore other critical perspectives on your own, perhaps beginning with a consideration of her attitude to religion in 'Safe in their alabaster chambers'.

Section B: Drama before 1770

The dominant Assessment Objective in this section is AO5ii. In other words candidates are expected to evaluate the significance of cultural, historical and other contextual influences on literary texts and study.

This Assessment Objective has been outlined in the Introduction (pages v–vi), but here is a reminder of the seven central types of context mentioned in the Specification:

- the context of period or era, including significant social, historical, political and cultural processes

- the context of the work in terms of a writer's biography and/or milieu (milieu refers to the particular environment in which the writer lived and worked, such as social, academic or professional environments)

- the context of other works, including other works by the same author

- the different contexts for a work established by its reception over time, including the recognition that works have different meanings and effects upon readers in different periods; this could overlap with AO4 in consideration of the different critical responses

- the context of a given or specific passage in terms of the work from which it is taken (a part-to-whole context)

- the literary context, including generic factors and period-specific styles

- the language context, including relevant and significant episodes in the use and development of literary language: this includes imagery (for example, the use of certain common images in a Revenge Tragedy) and matters of style, the use of colloquial language and dialect.

You will see the different contexts embodied in the questions on all of the texts in this section. It would therefore be worth looking at the questions relating to texts you are not studying in order to see how the different contexts may be tested.

The difference between Advanced Subsidiary Level and A2 Level is that you are now required to 'evaluate the significance' of the context. In other words, you are required to consider the context as well as the text. This is not the same as saying that you must spend excessive time studying the actual context. But it is essential that you understand the links between the context and the text in terms of a writer's ideas and manner of expression.

Note: candidates who have studied *Measure for Measure* in Unit 3 must not study it in Unit 5.

An example of 'evaluating the significance' of a given context

The genre of Comedy provides a literary context for Goldsmith's play *She Stoops to Conquer*. Later in this section you will look at the characteristics of **farce** as a type of comedy, and then assess how an individual play has developed this **sub-genre** (see page 143). In this way, you will 'evaluate the significance' of farce as a type of comedy in your response to an individual play.

Exploring contexts for Section B

For each drama text, you are offered six contexts to explore. You will see how the context becomes apparent in the ideas of the drama, and how an individual context relates to a contextual frame. The word 'primary' is used to describe the particular context explored in each of the six sub-sections because, as you will see, there is very often overlap between contexts.

Edward II – Christopher Marlowe

Compared to Marlowe's earlier plays, *Edward II* is written in a style that is much plainer and much more muted in tone. His drama had moved from the presentation of powerful heroic characters to the depiction of the personal struggle of a rather weak individual who is subjected to intense pressures by the inheritance of the crown.

The six contexts considered for the study of *Edward II* are:

- the historical context: kingship in *Edward II*

- the moral context

- the literary context I: *Edward II* as a **Morality Play**

- the religious context

- the literary context II: *Edward II* as a tragedy

- the language context.

Evaluating the significance of the contexts

One way of evaluating the significance of the contexts treated below is to compare what you would gain from them.

For example, an Elizabethan audience would probably have seen many plays that dealt with the subject of kingship. They would probably have known, for example, Shakespeare's *Richard II*, which was performed at about the same time. They would also have been aware that Elizabeth I had no heir and that the issue of who would succeed her was beginning to preoccupy the Court. So a consideration of the *historical context* can bring you close to some of the issues which may seem remote at the beginning of the twenty-first century, but which were of passionate interest to people of all social classes at the time the play was written and first performed.

Consideration of the *moral context* of the play could make you aware of the ethical issues that are important in any period – those of justice, loyalty, dishonesty, judging character against behaviour, and so on. But ideas, attitudes and values about crucial moral issues are often very different now from what they were in the sixteenth century; important examples include attitudes to homosexuality and the role and status of wives. In many Western cultures now, homosexuality is accepted and arranged marriages are frowned upon. But there are still many countries and cultures where arranged marriages are the norm and homosexuality is severely punished. A consideration of moral issues in *Edward II*, therefore, alerts us to the fact that while some issues are universal, attitudes and values relating to them may change profoundly during time and across cultures.

It also raises specific questions about the extent to which you think Marlowe might be arguing for change, and about what kinds of things he wanted to change.

A consideration of the two *literary contexts* – both of which raise questions relating to genre – will alert you to very different aspects of the play. Comparison with Morality Plays, for example, encourages you to think about good and evil, particularly in a religious context. By contrast, consideration of the play as a tragedy allows you to compare this play with quite different ones and so focus instead on what happens to the main character at the end of the play and also on how different audiences and different individuals might respond to the main character. Although there are aspects of *Edward II* that are episodic, (as in a Morality Play), there are other aspects which correspond to a tragedy.

Different contexts, therefore, draw our attention to different features of the play. They might also lead to different interpretations of the play. Which context you find the most helpful or useful will, therefore, depend upon what you see as the most interesting and significant features of the play. However, remember that AO5ii asks you to consider a range of different contexts, to think about how each of them might be important, and to assess how far each of them illuminates your interpretation.

The historical context: kingship in Edward II

Marlowe's consideration of kingship differs in many ways from that of other Elizabethan writers. Generally, the Elizabethans accepted the theory of the **divine right of kings**, according to which God chose the king independently of the wishes of the nation's subjects, this right to rule being passed down through generations.

In *Edward II*, Marlowe seems to explore what it is that gives a king the right to rule, but the ideas he offers may not be concerned with divine right.

What sort of a king is Edward II?

At the start of the play Scene 1, Edward is introduced through Gaveston's words:

> 'My father is deceased; come Gaveston,
> and share the kingdom with thy dearest friend.'
> Ah, words that make me surfeit with delight!
> What greater bliss can hap to Gaveston,
> Than live and be the favourite of a king?   (lines 1–5)

ACTIVITY 1

- What might Edward's priorities be when he takes over the kingdom?

- Do you think that a king should have favourites?

- What do you make of Gaveston's attitude here?

The Barons believe that Edward neglects his kingdom because of his relationship with Gaveston, and demand that he renounce his friend. Edward replies:

I cannot brook these haughty menaces:
Am I a king and must be overruled?   (lines 133–134)

ACTIVITY 2

- What is Edward's attitude to the Barons and to his own powers?

Shortly afterwards (Act 1, Scene 4), Mortimer makes a clear threat that if the King does not give up his favourite, the Pope will have to:

Curse him if he refuse, and then may we
Depose him and elect another king.   (lines 54–55)

ACTIVITY 3

- Why should the Pope oppose Edward's wishes?

- Who is now seen to have the right to elect the king?

Edward, however, is seen to be reconciled with the Barons when he appears to make peace with his queen, Isabella, and most of the Barons offer loyalty:

EDWARD: Once more receive my hand, and let this be
            A second marriage 'twixt thyself and me.
            ...
LANCASTER: This salutation overjoys my heart.
            ...
WARWICK: Slay me, my lord, when I offend your grace.   (lines 335–350)

ACTIVITY 4

- Why do you think Edward makes peace with Isabella?

- Do you think he has 'won over' the Barons at this point?

In the course of the ensuing battles, Edward, supported by the Spencers, crowns himself afresh in what is a very dramatic moment, saying (Scene 11):

[*Kneeling*] By earth, the common mother of us all,
By heaven and all the moving orbs thereof,
By this right hand and by my father's sword,
And all the honours 'longing to my crown,
I will have heads and lives for him …   (lines 128–132)

ACTIVITY 5

- This is like Edward's coronation service; what are his motives in repeating this service here?

- Why might Marlowe use such noble language, and refer to 'heaven'?

- Are Edward's motives here worthy of a king?

The decline of Edward II as a king

In Scene 17, Isabella explains how Edward might be regarded:

Misgoverned kings are cause of all this wrack;
And Edward, thou art one among them all,
Whose looseness hath betrayed thy land to spoil
And made the channels overflow with blood.   (lines 9–12)

ACTIVITY 6

- What problems might a weak king cause?

- Do you think that the description 'a weak king' might apply to Edward?

- Do you trust Isabella?

Edward cannot help his affections for his favourites. In the course of the play you see Edward arrested, imprisoned, degraded, tortured and finally killed. He therefore sees the reversal of his ideas about kingship and of his earlier hopes. When Lightborn comes to kill him (Scene 24), Edward says:

> Know that I am a king – O, at that name,
> I feel a hell of grief. Where is my crown?
> Gone, gone. And do I remain alive? (lines 88–90)

ACTIVITY 7

- Do you see a reversal in Edward's language from that quoted before (Activity 5)?

- Why might Marlowe use the word 'hell'?

- Is there anything in life left for Edward if he is not a king?

Here are some questions you might consider in order to evaluate the significance of this context:

- Who is seen to have a right to elect kings? Is it God?

- What do you think might be the qualities of a good ruler?

- How does Edward match up to these qualities?

The moral context

To consider this context you could look at two areas:

- the moral framework of the play

- how other characters fit into the moral scheme of the play.

The moral framework of the play

You have already seen in the discussion of kingship how the right of electing a king shifted from being the responsibility of God to being that of man.

At the end of the play (Scene 25), Mortimer Junior speaks what might be considered the 'moral' of the play:

Base Fortune, now I see that in thy wheel
There is a point to which, when men aspire,
They tumble headlong down; [...]   (lines 59–61)

ACTIVITY 8

- Is there any reference to God or morality here?

- Does Mortimer Junior suggest that life is ruled by fate and chance?

The new king, Edward III, makes reference to 'grief and innocence', but probably does not draw any further moral conclusion. Marlowe often made comments about his own atheism, such as 'The only beginning of religion was to keep men in awe'. Do you think that it is possible that he deliberately offered a play in which there are no moral rules stemming from divine law?

How other characters fit into the moral scheme of the play

The characters to be considered here are Gaveston, Mortimer Junior and Isabella (but you could consider others for your own study).

Gaveston

You have already looked at Gaveston's words when he asked what 'greater bliss' there could be than to be a king's 'favourite' (Activity 1).

Later in Scene 1, Gaveston arranges entertainment for the king, saying that he:

May draw the pliant King which way I please.
Music and poetry is his delight;   (lines 52–53)

ACTIVITY 9

- What do these words suggest about Gaveston? Might he be cunning?

- Is he governed by any concern for the King's well-being?

- Remember the King's words about why he loves Gaveston: 'Because he loves me more than all the world' (Scene 4). Do you think that Gaveston is a manipulator? A **Machiavellian** figure?

- Do you think Gaveston is rather shrewd in his analysis of the King?

Mortimer Junior

Mortimer might have some justification for being angry with the King. But does this anger justify his ambition to plot with Isabella and overthrow the King? In Scene 18, his feelings are made clear:

> [*Aside to* ISABELLA] I like not this relenting mood in Edmund,
>
> ...
>
> Your King hath wronged your country and himself,
> And we must seek to right it as we may.   (lines 47–77)

ACTIVITY 10

- What do you make of Mortimer Junior's aside to Isabella?

- Is he interested in reaching a peaceful solution?

When you consider his final words (which you looked at in Activity 8), you might consider whether Mortimer Junior had any moral purposes at all, or whether ultimately he, like Gaveston, was just out to better himself.

Isabella

In the scene where Edward makes peace with Isabella (Activity 4), you might feel sorry for her. But think about what happens in Scene 8, where Isabella and Mortimer join forces:

> MORTIMER JUNIOR: Madam, I cannot stay to answer you;
> But think of Mortimer as he deserves.
> ISABELLA: So well hast thou deserved, sweet Mortimer,
> As Isabel could live with thee forever.   (lines 58–61)

ACTIVITY 11

- How do you respond to Isabella now? Do you still feel sympathy?

- Do you think that she, too, might be self-interested?

- Might she be out for revenge?

To evaluate the significance of this context, you might consider if there are any moral rules established in the play. You could ask yourself whether any of them think of anything other than themselves. Do you think there might be some real love shown by Edward and his two lovers, who are both finally willing to die for him?

The literary context I: Edward II *as a Morality Play*

Morality Plays were popular in the Middle Ages, dramatising mankind's journey through life with all its temptations. Moral qualities of evil and goodness were presented on stage, and there were 'good' and 'bad' angels. The **Mystery Plays** developed a similar theme using stories from the Bible, playing out the whole of mankind's story from the fall to redemption through the birth of Jesus Christ.

There might be echoes of the Morality and Mystery Plays in the presentation of Lightborn in *Edward II*. When the audience first sees Lightborn (Act 5, Scene 4), he describes his 'apprenticeship':

'Tis not the first time I have killed a man.
I learned in Naples how to poison flowers,
To strangle with a lawn thrust through the throat,
To pierce the windpipe with a needle's point,   (lines 29–32)

ACTIVITY 12

- Read through the discussion of the genre of Revenge Tragedy on page 133. How might Lightborn be seen as a Machiavellian figure?

This speech might establish Lightborn as a villain, but there are references that link him, as a character, with Morality Plays. His name is taken from the name of a Devil in the Chester Cycle of Mystery Plays. The name 'Lightborn' is Lucifer, the name of the Devil, anglicised. In his scenes in the dungeon with Edward, certain significant references are made (Scene 24):

This dungeon where they keep me is the sink
Wherein the filth of all the castle falls.
...
My mind's distempered and my body's numbed,
And whether I have limbs or no, I know not.   (lines 55–64)

ACTIVITY 13

- Look at the language register here and in the dungeon scenes – darkness, rats, damp, dungeon, deprivation of the senses, Lightborn as Lucifer: might Marlowe be suggesting that Edward is in hell on earth?

To evaluate the significance of this context you might consider whether Marlowe created a drama with some suggestion of a Christian framework, but without drawing a Christian moral.

The religious context

To assess this context you could re-order material assembled in Activities 12 and 13 above, and interweave the material for the second context, the moral context.

ACTIVITY 14

- Might the Morality Play elements imply a religious context?

- Are there the suggestions of Lightborn as a devil, and of damnation?

- Might Edward be seen to endure the tortures of hell on earth?

- Do you think Marlowe suggests that there are consequences for mankind's wrongdoing, other than punishment here on earth?

- Is there in the play any sense of reward or punishment in an afterlife?

- Are there any 'judges' for Edward, other than his fellow men?

- What might Mortimer Junior's words about the 'Wheel of Fortune', at the end of the play, suggest about certain views of mankind's destiny?

- Is the 'Wheel of Fortune' a Christian concept?

The literary context II: Edward II *as a tragedy*

To assess this context you could consider three types of tragedy:

- the tragedy of a king's fall from grace: Edward

- the tragedy implicit in the concept of the 'Wheel of Fortune': how a person may apparently achieve wealth or fame, and then suddenly lose everything

- the personal tragedy of Edward himself.

ACTIVITY 15

To consider a king's fall from grace, think about the following:

- What does Marlowe suggest about the divine right of kings?

- Should a man be entitled to rule because he is from a certain family?

- Alternatively, should he have particular qualities that entitle him to rule?

The language context

To assess this context, think about the plainness of the language of this play, unusual for a drama of its time. There is a limited use of 'elevated' language, so when it appears in this play, you need to consider Marlowe's reasons for including it. You have seen the use of noble language in Activity 5 (page 114).

- Why does Marlowe make Edward speak in this noble way here? How does this language affect your response to Edward?

- Why do you think the language is generally so plain? (You might think about what Marlowe could be suggesting about a 'new' sort of king.)

- Is he a king in an age that is less heroic than that presented in other dramas of the period?

- Might he be a non-heroic king for a non-heroic age?

You might also consider Isabella's lofty speech to the troops (Scene 17). Mortimer Junior cuts the speech down:

> Nay Madam, if you be a warrior,
> Ye must not grow so passionate in speeches.   (lines 14–15)

ACTIVITY 16

- How does this language affect your response to Isabella? Does it change your sympathies for her?

- What might Marlowe be implying in Mortimer Junior's rebuff to Isabella?

- Might Mortimer Junior be a better politician and tactician than Isabella is, aware of the needs of troops? Aware of how language must be adapted to suit situations?

Conclusion

You have now worked through six contexts relating to *Edward II*. Using this model framework, you can go on to address other contexts on your own, perhaps beginning by considering *Edward II* as a history play, exploring Edward's conflict with the Barons.

Measure For Measure – **William Shakespeare**

In the development of *Measure for Measure* and in its conclusion – when a reformed society based on sound principles of law and justice is established after a period of chaos – the play may be classed as a comedy. However, some critics label *Measure for Measure* one of Shakespeare's 'problem plays'. This may be partly because of the extreme cruelty evident at times, which could put the play in the genre of tragicomedy, and partly because the play varies in its methods of presentation between realistic and non-realistic methods. You should not quibble if certain events or situations seem unlikely, but rather accept that they are there for specific dramatic purposes. If you accept the conventions of the play and 'suspend your disbelief', you can see many possible areas to explore, including that of the nature of just government. These three contexts – of comedy, of a 'problem play', and of an enquiry into the nature of just government – will be explored in the following pages.

The six contexts considered for the study of *Measure for Measure* are:

- the social context: an enquiry into the nature of just government

- the moral context: the development of self-knowledge

- the context of genre I: *Measure for Measure* as a comedy

- the dramatic context: the interlinking of two social classes

- the language context

- the context of genre II: *Measure for Measure* as one of the 'problem plays'.

Evaluating the significance of the contexts

One way of evaluating the significance of the contexts treated below is to compare what you would gain from them.

For example, enquiring into the *social context* of the play will enable you to think about issues relevant both to the time when the play was written and also, more broadly, to any society. More specifically, it might help you to consider the way society is organised and to reflect on the limits of legal justice.

But Shakespeare is not writing a tract about the way the law operates; he is also interested in that uncertain line between legal justice and moral justice. Evaluating the significance of this social context, therefore, might lead you to the conclusion that a consideration of the social context alone does not really get to the heart of the moral issues that Shakespeare was exploring in *Measure for Measure*. Similarly, whereas a consideration of the laws about pregnancy outside marriage gives some idea of the nature of the society Shakespeare chose to write about, a study of the *moral context* might show more about the issues that people are faced with in their daily lives.

Contemporary audiences would probably have been thinking about similar plays they had seen, and would thus have been particularly alert to what Shakespeare was doing in his play. So a consideration of the play as a comedy – its *literary context* – would enable you to highlight some of those things in *Measure for Measure* that an audience would find particularly striking. The audiences of Shakespeare's day would be well aware that a comedy was a play in which no one died, and so they would have been prompted to think especially hard about the cruelty surrounding the report that Claudio had been killed.

A modern audience, perhaps brought up on twentieth-century feminist ideas, would react strongly to the ending of the play; a consideration of the play as a comedy would allow you to think in particular about whether the ending is a happy one. But there is no clear answer to this; Shakespeare leaves the audience to decide for themselves whether Isabella and the Duke are going to live 'happily ever after'. Thinking about *Measure for Measure* as one of Shakespeare's 'problem plays' (again a *literary context*) means that you can compare it with 'darker' plays, such as *Hamlet*, or *The Merchant of Venice*, and therefore concentrate on features very different from those you might have looked at had you been comparing it with other comedies.

The different contexts, therefore, draw our attention to different features of the play. They might also lead to very different interpretations of the play. Which context you find the most helpful or useful will therefore depend on what you see as the most interesting and significant features of the play. However, remember that AO5ii asks you to consider a range of different contexts, to think about how each of them might be important, and to assess how far each of them illuminates your interpretation of the play.

The social context: an enquiry into the nature of just government

You could consider three characters here: Angelo, Escalus, and the Duke. You might discover that each character has a different view of how to govern.

Angelo

The Duke makes Angelo his deputy in his absence, and Angelo starts off by reviving an old law relating to fornication. The result of this is that Claudio is condemned to die. The Duke knows Angelo's character (Act 1, Scene 3):

> … Lord Angelo is precise;
> Stands at guard with Envy; scarce confesses
> That his blood flows; or that his appetite
> Is more to bread than stone. …

Angelo believes that 'we must not make a scarecrow of the law'.

ACTIVITY 1

- What sort of a person is Angelo? What are his attitudes?

- What might be the significance of the word 'precise', both here and in Act 3, Scene 1?

- Might it suggest that Angelo is an absolutist, seeing things in black and white, and not allowing for grey areas?

It would be helpful here to read through the two dramatic confrontations between Angelo and Isabella in Act 2, Scenes 2 and 4. You might ask yourself whether Angelo has fallen into a trap through his view of justice.

ACTIVITY 2

- Should Angelo take into account an individual case, such as Claudio's?

- If he were to give in to Isabella, and pardon Claudio, would he still be impartial in carrying out the law?

- If he were to go ahead and execute Claudio, would he be inhumane?

- Does this suggest that there is a problem in his type of justice?

Escalus

Escalus is exactly the opposite. In Act 2, Scene 1, he is asked by his constable, Elbow, to arrest Pompey for being a bawd. Angelo leaves him to take the case, and Escalus comments to Elbow:

Truly, officer, because he hath some offences in him that thou wouldst discover if thou couldst, let him continue in his courses

...

So for this time, Pompey, fare you well.

ACTIVITY 3

- What do you make of Escalus's view of justice?

- Might he take too much notice of the individual?

- Might he undermine the idea of the necessity of rigorous laws?

The Duke

Perhaps the Duke is not completely blameless in his rule of Vienna. Perhaps he has let the law drift, and not made his presence strongly felt? Do you think this may be the reason why Lucio refers to him twice as the 'dark' Duke (Act 2, Scene 2; and Act 4, Scene 3)? Might there be another reason?

He has seen the lawlessness of Vienna: '... I have seen corruption boil and bubble / Till it o'errun the stew' (Act 5, Scene 1). Perhaps he has let the law drift because he knows that it may be too harsh if applied to the letter. Perhaps he wishes to establish a *balanced* form of justice tempered by mercy.

Overall, the Duke might be seen to represent both justice and mercy in the sentences he hands out in Act 5, Scene 1, where he 'punishes' Angelo, Claudio and Lucio.

ACTIVITY 4

- What are these punishments? Are they 'negative' punishments, or are they designed to reform the 'sinners'?

- Was Pompey's earlier punishment negative or redemptive?

Perhaps there is a justice in which the law works through wisdom and mercy, to reform and not just to punish. To evaluate the significance of this context you could compare the sort of justice meted out by Angelo and Escalus to that of the *balanced* judgement of the Duke.

The moral context: the development of self-knowledge

To assess this context, consider the moral character of Angelo, Isabella and Claudio.

Angelo

You read on page 122 a description of Angelo by the Duke. Other characters in this play, such as Justice, think that Angelo is 'severe' (Act 2, Scene 1). Angelo himself thinks that he is faultless:

When I that censure him do so offend,
Let mine own judgement pattern out my death.

ACTIVITY 5

- What do you think of Angelo's attitude here? Is it rather smug?

- Would you know at this stage that he himself has had a love affair?

To consider the ways in which Angelo gains self-knowledge, and therefore can improve himself, you could consider two areas:

- his 'espousal' to Mariana

- his dealings with Isabella.

Angelo's 'espousal' to Mariana

The Duke is aware of this relationship, which he reveals in his plan to Mariana – 'he is your husband on a pre-contract' (Act 4, Scene 1) – so he sees that Angelo is morally flawed. In Act 3, Scene 1, the Duke explains why she was abandoned by Angelo before the marriage agreement was finalised:

> Between which time of the contract and limit of the solemnity, her brother Frederick was wracked at sea, having in that perished vessel the dowry of his sister.

ACTIVITY 6

- Angelo was *legally* entitled to break his espousal, but do you think he acted morally?

- What do you think his motives were? What might this suggest?

- When you compare Angelo's actions to those of Claudio, who was also 'espoused', who do you think is the better man? Is there any irony here?

Angelo's dealings with Isabella

But Angelo is presented as more than just a hypocrite, as you can see in his dealings with Isabella. In Act 2, Scene 4, he offers to waive Claudio's death penalty on condition that she:

> ... to redeem him,
> Give up your body to such sweet uncleanness
> As she that he hath stain'd?
> ...
> Might there not be a charity in sin

ACTIVITY 7

- What do you think of Angelo now?

- Why do you think Shakespeare uses words such as 'redeem', 'charity', and 'sin'?

Then Angelo gives the matter another twist. He plans to deceive Isabella after he has slept with her by ordering her brother's execution – in case Claudio might 'have ta'en revenge' (Act 4, Scene 4).

Isabella

When you first see Isabella she is about to become a novice nun. Even at this stage you can see that she is an extremist, who wishes 'a more strict restraint' on nuns (Act 1, Scene 4).

Shakespeare ensures that, as with Escalus and Angelo, the moral principles of Isabella are put to the test. You may see this in her two confrontations with Angelo in Act 2, Scenes 2 and 4, where she too faces an impossible choice. In the first confrontation, she works through four stages:

1. That Claudio should condemn the fault but not her brother (from line 34).

2. She then makes a plea for tolerance for all sinners (from line 88).

3. She now moves to the idea of mercy in law, asking Angelo to 'show some pity' (from line 100).

4. When all these pleas fail, she attacks all human authority: 'man ... like an angry ape plays such fantastic tricks before high heaven.'

ACTIVITY 8

- Pick out the different stages of Isabella's argument, and Angelo's counter-arguments, as you read through the scene.

In the second confrontation, in Act 2, Scene 4, Isabella responds to the deadly choice of either sleeping with Angelo and so saving her brother's life, or keeping her virtue and letting him die:

Th'impression of keen whips I'd wear as rubies,
And strip myself to death as to a bed
That longing have been sick for, ere I'd yield
My body up to shame.

ACTIVITY 9

- Why might Shakespeare give Isabella such very **sensuous** language here?

- What do you make of her choices: that she must let her brother die or give up her virginity?

- Is that choice consistent with the Christian ideas of love and sacrifice to which she claims she wishes to adhere as a nun?

- Should she break her own pledge as a nun and lose her chastity?

Claudio

Claudio has rather different weaknesses. Technically, he has offended state and moral law by sleeping with Juliet before they were married, but Claudio has other moral difficulties, as you may see in the scene with the Duke in prison (Act 3, Scene 1). Claudio may be seen to veer wildly in his responses to the Duke. When the Duke offers the advice 'Be absolute for death', Claudio seems heartened and resolute:

> I humbly thank you.
> To sue to live, I find I seek to die,
> And seeking death, find life. Let it come on.

But then Isabella reveals Angelo's offer, and in Act 2, Scene 1, when Claudio thinks about the terrors of death, his resolution fails:

> Death is a fearful thing.
>
> ...
>
> Ay, but to die, and go we know not where;

ACTIVITY 10

- How do you respond to Claudio at this point?

- Might it be thought that just as Angelo was too absolute in his morality, so here Claudio wavers too much? That he is not resolute enough?

The Duke may be seen as the moral ideal, with the themes of morality and justice being drawn together in one of his speeches (Act 3, Scene 2):

> He who the sword of heaven will bear
> Should be as holy as severe:
> ...
> Twice treble shame on Angelo.

ACTIVITY 11

- How does Shakespeare link morality and justice here?

- Why might the Duke be made to refer to 'the sword of heaven'?

To evaluate the significance of this context, you could:

- assess how each character has gained moral self-knowledge through experiencing 'new' and difficult situations, and

- measure each character against the 'ideal' standard of the Duke.

The context of genre I: Measure for Measure *as a comedy*

It has been suggested that in this distinctive form of social comedy there are three stages: (1) it opens with an unsettled society governed by a harsh or irrational law; (2) there is then a temporary loss of identity; and (3) finally there is the discovery of a new identity and a reconciliation. This structure seems to suit the development of *Measure for Measure*.

An unsettled society governed by a harsh or irrational law

At the beginning of the play, you can see the result of reviving the old fornication law in Claudio's arrest. In Act 1, Scene 2, the Duke says:

> We have strict statutes and most biting laws,
> The needful bits and curbs to headstrong jades,
> Which for this fourteen years we have let slip.

ACTIVITY 12

Do you think that this society is unsettled? Why might this be?

A temporary loss of identity

In exploring the first two contexts you have already identified the confusion in both events and moral attitudes.

The discovery of a new identity and a reconciliation

You could explore the ending of the play to see how the processes of self-discovery and reconciliation are achieved. You have already discussed 'punishment' and redemption in Activity 4 (page 124), so to complete the exploration of this context, you might 'flesh out' the full evidence under these three headings in your own time.

The dramatic context: the interlinking of two social classes

To assess this context you could consider how the lower-class characters counterpoint or illuminate the issues related to the higher-class characters. You can look at Pompey, Lucio and Barnardine.

ACTIVITY 13

Pompey and his attitude to law

- Does Pompey seem to talk good sense at times, for example when he points out the folly of closing all the brothels in the Dukedom?

- Might he be seen as a character of commonsense?

- Why is he made to make Escalus look foolish?

- How is his behaviour reflected by those of a higher class?

- Does he provide humour in the play?

- How does his punishment fit into the final mood of the play?

Lucio

- Does Lucio seem at first to represent and parallel the Duke?

- Does he too seem to exhibit common sense? What effects does this have?

- Does he seem to be treated more harshly as the play goes on?

- How does this affect the mood of the play?

- How does his punishment fit into the final moral scheme of the play?

Barnardine

- Does Barnardine deny the Duke's right of dispensing law to every citizen when he refuses to be executed?

- What effect does this have on your perception of the Duke?

The language context

To assess this context you could explore two of the different registers evident in *Measure for Measure*. There are two central registers operating in the play, each carrying certain values:

- the register linked to moral virtue, established by such words as 'redeem, grace, charity'; this register introduces the theme of morality and virtue

- the register linked to the title of the play, *Measure for Measure*, in other words language linked to weighing, testing, balancing; this register brings together the ideas of morality and justice.

ACTIVITY 14

- How might the register to do with grace and Christian virtue interlink with that of testing?

- Might they come together in the idea of Christian mercy?

- Might this be part of the exploration of the nature of justice in the play?

- Might the Old Testament idea of justice – of testing and weighing a person's deserts and then meting out punishment – need to be balanced with a New Testament concept of Christian grace in order to achieve a new sort of justice based also on mercy?

The context of genre II: Measure for Measure *as one of the 'problem plays'*

ACTIVITY 15

- Which issues are too serious for comedy?

- Is the Duke right to abuse Isabella and pretend that her brother is dead?

- Is Angelo's seduction of Isabella – a nun – appropriate for comedy?

- Is Claudio's attempt to prostitute Isabella in order to save his own life a proper subject for comedy?

- Does the constant threat of death which hangs over several characters seem right for comedy?

- Is the ending of the play completely convincing?

- Might this play, with its dark and complex themes and its threats of death, be best defined as a tragicomedy – a blend of two genres?

Do you think that the different types of characterisation might cause an audience some difficulty? To answer this, work through the next activity:

ACTIVITY 16

- Does Shakespeare present some characters, such as Angelo, Isabella and Claudio, with any psychological realism?

- Is the Duke a difficult character to assess because he is not fully rounded, but indeed part realistic and part a stock 'type' issuing moral statements?

- Does he hold up the pace of the play with his long speeches?

You might think about whether you are being asked to suspend disbelief and accept these presentations of character and situation without quibbling too much about the way in which Shakespeare has chosen to present certain ideas.

Conclusion

You have now worked through six contexts relating to *Measure for Measure*. Using this model framework, you can now go on to address other contexts on your own, such as the links Shakespeare makes between self-knowledge, mercy, compassion, morality and justice.

The Changeling – Thomas Middleton

The Changeling is an example of the genre of Revenge Tragedy, but Thomas Middleton and William Rowley (who contributed to the writing of the play) create a very complex play out of this type of drama. It is generally thought that Rowley's main contribution was the comic **sub-plot**, with Middleton responsible for most of the tragic main plot. As the title of the play suggests, there is an exploration of changes in character brought about by choices: how making bad decisions based only on self-interest leads to disaster; Middleton presents the idea of 'the deed's creature' to show this. Although the play was written early in the seventeenth century, Middleton develops the genre of Revenge Tragedy by exploring psychological motivation in a markedly modern way, something you may also see, for example, in Shakespeare's *Hamlet*.

Thomas Middleton was a Calvinist. Calvinists believed that each individual is sinful, and can only be redeemed through God's grace; and moreover that each individual is predestined to salvation or damnation. This could in part explain Beatrice Joanna's apparent helplessness as she inevitably falls into grave sin and faces damnation.

The six contexts to be considered for the study of *The Changeling* are:

- *The Changeling* as a Revenge Tragedy

- the moral context

- the psychological context

- the dramatic context: the use of the sub-plot

- the religious context

- the language context: imagery and register.

Evaluating the significance of the contexts

One way of evaluating the significance of the contexts treated below is to compare what you would gain from an understanding of them.

A consideration of the moral context might make you aware of the relationships between the characters, their morality and their motivation. It will alert you to the codes that the characters do or do not live by, and encourage you to think about a world where some people live their lives outside any kind of moral law.

Middleton gives the moral context a religious dimension. Consideration of this religious context will in turn raise questions about Middleton's purposes in choosing a setting in Roman Catholic Spain. Was this because he wanted to say something about Catholicism at a time when the Puritans were gaining strength in England? Or was it because he could say things about contemporary society in England by setting the play abroad? The social, historical and cultural context of aristocratic life would have encouraged contemporary audiences to think about the court that they knew, that of James I, and about changes that had occurred since the death of Elizabeth I in 1603.

Consideration of the dramatic and generic contexts – *The Changeling* as a Revenge Tragedy – draws attention to very different features. The elements of the play that you look at in terms of the dramatic context concern the ways in which the author provides spectacle and variety for his audience. In terms of dramatic context, the play can be seen both as a structure and as an entertainment. The generic context of the Revenge Tragedy invites a comparison with other Revenge Tragedies, perhaps *The Spanish Tragedy* by Thomas Kyd or Shakespeare's *Hamlet*. You do not necessarily have to read any other Revenge Tragedies, but you do need to be aware of the central features of the genre. In this way you will also appreciate Middleton's innovation as he explores psychological motivation.

The different contexts, therefore, draw our attention to different features of the play. They might also lead to other interpretations of the play. Which context you find the most helpful or useful will, therefore, depend upon what you see as the most interesting and significant features of the play. However, remember that AO5ii asks you to consider a range of different contexts, to think about how each of them might be important, and assess how far each of them illuminates your interpretation of the play.

The Changeling *as a Revenge Tragedy*

This play has many of the characteristics of a Revenge Tragedy. The Elizabethan and Jacobean audiences had mixed views about revenge, and an ambiguous attitude towards those seeking revenge. Whilst it was acceptable to avenge the murder of a blood relative, or a very brutal murder, or a murder in circumstances where the victim could not get legal redress, nevertheless it was an offence in the eyes of God to kill another human being.

The genre of Revenge Tragedy has certain characteristics that you could apply to *The Changeling*; think about the following questions:

- There will be one or more revengers. Who are they, and what are their motives?

- There is usually an Italian or Spanish setting. Where is *The Changeling* set? Could this be England in disguise?

- There is usually a discontented central character who comments on the action. This is often a Machiavellian figure, who cynically manipulates events for his own ends. Who is this in *The Changeling*?

- There is intrigue, violence, poisoning, death. Are there any of these in *The Changeling*?

- Disguise is often used to create confusion. Is this evident in *The Changeling*?

To take this enquiry further and *evaluate the significance* of this context, you might ask yourself exactly how Middleton uses the Revenge genre. For example you might consider:

ACTIVITY 1

- Does (do) the revenger(s) retain your sympathy? Is a better society established after revenge has been taken?

- Is there any other sort of 'vengeance' evident in the play? You could think here about Alsemero's words:

> O the place itself e'er since
> Has crying been for vengeance, ...   (Act 5, Scene 3)

- You might want to explore the idea of disguise further: there is actual disguise when Diaphanta wears the black mask to deceive Alsemero on his wedding night. But there is also metaphorical disguise: is Beatrice Joanna really what she seems to be? Or De Flores? Are the characters of the main plot any saner than the madmen of the sub-plot, or are they madmen in disguise?

- Might Middleton use this genre to address contemporary problems, including: (a) questions of personal honour and morality? (b) social/political problems related to the use and abuse of power? (c) questions of divine law in society? (d) questions relating to human frailty or evil?

The moral context

In the society of the play there would seem to be moral anarchy; some characters generally behave according to their own desires, without apparent reference to a governing moral law. In exploring this theme you might consider Beatrice Joanna and De Flores. Middleton offers a clear scheme: Beatrice Joanna is *amoral*, without any sense of a moral code. De Flores, on the other hand, is **immoral**; he is aware of sin and punishment, but rejects his conscience for the sake of his obsession with Beatrice Joanna. He says at the end of the play, 'I loved this woman in spite of her heart'. (Act 5, Scene 3)

Beatrice Joanna

Beatrice's faults are clustered around her selfishness; she has no concern for the rights or needs of others, believing that she can manipulate everybody to achieve her own desires. We first see Beatrice as she meets Alsemero after going to church and falls for him, 'I shall change my saint, I fear me, ... (Act 1, Scene 1). She persuades her father to postpone her wedding to her fiancé, Alonzo de Piracquo, and later thinks:

> ... what's Piracquo
> My father spends his breath for?   (Act 2, Scene 1)

ACTIVITY 2

Think about Beatrice's words here: is her attitude honourable? Does she show any concern for the feelings of her fiancé? Or for her father?

So, she has a problem: how can she break the relationship with Piracquo, and court Alsemero? Being honourable, Alsemero offers a duel, which won't do, in case her new love is hurt. It is at this point that she becomes involved in sin, and the idea of murder, when she thinks of death as the solution, and links the idea to her servant De Flores:

Blood-guiltiness becomes a fouler visage,
[*Aside.*] And now I think on one –   (Act 2, Scene 2)

ACTIVITY 3

In Act 2, Scene 1 Beatrice had planned to have De Flores 'quite discarded'; she changes her mind:

- What has passed through Beatrice's mind here?

- Can you see how she is manipulating four people here: her father, Alsemero, Piracquo, and De Flores?

- Does she express any horror at the idea of murder, even if it is by a duel?

Beatrice has her meeting with De Flores, stressing that 'There's horror in my service, blood and danger;' (Act 2, Scene 2), and the murder is planned. But she reacts most strangely to the outcome in the crucial Act 3, Scene 4. The murder complete, De Flores shows Beatrice the severed finger with the ring she gave her fiancé. She is shocked: 'Bless me! What hast thou done?', but Beatrice continues to try to pay off De Flores:

Look you, sir, here's three thousand golden florins:
I have not meanly thought upon thy merit.   (Act 3, Scene 4)

ACTIVITY 4

What do you make of Beatrice's responses here? Has she any moral sense at all? How does she view the murder, and also De Flores?

Beatrice seems more concerned that De Flores is 'the murderer of my honour', (Act 3, Scene 4), than that she is involved in murder herself; do you think that she has realised her guilt yet? De Flores makes sure that she does realise: 'A woman dipp'd in blood, and talk of modesty?' In this dramatic scene, the audience watches the changes in Beatrice, until it becomes clear even to her what has occurred. De Flores taunts her:

> You must forget your parentage to me:
> Y'are the deed's creature; by that name
> You lost your first condition, …
> And made you one with me.

ACTIVITY 5

This is a key moment in the play, underlined when Beatrice kneels to De Flores. You might think about the following:

- How has Beatrice 'lost her parentage' and her 'first condition'?

- What might De Flores mean by the phrase 'the deed's creature'?

- What is Beatrice's status now morally and socially? What are her chances of a happy future?

As the play progresses, Beatrice continues to remove obstacles in her path, for example, by substituting Diaphanta in her wedding-night bed. However, the maid stays too long, as Beatrice says to De Flores: 'This whore forgets herself' (Act 5, Scene 1). Naturally, De Flores comes up with a plan to get Diaphanta out of the room, and to kill her. But Beatrice is not alarmed, saying:

> I'm forc'd to love thee now,
> 'Cause thou provid'st so carefully for my honour.   (Act 5, Scene I)

ACTIVITY 6

What do you make of her attitude here? What does Beatrice mean by the word 'honour'? Are there any moral connotations, or is it used in a purely social sense?

To see another statement like this, look at Act 5, Scene 2, where Beatrice explains her actions to Alsemero, thinking that adultery is a worse sin than murder.

Does Beatrice ever gain a moral sense? Perhaps she might at the end of the play. Look at her final speech, when she talks to Vermandero:

> O come not near me, sir, I shall defile you:
> I am that of your blood was taken from you
> For your better health; ...   (Act 5, Scene 3)

ACTIVITY 7

Here, you might see that images are clustered together to expand the meaning of her words. What do you make of Beatrice now?

- Why does the author use the image of **blood-letting**?

- How does Beatrice respond to her life and her crimes now?

- Might there be a sense of purification?

De Flores

De Flores is immoral, aware of the consequences of his evil actions, but so obsessed with Beatrice that nothing else matters to him.

On his first appearance, the author makes all of this very clear. An **opportunist**, De Flores picks up the glove intended for Alsmero, and says:

> She had rather wear my pelt tann'd in a pair
> Of dancing pumps, than I should thrust my fingers
> Into her sockets here. ...   (Act 1, Scene 1)

ACTIVITY 8

What does this short speech tell you about De Flores? You might consider the following:

- The sexuality of the word 'thrust': what image is created?

- How well does he understand Beatrice?

- How would you assess his character already?

Indeed, De Flores never wavers in his purposes from this point on. But he is aware of the evil he is committing. In Act 3, Scene 4 he taunts Beatrice: 'Twill hardly buy a capcase for one's conscience, though,' and later reminds her how his 'conscience might have slept at ease', if he had not carried out the murder for her sake.

Later, in Act 5, Alonzo's ghost appears, and De Flores says:

> Ha! What art thou that tak'st away the light
> 'Twixt that star and me? I dread thee not;
> 'Twas but a mist of conscience – all's clear again. (Act 5, Scene I)

ACTIVITY 9

Examine these words carefully, and think about what they reveal about De Flores and his beliefs:

- Why might he see a ghost?

- Why should the ghost block out the light of a star? What might this suggest?

- Why might he say that all is clear again? What do you think might be 'clear'?

- Why do you think Beatrice cannot see the ghost?

De Flores is unnerved a little when Tomazo speaks to him, and feels:

> Guilt must not walk so near his lodge again;
> He came near me now. (Act 5, Scene 2)

Do you think that this might show some sort of self-knowledge or honesty? Think about his words as he is about to die and thinks of his lovemaking with Beatrice:

> But that pleasure; it was so sweet to me
> That I have drunk up all, left none behind (Act 5, Scene 3)

Is there any sense of regret for his evil deeds evident here? Is there any fear of an afterlife? Do you find that you have rather a strange response to De Flores? Perhaps Middleton has created a very complex character. He is wicked, certainly in his murders. But think about the way he rushes to Beatrice when he hears of her fate; and also re-read his dying words to her.

Is it possible that he is honest in his love to her, that the strong love he feels has more energy, more spirit than that of other men in this play? If you feel that this is so, perhaps Middleton has set a moral trap here, to show the reader how it was that Beatrice succumbed to his love?

The psychological context

Middleton explores the inevitability of the fatal outcomes which occurs when a character makes bad decisions, is insensitive to the rights of others, and has a very strong will. The play grimly and ironically follows the reversal of fortunes for Beatrice Joanna, and the effects for De Flores. Obviously there will be an overlap in the evidence used in the previous section above, but there are some key moments worth exploring.

Almost at the beginning of the play, the audience sees Beatrice wrangling with her father' who insists that she marry de Piracquo:

VERMANDERO: He shall be bound to me, …

                                I'll want my will else.

BEATRICE [aside]: I shall want mine if you do it.   (Act I, Scene I)

ACTIVITY 10

Think about this exchange, and what it reveals about Beatrice. What do you learn of her character here? Why might she speak in an aside? Is she like her father here?

You have already looked at Act 2, Scene 2 in Activity 2 above; here it is relevant to recall that De Flores kneels to pledge his service to her. This is the start of his psychological manoeuvring of her; at this stage Beatrice is the princess and De Flores her subject.

You have seen how De Flores stripped Beatrice of her dishonesty and pretence about committing murder, and the movement ends in Act 3, Scene 4. De Flores has taunted Beatrice as 'the deed's creature', and suddenly she changes her tone when he persists in making her see herself as she really is:

DE FLORES: As peace and innocency has turn'd you out,
            And made you one with me.

BEATRICE: With thee, foul villain?

DE FLORES: Yes, my fair murdr'ess; …

ACTIVITY 11

Think about this stark and abrupt exchange:

• Does Beatrice respond as a 'princess' or as an equal now?

• Why do you think Middleton makes them share a line?

• Why does De Flores use the word 'my'?

At this stage, Beatrice is almost parallel, an equal, to De Flores, but the dramatic movement is not quite complete yet. Finally, later in the scene, Beatrice kneels to him. At this point her downward spiral is complete.

However, is it possible to say that De Flores is equally bound by his own needs, his own desires for Beatrice? Think about his words when Beatrice taunts him near the beginning of the play, and he says:

> Wrangling has prov'd the mistress of good pastime;
> As children cry themselves asleep, I ha' seen
> Women have chid themselves abed to men.

Elsewhere, he says 'I'm up to the chin in heaven' when she approaches him, (Act 2, Scene 2).

ACTIVITY 12

- Is De Flores being truly honest with himself, do you think? Or is he trying to persuade himself because he is desperate?

- Why do you think he is made to use the word 'heaven'?

- Might De Flores be as obsessive and strong-willed as Beatrice, and a little more clear-sighted?

- Could that be why they are called 'twins of mischief' (Act 5, Scene 3)?

In her last speech Beatrice claims that 'beneath the stars, upon yon meteor / Ever hung my fate;' but when you consider choices made and paths followed, do you believe that the outcome is due to fate? Could it be that the characters themselves have brought about their own ends, or is it that 'murder, the deed will out', as De Flores says? Do you think that it is due to a combination of all these factors?

The dramatic context: the use of the sub-plot

The sub-plot does not appeal to everybody who reads or sees this play. This is perhaps because the humour at the sight of madmen is not attractive any more; an original audience might have felt differently. But there are close links between main and sub-plots. Here are a few for you to think about:

ACTIVITY 13

- Work out the actual overlaps in the action, the invitation to the wedding as entertainment; the appearance there; the combination of characters at the end.

- Characters: how might Isabella be compared to Beatrice? Lollio to De Flores? Alibius to Alsemero? Antonio to Alsemero?

- Events: think about the 'test' in each plot, and the decisions and outcomes.

- Language: work out the echoes, such as the game of barley break, the words 'change' and 'conscience'.

Many critics believe that the sub-plot is the exact reverse of the main plot, that there is a comic working-out with no deaths and subsequent happiness compared to the main plot. In this way, it might be possible to contemplate how things might have been if characters had acted with integrity and honour.

The religious context

There is an overlap between the moral and religious contexts, but there are fresh points to be made here. How might you approach this context? Here are some ideas to start you off:

ACTIVITY 14

- Might Alsemero represent the Christian viewpoint? Look at his last speeches, 'justice hath so right / The guilty hit' (Act 5, Scene 3) and see how he offers renewal, with no looking back in his Epilogue. How persuasive do you find this?

- Think about Christian references in the play, such as the Church at the beginning. Is a Christian register used to show how characters misbehave?

- Is Beatrice's repentance a Christian element, and also De Flores's references to conscience?

- Beatrice was the name of **Dante**'s beloved; Dante wrote a poem in which hell was called the *Inferno*, and was seen as circles spiralling down. Might the castle, with its 'narrow descent' and its 'secrets' be a representation of hell on earth? And the flames that sweep the castle during the fire a glimpse of hell?

As you read the play, it is worth noting the words of Christian context, such as sacred, holy and blest, to see how Middleton matches these ironically to events going on.

The language context: imagery and register

There are several key words used in *The Changeling*, each related to one or more themes of the play, each driving home the authors' purposes.

To evaluate the significance of this context, you could relate these sets of words to the themes and actions of the play. Here are some of the words you might think about which are used over and over again in the play as motifs:

ACTIVITY 15

Consider these words:

- 'blood', with four meanings: relationship, high birth, temperament and the hot blood of a sexual relationship, for example: 'I am that of your blood was taken from you' (Act 5, Scene 3)

- 'service': to Beatrice, a servant's duty *initially*; to De Flores, the connotations are sexual as he plays with Beatrice's words for example in Act 2, Scene 1, 'True service merits mercy.'

- 'poison': as Beatrice talks of the murder to Alsemero she says: 'I have kiss'd poison for't,' (Act 5, Scene 3). Perhaps there is an indication of the infection caused by the sin of murder? Might that idea be linked to Beatrice's words to her father above?

- 'change': this word frequently appears in the main and sub-plot, for example in the closing scene of the play. How might it remind you of the play's themes?

You will build up many examples of these words; each time they are used meanings are accumulated, so that each word carries several ideas with it to evoke the themes of the play at once.

ACTIVITY 16

- Consider some of the dramatic moments such as the key scenes, Act 2, Scene 2 and Act 3, Scene 4 with their dramatic reversal, and the horror of Piracquo's severed finger, the dumb show, the animal-like madmen – is this what happens when sexuality is not disguised?

- Think about the setting: the castle as hell, or maybe even a journey into the mind as well, and the closing down of settings for Beatrice and De Flores as they are locked in a closet. How might this develop the themes of this complex and exciting play?

Conclusion

You have now worked through six contexts relating to *The Changeling*. Using this model framework, you can now go on to address other contexts on your own, perhaps beginning with the *dramatic context* in terms of staging and setting.

She Stoops to Conquer – **Oliver Goldsmith**

She Stoops to Conquer, Oliver Goldsmith's second play produced in 1773, was immediately a great success. Goldsmith had very clear ideas about the sort of drama he wished to create, and in *The Westminster Review* of 1773 he wrote an article called 'A Comparison between Laughing Comedy and Sentimental Comedy' explaining his ideas.

He felt that the 'Sentimental Comedy' of the time did little to expose the vice and folly of mankind, and was not even funny. So, in his 'Laughing Comedy' he intended to provoke laughter as he exposed and ridiculed these human flaws.

As a result, *She Stoops to Conquer* is a mixture of sentimental comedy in the Kate/Marlow relationship for example, of satire centred on the character Tony Lumpkin, and farce in the humour of absurd situations.

It is fair to say that Goldsmith was an innovator in most areas, modifying older traditions and developing newer types of comedy. For this reason, *She Stoops to Conquer* is a useful text to study as there is much material for you to work on as you evaluate the significance of the contexts.

Evaluating the significance of the contexts

Oliver Goldsmith drew on past traditions, and developed new forms of drama, so the study of the *generic context* of comedy is a fruitful area to think about.

In a way Goldsmith stands at a watershed. From the past, he drew on very old traditions to establish farce as a strong dramatic form. Originally the name came from medieval drama, when individual cast members improvised in their roles. So the name 'farce' comes from the French word meaning 'stuffing', as these characters extended their roles and therefore filled out the performance. Then a great French writer of the seventeenth century, Molière, helped establish this sub-genre in his plays such as *The Hypochondriac,* where he ridiculed human vices.

Goldsmith developed this form so that several characteristics were established which are recognisable in today's farces. These include: the presentation of ridiculous situations, problems arising from mistaken identity, and marital problems, all played with split-second timing. You might recognise some of the modern successors to Goldsmith's drama, which include the plays of Michael Frayn, Ben Travers and Joe Orton, and in a different medium, TV programmes such as *Fawlty Towers*, *Absolutely Fabulous* and *Blackadder*.

From the slightly earlier Restoration Drama, Goldsmith inherited key motifs including: conflict between town and country, the idea of the country bumpkin as a fool, the central character of the **Restoration Rake,** and problems of parenting and inheritance. In each area, Goldsmith made innovations, so the significance of the context is clear to evaluate through the ways in which Oliver Goldsmith made changes to what was handed down.

In the larger scheme of *social comedy*, Goldsmith again made alterations to the way in which the problems within a society were exposed and resolved because he varied the outcome for different characters.

In the *social and moral contexts* there are several areas worth investigating. These include:

- the establishing of balanced relationships between lovers

- the moral growth of a rakish youth at the hands of a good woman and the need for prudence in another young man

- problems of justice in terms of parenting and the legal question of inheritance

- social issues of town versus country conflict

- the area of women's rights.

This text is rich ground for feminist readings, with a study of the views and behaviour of the two central female characters. However, after you have read the text you should decide whether you think that Oliver Goldsmith is truly radical in his attitude to women and their rights, or in fact finally supports the situation which existed in the society of his age.

Of the many interesting contexts available, these are the six to be considered here:

- the generic context of comedy and the dramatic context

- the social and moral contexts of comedy as a means of redefining society

- the social and moral contexts of women's rights

- the social and moral contexts of love

- the social and moral contexts of parenting

- the moral, social and legal contexts of inheritance.

The generic context of comedy and the dramatic context

Earlier in the introduction there was a reference to Oliver Goldsmith's skill in developing farce as a central feature of a newly popularised form of drama. To make farce acceptable and credible Goldsmith carefully prepared the audience to accept without quibbling the often preposterous situations presented on stage. He used several techniques to achieve this, including:

- the use of **alienation**

- very careful, tight plot structuring

- very funny situations which helped the audience to drop their guard, his so-called 'Laughing Comedy'

- other dramatic effects.

The use of alienation

Alienation is a technique used to persuade the audience to 'suspend disbelief'; in other words, to lose expectations of realistic presentation of characters and events, and for the time being, to accept wholeheartedly what the playwright suggests, even if in 'real life' it would be absurd. Goldsmith partly achieves this through the use of a Prologue.

The Prologue was spoken by one of the actors in the play, who explained Goldsmith's belief to the audience that a new kind of comedy was needed:

> The Comic muse, long sick, is now a-dying!

Through the speaker Goldsmith used the image of comedy as a sick maiden, and explained that he offered:

> A kind of magic charm – for be assur'd,
> If you will swallow it, the maid is cur'd: ...

ACTIVITY 1

Think about what Goldsmith is doing in the Prologue, and work out:

- what sort of case Goldsmith is making

- how he tries to win the audience over

- what might be new in the playwright's view of comedy.

Careful plot structuring

Oliver Goldsmith created a very tight structure to his play. The remarkably complex plot is contrived so brilliantly that each fresh situation appears to arise naturally from previous events, so the play has a strong internal logic.

Therefore, it seems sensible to begin by looking at some of the ways in which Goldsmith prepares the audience for some of the farcical situations of the play. In this way, you will be 'evaluating the significance of the context' as you explore the innovations which Goldsmith brings to comedy.

As soon as the play opens, Goldsmith sets up the possibility for confusion in Mrs Hardcastle's second speech in Act 1, Scene 1:

Here we live in an old rumbling mansion, that looks for all the world like an inn, but that we never see company.

ACTIVITY 2

This extract shows how economical Goldsmith is in his methods. You have to read this play very carefully, for all the speeches seem to count. You might think about this speech and consider:

- how it prepares the way for the confusions of place and identity which are so funny

- how these few words let you know a little about the character of Mrs Hardcastle.

You will realise that because the audience has been prepared for confusion, it will be easier for them to accept later farcical developments in the plot. A similar example occurs in Act 1, Scene 2 when Tony Lumpkin misleads Marlow and Hastings as he describes 'Mr Hardcastle's' of 'Quagmire Marsh' as an inn, the 'Buck's Head', and continues:

He'll be for giving you his company, and ecod, if you mind him, he'll persuade you that his mother was an alderman, and his aunt a justice of the peace.

ACTIVITY 3

Again, Goldsmith makes sure that a lot of things are going on here. You might think about:

- how this prepares the audience for the confusion of place and situation

- how this sets up confusion of identity

- in terms of ideas, what these confusions might suggest about the shallowness of a class system that lays so much store on name and rank.

Here is a third and final example for you to think about. As early as Act 1, Scene 2 you hear of Marlow's 'unaccountable reserve'. This is taken further in Act 2 when Marlow is about to meet Kate Hardcastle, and complains to Hastings:

... But for the rest, I don't think I shall venture to look in her face, till I see my father's again.

Again, this is a neat and economical method of plot building. What do you think Goldsmith prepared you for here?

ACTIVITY 4

You might explore the significance of these words and think about the following:

• How does Marlow's admission make later events with Kate credible?

• How do they help create more confusion of identity?

• How does Goldsmith cleverly build up character here?

• How does Goldsmith have another swipe at the rules of this stuffy society?

These are just three of the many examples of clever and careful plotting in the play. You might go on, for example, to think about Mrs Hardcastle's belief in the Tony/Charlotte engagement, near the end of Act 2 and of Kate changing her dress at her father's command, at the beginning of Act 3. You might explore the ways in which Goldsmith neatly intertwines the main Marlow/Kate plot with the jewellery plot later in the same act. It might be helpful for you to have a clear chart of all of the instances where Goldsmith prepares for later developments in the play.

Goldsmith's 'Laughing Comedy'

Throughout the play there is great fun and much laughter, such as the exchanges between the confused Marlow, Hastings and Mr Hardcastle as they discuss the dinner menu, for example, near the beginning of Act 2. Similarly, there is the fun of Mrs Hardcastle seeing her husband as a highwayman in Act 5, Scene 2. Again, you might find it helpful to list all these comical scenes, and think about how a good laugh might charm an audience and lull the sense of outrage at the impossibility of what is happening on stage.

Other comic effects

Oliver Goldsmith adds other techniques to vary the effects of the play. There is the knock-about humour of Mr Hardcastle trying to train his hopeless servants at the beginning of Act 2 when the audience can see that this is probably a lost cause. You might think here whether Marlow's 'posher' servants are really seen as any better than Mr Hardcastle's country servants at the beginning of Act 4. All the way through Goldsmith uses **dramatic irony** when the audience is fully aware of what is really going on although the characters are fooled by disguises. There is also irony, for example when Marlow misguidedly gives Charlotte's jewels to Mrs Hardcastle to look after in Act 4, and tells Hastings:

I have sent it to the landlady to keep for you.

To the landlady!
The landlady!

You did?

I did.

ACTIVITY 5

- How does the exchange here develop the situation?

- How effective is the pace of the dialogue, and the repetition?

- How does this exchange remind the audience of Mrs Hardcastle's moral flaws, her greed and dishonesty?

There is also the *pace* of the play, which rattles along at a great speed. Look carefully at the mistake of thinking the house is an inn in Act 2: for how long does Goldsmith let this go on? Do you think he carefully judges how much an audience will take of any absurd situation?

Perhaps the best example of pace occurs at the end of Act 3, when Mr Hardcastle allows Kate just one hour to prove that Marlow is a worthy suitor. Interestingly, this runs very close to real time in the span of the play, and will surely help to create tension as the internal clocks of the audience will immediately start ticking away. All in all, Oliver Goldsmith was very careful in his preparation and plotting, extremely funny, and used a wide repertoire of tricks to lull or amuse his audience into accepting the farcical situations developed. That is what Goldsmith brought to the genre of comedy.

The social and moral contexts of comedy as a means of re-defining society

Dr Samuel Johnson, Oliver Goldsmith's good friend, wrote: 'No man was more foolish when he had not a pen in his hand, or more wise when he had.' You might think about whether this is a just comment, and whether Goldsmith seemed to have a keen sense of social justice mixed with a fair degree of common sense. You might see this as Goldsmith surveys the society of the age, and assesses how it could be improved, which he presents in comic terms.

In this type of comedy three different stages have been noted:

- the existence of an unsettled society governed by a harsh or irrational law under which people are unhappy

- temporary loss of identity as confusion reigns

- the discovery of a new identity as a well-balanced society is re-formed and the characters take their rightful places in society.

Three characters will be considered here: Tony Lumpkin, Mrs Hardcastle and Marlow. You might go on to explore other characters in your own time.

The existence of an unsettled society governed by a harsh or irrational law

When you meet Tony Lumpkin he is in an inn enjoying himself. Hastings explains at the end of Act 2 that he knows that Tony prefers this sort of company, and does not want to marry Charlotte. Tony seems to be unsettled, and perhaps much of this is due to Mrs Hardcastle, who explains to her son how she has brought him up near the end of Act 2:

Did I not work that waistcoat to make you genteel? Did I not prescribe for you every day, and weep while the receipt was operating?

ACTIVITY 6

What does this reveal about the lack of common sense of Mrs Hardcastle's aims? You might think about the following:

- What social rank was his father, Mrs Hardcastle's first husband? How did he behave?

- Are Mrs Hardcastle's ambitions for her son reasonable? Do they make him happy?

- What do you think her real motives are?

Then there is Marlow, who, as you saw on page 146, cannot cope with the social niceties of courtship.

Temporary loss of identity

This section needs little explanation as all the characters are confused in one way or another. However, you might explore the ways in which Goldsmith varies the usual formula by making Tony actually a leader in his wisdom and quickwittedness, saving the day for the four lovers with his plans. He really is no country fool, is he?

Discovery of a new identity

In this area Goldsmith also pops in some surprises. Marlow is the most conventional, a Restoration rake who reforms. However, Goldsmith modifies this so that you see his genuinely good nature when he refuses to seduce Kate-as-barmaid in Act 4: 'I can never harbour a thought of seducing simplicity ...'. He seems to be truly a nobleman, especially when he admits his stupidity in Act 4.

You can see how Goldsmith modifies the outcome as far as Mrs Hardcastle and Tony are concerned. Throughout the play Goldsmith has manipulated the audience's responses to Mrs Hardcastle as her greed and vanity become clear. At the end of the play husband and son turn on her:

ACTIVITY 7

Remind yourself of the exchanges in Act 5, Scene 3, when Tony discovers that he is actually of age, and takes delight in spiting his mother: 'Then you'll see the first use I'll make of my liberty', as he refuses Constance. Mr Hardcastle has been surprised by her greed over the jewels: 'Sure, Dorothy, you would not be so mercenary?'

- What do you think of Mrs Hardcastle now?

- How does she come out at the end of the play? Does she achieve her ambitions, or does she get what she deserves?

As far as Tony is concerned, Goldsmith provides an unusual outcome. You may well find that you have grown to approve of him during the course of the play. Perhaps you think that he is kind and rather wise. Then he is given a moving speech, about men not letting quarrels last – a lesson he delivers to Marlow and Hastings in Act 5, Scene 2:

After we take a knock in this part of the country, we kiss and be friends.

ACTIVITY 8

Think carefully about this short speech, and consider the following:

- What sort of friendships and relationships does Tony appear to have in his own group?

- How might this compare with the bickering of those socially superior?

- Do you think that in a way Tony might be wise in rejecting the higher society for truer friends?

So at the end of the play Goldsmith has redefined a society in which there is stability and in which people have found their true place, and have been rewarded according to what they deserve.

The social and moral contexts of women's rights

This is rather a tricky matter to deal with in *She Stoops to Conquer*. You need to weigh the evidence very carefully, for some people believe that Goldsmith is sympathetic to women's rights and their restricted roles in society. However, others believe that although he seems to be very supportive about the case for improved rights and roles for women, nevertheless at the end of the play the existing social structure is reinforced. You might think about:

- the roles the women take on in the play

- social attitudes and their implications

- Goldsmith's attitude towards women in society.

The roles the women take on in the play

Perhaps Kate makes the case clearly about how she sees male/female relationships when she talks of her attempts to win Marlow over in Act 3:

> But my chief aim is to take my gentleman off his guard, and like an invisible champion of romance examine the giant's force before I offer to combat.

ACTIVITY 9

Think carefully about what Kate is saying here, and how she expresses her ideas:

- She thinks of herself as a medieval knight in combat defending 'romance'; but why 'invisible'? What might this suggest about her status in society?

- Why might she describe the male as a giant?

- Do you think she stands a chance of winning? Why?

Might this suggest that Kate is very clear-minded? Is Marlow?

Further evidence of Kate's clarity of vision is the way she describes what she needs to do to win her man:

ACTIVITY 10

Kate states in Act 5 that she needed to 'stoop to conquer' Marlow. You will have seen how their courtship was not conventional or open because of Marlow's social inadequacy and his reserve. Also, Kate needed to manipulate her father by hiding behind a screen to engage Marlow in courtship in disguise as a barmaid.

What do you think this tells us about the balance of power between the two sexes?

However, there is a discussion about society and the expectation of dowries for women, when Sir Charles Marlow dismisses Mr Hardcastle's worries about Kate's lack of wealth in Act 5, Scene 1:

Why, Dick, will you talk of fortune to *me*? My son is possessed of more than a competence already, and can want nothing but a good and virtuous girl to share his happiness and increase it.

ACTIVITY 11

- What sort of viewpoint is Goldsmith suggesting here?

- What might be seen as the ideal basis for marriage?

Social attitudes and their implications

Constance offers a slightly different viewpoint. Think about how she behaves in Act 2 when Hastings impetuously wishes her to elope. She says to him:

I have often told you, that though ready to obey you, I yet should leave my little fortune behind with reluctance.

ACTIVITY 12

- Do you think that there is a difference in Constance's attitude to marriage from Kate's?

- Why might she be reluctant to lose her fortune?

- Might she be more socially **conformist** than Kate?

This conformity is partly explained in Act 5, Scene 3 when Constance explains why she had to deceive her aunt over the relationship with Tony Lumpkin after her father's death:

Since his death, I have been obliged to stoop to dissimulation to avoid oppression.

ACTIVITY 13

What do you think are the differences between Kate's and Constance's attitudes? You might consider:

- how their social levels are different

- whether one woman is luckier than the other

- whether one is more conventional than the other.

Goldsmith's attitude towards women in society

What do you think about the outcomes for the two women? How much power do they have socially? What are their probable roles in marriage? Has Goldsmith come up with anything new or unconventional, or does he pretty much let the status quo stand? That is something you must decide for yourself as you look further into the presentation of the two women in this play, and extend your thoughts to include other minor female characters.

The social and moral contexts of love

To assess this context you might consider all the male/female relationships in the play, although the two main female characters, Kate and Constance, are the most significant.

ACTIVITY 14

- Begin by comparing the differences in the ways in which Marlow treats Kate as Mr Hardcastle's daughter, and as a barmaid. You will be able to draw several conclusions from this.

- Move outwards and compare this relationship with that of Constance and Hastings.

The social and moral contexts of parenting

This is a rich field of study, as there are several examples of parent–child relationships.

ACTIVITY 15

- Begin with the absurd relationship which Oliver Goldsmith so cruelly satirises between Mrs Hardcastle and her son Tony Lumpkin, remembering that beneath the humour some serious moral points are being made.

- Move your focus out to compare this with the possibly equally indulgent but perhaps sounder relationship between Kate and her father.

The moral, social and legal contexts of inheritance

This is a large context as so many social issues are drawn in. You should bear in mind that money and dowry mattered very much at the time.

ACTIVITY 16

- Begin by thinking about the entrusting of Constance's welfare to Mrs Hardcastle, and what nearly happened.

- Use this as a basis for comparing attitudes to money. It might be worth comparing Tony's attitude to his inheritance, with his casual generosity, to Constance's really earnest awareness of her need to make sure that she received her rightful inheritance. What do you think the differences are in these two attitudes?

Conclusion

This concludes the study of six contexts in Oliver Goldsmith's play *She Stoops to Conquer*. You must remember that you need to do more work on each of these contexts, and then develop your own ideas about some contexts of your own choice. As you will have discovered, one of the great pleasures of this play is the laughter it generates. You will smile as you read – and that is a great plus for an A2 level text!

The Rover – Aphra Behn

Restoration Drama is so called because theatres that had been closed by the Puritan Oliver Cromwell were reopened to the public in 1660 after the restoration of Charles II to the throne. However, although public performances had been banned, plays had still been read and performed privately. So the Restoration dramatists had no sharp break with past traditions, and in the reopened theatres older plays, such as the Revenge Tragedies, were very popular. It is no surprise, therefore, that Aphra Behn may have used some of the conventions of the Revenge Tragedy in her play *The Rover*. But *The Rover* has been linked to many genres: comedy, tragicomedy, drama of intrigue, farce, and history play, to name but a few.

Aphra Behn was vilified over the publication of *The Rover*, apparently because she was a woman who dared to enter a man's field. She was unmarried, and supported herself by her own writing. Concern for women and their roles and rights is therefore very important in this play.

As Aphra Behn's *The Rover* is a Restoration Comedy, you might find it helpful to look at the characteristic features of the genre listed on page 163.

The six contexts considered for the study of *The Rover* are:

- the literary and social contexts of comedy

- the social context: the female perspective

- the social context: the male perspective

- the literary context: the Revenge Tragedy

- the dramatic context: the carnival setting

- the psychological/dramatic context.

Evaluating the significance of the contexts

One way of evaluating the significance of the contexts treated below is to compare what you would gain from them.

Aphra Behn wrote her play at a time when women were just emerging as playwrights, and so it might well be assumed that she would have something to say about gender and the roles and behaviour of men and women. Consideration of the *social context* from both the female and the male perspective might well draw attention to issues the dramatist was particularly interested in. It would still have been something of a novelty for audiences to see a play written by a woman. Gender is also a major issue for audiences today, and so consideration of these contexts allows modern readers and audiences to draw some conclusions as to the similarities and differences between their own attitudes and values and those of Restoration society.

Consideration of the *literary context* of comedy, however, will draw your attention to those elements of *The Rover* that were conventional at the time it was written. It could indicate which aspects of Aphra Behn's craft might have seemed novel to an audience and which would have been familiar. But Aphra Behn is also mixing genres in this play, and consideration of the play in the context of the Revenge tradition would draw attention to its darker and more sinister aspects.

Similarly, consideration of the carnival setting draws attention to the stagecraft employed by Aphra Behn and to those aspects of 'entertainment' that a contemporary audience might particularly have enjoyed (this is a *dramatic context*). Disguise was a common feature of plays of the period and so contemporary audiences would have been able to think about the treatment of disguises in *The Rover* by comparing it with the use of disguises in other contemporary plays.

Consideration of the *psychological/dramatic context* can focus attention on two main areas of the play – the extent to which the characters are fully rounded or mere 'types', and the extent to which Aphra Behn is concerned to show us the thought processes of the characters. This will allow you to identify which characters appear to be most fully developed, in other words those to whom she wanted the audience to pay particular attention. You could go on to think about what aspects of motivation and behaviour she wanted the audience to consider.

The different contexts, therefore, draw our attention to different features of the play. They might also lead to different interpretations of the play. Which context you find the most helpful or useful will, therefore, depend on what you see as the most interesting and significant features of the play. However, AO5ii asks you to consider a range of different contexts, to think about how each of them might be important, and to assess how far each of them illuminates your interpretation of the play.

The literary and social contexts of comedy

As you saw when looking at Shakespeare's *Measure for Measure* (see page 128), it has been suggested that there are three successive stages in a social comedy: (1) first, an unsettled society governed by a harsh or irrational law; (2) a temporary loss of identity; and finally (3) the discovery of a new identity and a reconciliation. This structure seems to suit the development of *The Rover*.

An unsettled society governed by a harsh or irrational law

You can see immediately that the members of society shown in *The Rover* are very unsettled. It has been decided that for the sake of family honour, Hellena must become a nun. She gives her view on this in Act 1, Scene 1:

> And dost thou think that ever I'll be a Nun? Or at least til I'm so old, I'm fit for nothing else. Faith no, Sister; ... nay, I'm resolv'd to Provide my self this Carnival,

ACTIVITY 1

- What is Hellena's attitude towards her intended life?

- What sort of person does she seem to be?

Florinda is no happier. She has had one fiancé, Don Vincentio, selected for her by her father without consultation. She talks about him to Hellena (Act 1, Scene 1):

... and how near so ever my Father thinks I am to marrying that hated Object, I shall let him see I understand better what's due to my Beauty, Birth and Fortune, and more to my Soul, than to obey those unjust Commands.

ACTIVITY 2

- What might be the reasons behind Florinda's rejection of this proposed marriage?

Her brother, Don Pedro, hears her complaints, and suggests another fiancé instead, his friend Antonio. Florinda explains why she will find it difficult to get out of this second match (Act 1, Scene 1):

I've no Defence against Antonio's Love,
For he has all the Advantages of nature,
The moving arguments of Youth and Fortune.

These words may explain the harsh or irrational law governing this society.

ACTIVITY 3

- Why has Florinda 'no Defence' in refusing Antonio's courtship?

- Why might the family be pleased with this marriage?

Florinda also talks to her brother, who will:

follow the ill Customs of our Country, and make a Slave of his Sister.

ACTIVITY 4

- Is Don Pedro's attitude towards his sister the same as his father's?

- What does this tell us about the role of women in society, and how they are perceived by men? Is this treatment of women just, or 'an ill custom'?

A temporary loss of identity

Dominated as they are by disguise and confusion, the carnival scenes establish this period of lost identity.

ACTIVITY 5

Remind yourself of the scene in Act 3, where Florinda, hoping to elope with Belvile, is accosted by Willmore, who is drunk.

- Might the drunkenness suggest confusion? Is it a form of 'disguise'?

- Is there a serious issue here about attitudes to women?

In Act 4, Scene 1, Florinda is again chased by Willmore, but she is captured by Ned Blunt, who is joined by Frederick. Later (Act 4, Scene 3) Blunt says:

... we must be better acquainted – we'll both lie with her, and then let me alone to bang her.

In Act 5, Scene 1, Willmore suggests that they 'draw cuts' for her.

ACTIVITY 6

- Do you think that this is a serious situation for Florinda?

- What might be the implications of the idea of disguise here?

- Could there be a suggestion that Florinda is, to the men, a mere animal-like convenience, and not a woman? Women 'disguised' as animals?

- Might the men seem to behave as though they were animals also, unconcerned with the rights of a woman? Men 'disguised' as animals?

The discovery of a new identity and a reconciliation

After the disguise and confusion of the carnival, Act 5 presents reconciliations and the foundation of a new and better society. In keeping with the traditions of comedy, this is achieved through marriage: Florinda and Belvile, the idealised 'Romantic' lovers, finally wed, as do Hellena and Willmore. But here Aphra Behn may present a realistic view when Willmore says (Act 5, Scene 1):

> ... I adore thy Humour and will marry thee, and we are so of one Humour, it must be a bargain – give me thy Hand –

Hellena later adds that she would rather spend her inheritance of three hundred thousand crowns 'in Love than in Religion'.

ACTIVITY 7

- Do you think that their relationship will be smooth or stormy?

- Has Aphra Behn been honest in showing that marriage requires courage?

- Has she been honest in showing that in this society money helps to achieve independence?

There are tragic tones at the end, related to Angelica and Moretta, which are considered in the next context. The significance of this context has been evaluated by considering *The Rover* within the genre of comedy.

The social context: the female perspective

This context was touched on above in Activities 1–4 (pages 157–8), when you assessed Florinda's and Hellena's reactions to the marriages proposed by their father and their brother. It is seen to be a patriarchal society, dominated by men and ruled by men's laws. Activities 5 and 6 explored the lack of value placed on women, and another perspective was touched on in the assessment of the comic outcome of the play, while also noting the tragic element introduced by Angelica, Moretta and Lucetta.

The problem for these three women may be that in this harsh society, a woman needed financial independence in order to live as she wanted to. It may have been all right for wealthy young women of powerful families, but what about women of a different social order? In Act 2, Scene 1, the men discuss Angelica's picture and her price as a prostitute. Belvile thinks she 'has rais'd the Price too high', but Willmore says:

> How wondrous fair she is – a Thousand Crowns a Month – by Heaven as many kingdoms were too little.

ACTIVITY 8

- Why do you think that Angelica has set such a high price?

- Do you think that she might have some pride in herself?

- How do you respond when Willmore has sex with her without payment?

Moretta, Angelica's assistant, is quite realistic about the future for women such as them. As she is dependent upon Angelica, she is dismayed when Angelica falls for Willmore (Act 2, Scene 1):

Oh Madam we're undone, a pox upon that rude Fellow, he's set on to ruin us:

ACTIVITY 9

- Why do you think that Moretta is so concerned for Angelica's actions?

- Do you think that she might be talking sense financially?

To consider the outcome of Angelica's love for Willmore, ask yourself the questions in the next activity.

ACTIVITY 10

- Do such women have a hope of improving their situations in Restoration society?

- Angelica and Moretta 'sell' their favours. Can you see any similarity to the ways in which wealthy fathers 'sell' their daughters in marriage?

- Is the difference social or moral? Willmore says about the carnival "tis a kind of legal authoriz'd Fornication' (Act 1, Scene 2). Might this be the truth?

- Might the situation of the prostitutes be seen as tragic?

- Might the audience, through Angelica's moving speeches in Act 5, Scene 1, warm to her?

To evaluate the significance of this context, you could assess the situation of the women in the society in which they lived; you could carry out the opposite exercise when you consider the male characters in the next context.

The social context: the male perspective

The men, in contrast, seem to have complete sexual freedom. Pedro offers to buy Angelica (Act 2, Scene 1); Ned Blunt tries to use Lucetta (Act 2, Scene 2); and Ned and Frederick both abuse Florinda (Act 4, Scene 3). Belvile seems to be unique in his faithfulness to Florinda. The central character of the play, Willmore, is 'the rover'. He is almost pathological in his need to pursue and conquer women. Belvile recognises this in Act 3, Scene 4:

... if it had not been Florinda, must you be a Beast? – a Brute, a senseless Swine?

ACTIVITY 11

- Why is Belvile so enraged with Willmore?

- Might he be making a point about Willmore's attitude to women generally?

But Willmore is a complex character who may well charm an audience. In Act 5, Scene 1, he is honest with Angelica about his fault:

I wish I were that dull, that constant thing,
Which thou woud'st have, and nature never meant me:

ACTIVITY 12

- How do you respond to Willmore's honesty here? Is he disarming?

- Do you find the honest Belvile or the wild Willmore the more attractive?

Willmore is 'reformed' to some extent by marriage, but Aphra Behn seems to indicate that married life will not be easy. Many critics point out the political context of the men. They are exiled Cavaliers, noblemen or upper-class gentlemen who fought on the side of the King in the English Civil War; they were defeated, made penniless for their efforts, and exiled by the new ruler, the Lord Protector of England, Oliver Cromwell. They are attractive and spirited, and accept the social climber Blunt because he is rich, 'his Purse be secure', which will provide the Cavaliers' 'whole Estate' (Act 2, Scene 1). Might Blunt be somewhat resented because, by avoiding fighting in the Civil War, he risked nothing? Might Aphra Behn feel some nostalgia for the glamorous past in a new, rather dull, less heroic England?

To evaluate the significance of this context, you could assess the situation of the men in the society presented in the play.

The literary context: the Revenge Tragedy

To consider this aspect, it might be helpful to think about the characteristic features of plays in the Revenge genre, such as:

- How many revengers are there in *The Rover*?

- Is there the usually foreign setting, such as Italy or Spain?

- Is there intrigue, violence, a poisoning, death?

- Is there a disguise to create confusion?

- Is there a bloodbath at the end?

- Is there a central character who can act as a commentator?

Now consider the questions in the next activity.

ACTIVITY 13

- Who are the revengers? Might Angelica and Blunt be considered as such?

- Is the need for revenge justified?

- Is the ending that of a Revenge Tragedy or that of a comedy?

- If any component parts of a Revenge Tragedy are omitted or altered, why might Aphra Behn have made that particular choice?

- What is it that she wishes to say about the society portrayed in the play?

The dramatic context: the carnival setting

Aphra Behn makes much use of this setting, and you can assess its implications by considering the questions in the next activity.

ACTIVITY 14

- Might the disguise help to create humorous situations for the audience?

- Does it allow for multiple action on stage?

- How does it allow the different layers of the plot to come together?

- Does the Naples setting allow for the introduction of characters such as Angelica, Moretta or Lucetta?

- What effects does the introduction of characters such as these women have on the breadth of the play's action and themes?

- Might this setting allow the sexual double standards of the society to be made clear? What are the differences in the rules of behaviour for men and for women?

- How does Aphra Behn undermine these codes of behaviour, and what does she achieve by this?

- Does the carnival allow for the reversal of the usual social situation, so that the sisters may become the pursuers instead of the pursued?

The psychological/dramatic context

To address this context you could consider the different types of character presented in *The Rover*. For example, you could distinguish between characters who have psychological motivation, and those who remain largely undeveloped. Examples here might be:

ACTIVITY 15

- Belvile: how much variety or development is created for him?

- Willmore: is he the central protagonist whom we see as a Restoration 'rake' or philanderer reformed?

- Are Hellena, Florinda and Angelica presented 'from the inside'?

- To what extent is Blunt a realistic character, and to what extent is he the stock 'country bumpkin' of Restoration Comedy?

- Might he be used as the main source of broad humour in the play?

- Are Lucetta and Moretta anything more than two-dimensional?

- Might they act as ciphers to allow Aphra Behn to develop her ideas?

Conclusion

You have now worked through six contexts relating to *The Rover* (remember that this list is not exhaustive). Using this model framework, you can go on to address other contexts on your own, perhaps beginning with a consideration of the play as a Restoration Comedy. The following checklist identifies some of the typical features of Restoration Comedy.

- What classes of society are presented in this play?

- How far is the play concerned with the issue of 'manners', of how to behave properly in society?

- Is the author interested in something that might seem rather more serious?

- Is there sexual intrigue?

- Are there attractive, high-spirited, noble gentlemen?

- Is there a character outside this charmed circle (from the country, for example) who is mocked or used as a source of humour?

- Might this 'gull' be mocked because he tries to be fashionable and wise like the hero, but becomes a fool in doing so?

- Is there a central hero who develops during the course of the play?

- How do you respond to the idea that the audience of the day saw in the hero a reflection of themselves, and in the fop or bumpkin a reflection of their neighbour?

- Do you think that the author has a serious moral purpose in writing the play?

The Way of the World – William Congreve

The Way of the World, like *The Rover* by Aphra Behn, belongs to the genre of Restoration Comedy, and it would be helpful to read through the discussion of this genre on page 163. Congreve's play is considered by many critics to be the peak of Restoration Comedy, and this context is the sixth context discussed below.

First staged in 1700, *The Way of the World* is concerned with the nature of society, and relationships within society. Congreve's interest, as he explains in the dedication, is with the 'affected' and 'false' wit that damages society. 'True wit' implies an intelligent and well-judged understanding of how to behave properly and elegantly in society. 'False wit' is characterised by affectation and pretence. Congreve may be seen to extend this criticism to include 'false' people who are not really what they appear to be, such as Fainall and Mrs Marwood. At first such people seem to thrive in the society of *The Way of the World*; but after the 'Proviso scene' between Millamant and Mirabell in Act 4, Scene 1, a new society, based on social justice and fairness, is established.

Because the concerns of Restoration Comedy were finally centred on the individual as a member of society, drama became secular; that is to say, religious themes such as sin and punishment are not included. This marks a major break with pre-Restoration drama.

The six contexts considered for the study of *The Way of the World* are:

- the philosophical context

- the social context

- the biographical context: the influence of Congreve's training as a lawyer

- the dramatic context: 'patterning' within the play

- the context of genre I: the play as a **Comedy of Manners**

- the context of genre II: the play as a Restoration Comedy.

Evaluating the significance of the contexts

One way of evaluating the significance of the contexts treated below is to compare what you would gain from them.

Consideration of the *social context* might lead you to think about the ways in which society is organised. This context in particular will allow you to compare attitudes and values as depicted in the play with the attitudes and values of the author's own time and society. It therefore leads you to think about the extent to which Congreve's play needs to be understood in terms of the time in which it was written, and the extent to which it deals with matters that transcend time. By looking at this context, characters' attitudes and values are identified and compared and some conclusions can be drawn about matters such as marriage and inheritance, as well as the laws which govern the passing of property from one person to another, particularly to a woman.

An understanding of the *philosophical context* places this exploration of different kinds of people in a wider context of ideas – those of Thomas Hobbes and John Locke – and so makes you aware that the play is part of a much wider concern with the period's with reason, sensation and society.

The *context of genre* allows you to make comparison not so much with the ideas prevalent in the Restoration period as with the kind of plays that were popular at the time. An exploration of the genre of Restoration Comedy will make you aware of *The Way of the World* within the context of what contemporary audiences would be familiar with, and what they might be expecting from a new play. The more these contexts are explored the more it becomes apparent that in this play Congreve introduced new elements into the comedy genre. A contemporary audience would have been particularly fascinated by Mrs Marwood, by the Proviso scene, and by the character of Millamant, and they would have been intrigued by how matters of inheritance are sorted out.

The context of *patterning* within the play allows us to appreciate more fully Congreve's craftsmanship. His skilful use of such patterning allowed him to construct what was thought at the time, and by many critics since, to be a 'well-made play'.

The different contexts, therefore, draw our attention to different features of the play. They might also lead to different interpretations of the play. Which context you find the most helpful or useful will, therefore, depend on what you see as the most interesting and significant features of the play. However, AO5ii asks you to consider a range of different contexts, to think about how each of them might be important, and to assess how far each of them illuminates your interpretation of the play.

The philosophical context

This context is made apparent in the contrast between Fainall and Mirabell. The character of Fainall may be evident in the opening scene, where he has won the card game, and says to Mirabell:

> … I'd no more play with a man that slighted his ill fortune than I'd make love to a woman who undervalued the loss of her reputation.

ACTIVITY 1

- What is Fainall's attitude here?

- Does he seem to care for anybody other than himself?

Throughout the play Fainall can be seen to treat life as he treats the card game, as a game of chance and opportunity. His response to other people is seen in his words about his wife, Mrs Marwood (Act 2, Scene 1):

… and wherefore did I marry, but to make lawful prize of a rich widow's wealth, and squander it on love and you?

ACTIVITY 2

- What do you think of his attitude here? What about the word 'squander'?

- Does he appear to think of anything but satisfying his own desires?

Mirabell can be seen as a contrast. He appears to think about other people, as you can see in the Proviso scene (Act 4, Scene 1). But he isn't perfect: he has arranged a marriage for a pregnant mistress and deceived Lady Wishfort, though at several points in the play he appears to feel sorrow for his past actions. He tries to make amends to Mrs Fainall (Act 2, Scene 1):

In justice to you, I have made you privy to my whole design, and put it in your power to ruin or advance my fortune.

And in Act 5, Scene 1, he apologies to Lady Wishfort with 'a sincere remorse and a hearty contrition'.

ACTIVITY 3

- How is his attitude towards other people different from that of Fainall?

- Which attitude do you think is a better basis for society?

What is the difference between these two sets of attitudes? Behind the presentation of these two characters, Mirabell and Fainall, there probably lie two contrasting seventeenth-century philosophies, those of Thomas Hobbes and John Locke. Hobbes believed we learn from experience and sensation, and that our 'appetites' let us gather experience through our own activities (Mrs Marwood refers to 'appetites' in Act 3, Scene 1). Does Fainall live to experience different sorts of pleasure entirely for his own satisfaction?

On the other hand, Locke suggested that we learn to work out our situation in society and the world as a whole through the application of our reason. Mirabell might be seen to represent a way of thinking drawn from the philosophy of Locke. In his *Essay Concerning Human Understanding* (1690), Locke argues that we can make sound judgements by using reason. In *The Way of the World*, Mirabell works through reason, through applying his judgement, so that his actions will no longer damage other people, as you saw in Activity 3 above. His responses to other people seem to be based on an idea of social justice, namely that people should think about others around them as well as of themselves.

ACTIVITY 4

- Which set of ideas do you think provides the better basis for society?

- Do you think Congreve believed in Hobbes or Locke?

- Which rules do you think govern the new society at the end of the play?

The social context

This context is related to the philosophical context, as the female characters in the play generally follow the same categories as the men. You may see Mrs Fainall and Millamant as characters in the Lockean sense, and Mrs Marwood as a Hobbesian character. Mrs Fainall seems to be a generous and caring character, as you can see when she replies to Millamant's question about marrying Mirabell (Act 4, Scene 1):

Ay, ay, take him, take him, what should you do?
…
Fie, fie, have him, have him, and tell him so in plain terms;

ACTIVITY 5

- How might Mrs Fainall have damaged Millamant's happiness here?

- What do you think of her as a person here? Is she generous? Forgiving?

Throughout the play, Millamant seems to be a sensible person, and she seems aware of the foolishness of those around her. Congreve might be thought to use Mirabell to point up Millamant's character, as in Act 2, Scene 1:

You would affect a cruelty which is not in your nature; your true vanity is in the power of pleasing.

ACTIVITY 6

- What sort of a character sketch of Millamant is presented here?

- Do you think that it is a fair judgement of Millamant overall?

- Do you see her hurt people?

Mrs Marwood is a different kettle of fish. She plots with Fainall (Act 3, Scene 1):

> You married her to keep you; and if you can contrive to have her keep you better than you expected, why should you not keep her longer than you intended?

ACTIVITY 7

- What sort of a person do you think that Mrs Marwood is?

- Does she care about the well-being of anyone else?

- Is she interested in anything more than money, and her own desires?

You could then consider the observations Congreve is making about society. You might ask yourself questions such as those in the next activity.

ACTIVITY 8

- What attitudes towards marriage are evident in this play?

- Are the rules of marriage rewritten in the Proviso scene?

- What are the attitudes towards money and love?

- Are money and love linked?

- Is the society represented in most of the play caring or just?

- What happens at the end of the play? Are any social rules reformed?

The biographical context: the influence of Congreve's training as a lawyer

Congreve had some training in law, having entered the Middle Temple to study law in 1691. This legal knowledge is evident in the Proviso scene in Act 4, when Mirabell and Millamant discuss what marriage means. Millamant begins, and Mirabell comments:

> Have you any more conditions to offer? Hitherto your demands are pretty reasonable.

Millamant continues her demands and says:

> … These articles subscribed, if I continue to endure you a little longer, I may by degrees dwindle into a wife.

ACTIVITY 9

- How is the legal metaphor presented in these exchanges?

- Is there a serious message beneath the playful tone?

- Would you say that it is sensible to think like this before marriage?

- Might there be a suggestion that, in using a reasoned approach to marriage, the marriage will be fairer for both people? Is this a right basis for marriage?

You might analyse the rest of the scene by exploring its legal imagery, such as 'imprimis', 'item', and the 'sealing of the deed'.

To evaluate the significance of this context, you could consider whether Congreve suggests that law and justice are as important in society as good manners, decorum, wit or social graces.

The dramatic context: 'patterning' within the play

Remember that this is just one part of the dramatic context of the play, but it is significant in evaluating the nature of Congreve's *The Way of the World*. There are five aspects of the patterning to be considered here:

- the implications of the idea of a card game

- the sequenced introduction of characters

- the echoes of the central Proviso scene

- the use of suspense and a cliff-hanger ending

- the repetition of the phrase 'the way of the world'.

The implications of the idea of a card game

References to the playing of a chance game of cards are to be found throughout the play. Consider the following examples: in the opening scene, when plotting about his wife, Fainall thinks that 'she might throw up her cards'; in the last scene (Act 5, Scene 1), Fainall's gamble has failed, and Petulant says 'how now, what's the matter? Whose hand's out?'

ACTIVITY 10

- To whom do most of the gaming images relate?

- How do these images suggest a certain view of the world?

- Do you think that it is a sensible or just viewpoint?

The sequenced introduction of characters

Congreve introduces his characters in a specific order. If you look at the introduction of both male and female characters into the play, you will notice a set pattern.

ACTIVITY 11

- The men: Mirabell, Fainall, Witwould, for example, are introduced in that order. Do you think this has something to do with the intelligence of each character?

- The women: Mrs Marwood, Mrs Fainall, Millamant: might this be in reverse order to the males? Why do you think Congreve does this?

The echoes of the central Proviso scene

The key scene between Mirabell and Millamant is echoed twice afterwards. First, there is the scene between Fainall, Mrs Marwood and Lady Wishfort (Act 5, Scene 1), in which Fainall lays down her terms.

ACTIVITY 12

- How might this scene echo that between Millamant and Mirabell?

- What are the similarities and what are the differences?

Second, there is a final echo in the last scene of the play, when Lady Wishfort says to Mirabell:

> … but on proviso that you resign the contract with my niece immediately.

These words begin the unravelling of Fainall's plots, and thus lead to the satisfying conclusion of the play.

ACTIVITY 13

- Might the echo be of a different nature here?

- Might the justice seen in the first Proviso scene now be extended?

The use of suspense and a cliff-hanger ending

The ending comes as a shock to some of the play's characters, and often also to some of the audience. But Congreve has laid down clues for his ending. You might look at Mirabell's words to Mrs Fainall in Activity 5 (page 167). Are any other clues offered?

The repetition of the phrase 'the way of the world'

In Act 3, Scene 1, Fainall thinks of Foible, of his wife, and of himself as a husband, as all 'rank', adding 'all in the way of the world'. But in Act 5, Scene 1, when Mirabell reveals the legal deed which will be Fainall's downfall, Mirabell throws this back at him: ''tis the way of the world, sir.'

ACTIVITY 14

- What is the difference between Fainall's and Mirabell's ways?

- Which 'way of the world' has finally prevailed?

The context of genre I: the play as a Comedy of Manners

In a Comedy of Manners, the dramatist presents mankind in relationship to society, so that individuals are examined as a product of the existing fashion, of birth, of custom and of existing codes of behaviour. You might look at the range of characters and think about the various levels in society which they represent.

ACTIVITY 15

- Place the characters in their different social levels.

- Does Congreve give each a particular way of speaking (look at Mincing, for example)?

- Might this be one of the sources of humour in the play?

You could take this enquiry further, and think about why manners are important and how they have a role in society. You might ask yourself questions such as those in the next activity.

ACTIVITY 16

According to the new eighteenth-century philosophy, society is a 'man-made machine'.

- What might the role of manners be in this view of society?

- Might the observations of manners be a way of making sure that this sort of society runs smoothly?

- Might good manners therefore be a new virtue for a new society?

- How does the idea of 'manners' relate to the idea of social morality?

- Do you think that Congreve is concerned to establish a link between manners and morality? Could he be suggesting that manners must not be merely skin-deep?

- Do you think that he succeeds in doing this?

The context of genre II: The Way of the World *as a Restoration Comedy*

Many critics agree that Restoration Comedy 'holds a mirror up to society', and the 'world' of the title is the world of society. Here again are some of the characteristic features of this genre. How do they relate to *The Way of the World*?

- What classes of society are presented in this play?

- How far is the play concerned with the usual Restoration Comedy issue of 'manners', that is, of how to behave properly in society?

- Is the author interested in something that might seem rather more serious?

- Is there sexual intrigue?

- Are there attractive, high-spirited, noble gentlemen?

- Might these qualities have appealed to the audience of the period?

- Is there a character outside this charmed circle (from the country, for example) who is mocked or used as a source of humour?

- Might this 'gull' be mocked because he tries to be fashionable and wise like the hero, but appears to be a fool in doing so?

- Is there a central hero who develops during the source of the play?

- How do you respond to the idea that the audience of the day saw in the hero a reflection of themselves, and in the fop or fool a reflection of their neighbour?

- Do you think that the author had a serious moral purpose in writing the play?

Conclusion

You have now worked through six contexts relating to *The Way of the World*. Using this model framework, you can go on to address other contexts on your own, for example the social context of marriage in *The Way of the World*.

Internet resources and select bibliography

INTERNET SITES

A range of useful websites can be accessed through the Heinemann website www.heinemann.co.uk/hotlinks. Just type in the express code for A2 English Literature for AQA B: 2326P.

CD-ROMS

The following are available from Headstrong Interactive, Magdale House, Lea Lane, Netherton, Huddersfield, HD4 7DL:

Silver Hooks and Golden Sands (an introduction to poetry and prose in English from 1360 to 1900)

The English Romantic Poets (for Coleridge)

BIBLIOGRAPHY

General Textbooks

Cambridge Companion to English Literature

The New Pelican Guide to English Literature, ed. Boris Ford

A Companion to Shakespeare's Works, ed. Richard Dutton and Jean Howard, Blackwell, 2003

POETRY

The General Prologue – Geoffrey Chaucer

The General Prologue to the Canterbury Tales, ed. James Winny, CUP, 2003

The Poet Chaucer, Neville Coghill, OUP, 1949

Chaucer and Chaucerians, ed. D. S. Brewer, Nelson, 1970

A Reading of the Canterbury Tales, T. Whittock, CUP, 1968

Selected poems – Gerard Manley Hopkins

The Poems of Gerard Manley Hopkins, ed. Catherine Phillips, Oxford World Classics, 1998

The Shaping Vision of Gerard Manley Hopkins, Alan Heuser, OUP, 1958, Repr. New York, 1968

Hopkins: A Collection of Critical Essays, ed. Geoffrey Hartman, Englewood Cliffs, 1966

All My Eyes See: The Visual World of Gerard Manley Hopkins, R. K. R. Thornton, Sunderland, 1975

Gerard Manley Hopkins: The Poems, R. K. R. Thornton, London, 1973

A Reader's Guide to Gerard Manley Hopkins, Norman H. Mackenzie, London, 1981

Gerard Manley Hopkins: New Essays on his Writing, Life and Place in Literature, ed. Michael E. Allsopp & Michael W. Sundermeier, Lampeter, 1989

Gerard Manley Hopkins and the Language of Mystery, Virginia Ridley Ellis, London, 1991

The Rape of the Lock – Alexander Pope

The Rape of the Lock, ed. Elizabeth Gurr, OUP, 2000

Alexander Pope and the Tradition of Formal Verse Satire, H. D. Winbrot, 1982

The World of Pope's Satires, P. Dixon, Methuen 1968

The Well Wrought Urn: Studies in the Structure of Poetry, Cleanth Brooks, Dobson, 1960

Alexander Pope: The Poetry of Allusion, Reuben A. Brower, Clarendon Press, 1959

Pope and Human Nature, Geoffrey Tillotson, Clarendon Press, 1958

Augustan Satire: Intention and Idiom in English Poetry, 1660–1750, Ian Jack, Clarendon Press, 1952

On the Poetry of Pope, Geoffrey Tillotson, Clarendon Press, 1950

The Rime of the Ancient Mariner – Samuel Taylor Coleridge

The Rime of the Ancient Mariner, Vintage, 2004

Samuel Taylor Coleridge's The Rime of the Ancient Mariner, ed. Harold Bloom, Chelsea House, 1986

Coleridge's Submerged Politics: The Ancient Mariner and Robinson Crusoe, Patrick. J. Keane, University of Missouri Press, 1994

Prescribed poems – *Alfred Lord Tennyson*

Tennyson: The Critical Heritage, ed. J. D. Jump, Routledge & Kegan Paul, 1967

Critical Essays on the Poetry of Tennyson, ed. John Killham, Routledge & Kegan Paul, 1967

Tennyson, Roger Ebbatson, Penguin, 1988

A Tennyson Companion, F. B. Pinion, Macmillan, 1984

Tennyson, Christopher Ricks, University of California Press, 1989

Prescribed Poems – *Emily Dickinson*

Poems and Letters of Emily Dickinson, ed. Robert N. Linscott, Anchor Books

Emily Dickinson, Personae and Performance, Elizabeth Phillips, Pennsylvania State University Press, 1988

The Years and Hours of Emily Dickinson, Jay Leyda, Yale University Press, 1960

The Poetry of American Women, Emily Stipes Watts, University of Texas Press, 1978

Literary Women, Ellen Moers, W. H. Allen, 1977

The Undiscovered Continent: Emily Dickinson and the Space of the Mind, Suzanne Juhasz, Indiana University Press, 1983

Drama

Edward II – Christopher Marlowe

Edward II, ed. Martin Wiggins and Robert Lindsey (New Mermaids, 2003)

Themes and Conventions of Elizabethan Tragedy, M. C. Bradbrook, CUP, 1980

Marlowe: 'Tambourlaine the Great', 'Edward II' and 'The Jew of Malta', ed. J. R. Brown, Macmillan, 1982

Christopher Marlowe: A Study of his Thought, Learning, and Character, P. H. Kocher, Russel & Russell, 1962

The Overreacher, H. Levin, Faber & Faber, 1965

Marlowe: A Critical Study, J. B. Steane, CUP, 1970

Christopher Marlowe and the Renaissance of Tragedy, Douglas Cole, Praeger, 1995

Measure for Measure – William Shakespeare

Measure for Measure, ed. J. W. Lever, Arden, 1965

The Problem of Measure for Measure, R. Myles, Vision Press, 1976

Themes and Conventions of Elizabethan Tragedy, M. C. Bradbrook, CUP, 1980

The Problem Plays of Shakespeare, Ernest Schanzer, Routledge, 1965

The Wheel of Fire, G. Wilson Knight, University Paperbacks, 1960

Aspects of Shakespeare's Problem Plays, ed. Kenneth Muir and Stanley Wells, CUP, 1982

Shakespeare's Problem Plays, E. M. W. Tillyard, Chatto & Windus, 1957

The Moral Universe of Shakespeare's Problem Plays, Vivian Thomas, Rowman & Littlefield, 1987

The Changeling – Thomas Middleton

Drama Classics, ed. Trevor R. Griffiths, Nick Hern Books, 2000

Themes and Conventions of Elizabethan Tragedy, M. C. Bradbrook, Cambridge University Press, 1969

Shakespeare's Tragedies and Other Studies in Seventeenth Century Drama, Clifford Leech, Chatto & Windus, 1950

Shakespeare's Contemporaries, Max Bluestone & Norman Rabkin, Prentice Hall, 1961

Woman as Individuals in English Renaissance Drama: A Defiance of the Masculine Code, Carol Hensen, Peter Lang, 1993

Societies and Politics in the Plays of Thomas Middleton, Swapan Chakravarty, Clarendon, 1996

English Drama 1586–1642 The Age of Shakespeare, G. K . Hunter, OUP, 1997

She Stoops to Conquer – Oliver Goldsmith

She Stoops to Conquer, ed. Trevor Millum, Longman, 1994

Oliver Goldsmith Revisited, Peter Dixon, Twayne Publications, 1991

Oliver Goldsmith, She Stoops to Conquer, Neil King, Longman Study Texts, Longman 1989

Multiple Personality and the Disintegration of Literary Character: From Oliver Goldsmith to Sylvia Plath, Jeremy Hawthorn, Palgrave Macmillan, 1983

She Stoops to Conquer, Paul Ranger, Macmillan Master Guides, Palgrave Macmillan, 1985

Goldsmith: The Critical Heritage, George S. Rousseau, Olympic Marketing Corporation, 1985

The Art of Oliver Goldsmith, Andrew Swarbrick, Rowman & Littlefield, 1984

The Rover – Aphra Behn

The Rover: Methuen Student Edition

Feminist Theatre and Theory, ed. H, Keyssar, Macmillan, 1996

The Passionate Shepherdess: Aphra Behn: 1640–89, Maureen Duffy, Methuen, 1989

Reconstructing Aphra, Angeline Goreau, Dial Press, 1980

Aphra Behn, F. M. Link, Twayre Publishers, 1968

The Way of the World – William Congreve

The Way of the World, ed. Brian Gibbons, New Mermaids

William Congreve, Mermaid Critical Commentaries, ed. Brian Morris, Benn, 1972

Congreve's Plays on the Eighteenth-Century Stage, E. L. Avery, New York, 1951

The Cultivated Stance. The Designer of Congreve's Plays, W. H. Van Voris, Dolmen Press, 1965

Restoration Theatre Production, Jocelyn Powell, Routledge & Kegan Paul, 1984

The aim of this final module is to test what you have learned during the course. It therefore tests all the Assessment Objectives, which are set out below.

ASSESSMENT OBJECTIVES

AO1 communicate clearly the knowledge, understanding and insight appropriate to literary study, using appropriate terminology and accurate and coherent written expression
(5% of the final A2 mark; $2\frac{1}{2}$% of the final A Level mark)

AO2ii respond with knowledge and understanding to literary texts of different types and periods, exploring and commenting on relationships and comparisons between literary texts
(10% of the final A2 mark; 5% of the final A Level mark)

AO3 show detailed understanding of the ways in which writers' choices of form, structure and language shape meanings
(10% of the final A2 mark; 5% of the final A Level mark)

AO4 articulate independent opinions and judgements, informed by different interpretations of literary texts by other readers
(10% of the final A2 mark; 5% of the final A Level mark)

AO5ii evaluate the significance of cultural, historical and other contextual influences on literary texts and study
(5% of the final A2 mark; $2\frac{1}{2}$% of the final A Level mark)

Introduction

These Assessment Objectives embody the skills that you use in reading and studying literary texts. In this module you have to show your ability to use these skills by working on (a) a set of pre-release materials, which you will receive three days before the examination, and (b) an unseen text, which will be in the examination paper itself. The key text might be prose, poetry or drama, and the other materials will relate to it: they might be articles or reviews, biography or autobiography, historical information or interpretation – in other words, materials relating to contexts and interpretations. The unseen text will bear some relation to the key text, too, and will be used as a comparative piece, to test AO2ii.

The examination paper will comprise two questions, each marked out of 40 marks, as follows:

- **Question 1** will test Assessment Objectives 2 and 3.

- **Question 2** will test Assessment Objectives 1, 4 and 5. This question will have an overarching theme but will be broken down into bullet points to help candidates organise their responses.

Most of this module will deal with how to look at the pre-release materials and at how to approach the examination questions. It ends with two sample examination papers that you can attempt; Paper 1 has sample responses for you to study.

Preparing for Module 6

The real preparation for this module is the rest of the course. When you sit this examination, you will have prepared for and taken five other modules in AS and Advanced Level, and in the course of that work you will have gained skills and experience in applying the Assessment Objectives to the texts that you have studied. The focus of any revision you might want to do, therefore, should be on the Assessment Objectives. If you haven't already attempted it, the activity on page xi of the Introduction to this book might be a useful reminder. The activities in Module 5 cover the full range of Assessment Objectives, while focusing chiefly on AO2ii, and further work on AOs 4 and 5ii can be found in Module 4.

This is the whole point of the synoptic unit. When looking at the texts you compared in Unit 4, and the Poetry text before 1900 in Unit 5 and the Drama text before 1770, you should have looked at far more than the texts themselves. Thinking and reading about the contexts of those texts, and about different interpretations, should have been a central part of your study too, and if you have done this, then the testing of how you apply these skills to other texts should be a natural progression – and that is exactly what Unit 6 is designed to do. Because the pre-release materials for Unit 6 contain writing about contexts and interpretations, looking at these materials should be a familiar part of the process for you. You could easily create a similar pack of materials about any of the texts you study in A2, and create some synoptic questions around it.

This unit, therefore, tests your skills as a reader, which is another reason why your reading during the whole Advanced Level course needs to be as varied as possible, so that you are used to reading and thinking about a range of types of text – after all, you will not know what the primary text for the examination will be until the weekend before, and you will then have to compare it with an unseen text in the examination. Part of Question 2 might also ask you a general question which centres on your own reading, and if this is confined to the four texts studied in A2 the range is obviously narrow. If you're wondering what to read, look for texts of different periods, genres and types – what do you have little experience of? Modern poetry might be a place to start; unless you chose a poetry text in Unit 4, you may well have read little during the course. Try a writer and explore.

What to do with the materials

You will receive the pre-release materials approximately three days before the examination. This gives you plenty of time to read the texts thoroughly, but it is important to keep in mind the reason for doing so – you have to look for the features which relate directly to the Assessment Objectives being tested in the two questions you will be asked. It is a good idea to make some notes as you read, but remember that you can make only brief marginal annotations on the material itself, as you'll be taking this into the examination room with you. Here are the rules from the Specification:

Such annotation should amount to no more than cross-references and/or the glossing of individual words or phrases. Highlighting and underlining is permitted. Annotations going beyond individual words or phrases, or amounting to *aides-mémoire* or notes towards the planning of essays are not permitted. Insertions of pages, loose sheets, 'post-its' or any other form of notes or additional material are not permitted.

You must stick to these rules. If you don't, you risk disqualification – but apart from that, it is best practice anyway. You don't know what the questions will be, so it would be foolish to try to write the answers in advance. There's the unseen element, too – the second text will be given in the examination itself, and so you can't know what the points of comparison with the first passage will be until you see it.

Here are the Assessment Objectives tested on each question, together with comments on what to look for as you work on the materials.

Question 1

This question will ask you to compare an extract from a text (Item 1 of the pre-release materials) with an unseen extract, which will be printed on the examination paper.

The Assessment Objectives tested here will be AO2ii and AO3. As stated above, you won't know what you have got to compare (AO2ii) until the day of the examination, but you can work on AO3 with the pre-release extract. In other words, you can identify the features of 'form, structure and language' that 'shape meanings'. As this isn't a text that you've worked on before, you need to think about what the writer's meanings seem to be, and how the writer has shaped them. Underlining, highlighting or writing brief marginal annotations will allow you to provide reminders for yourself of what you've seen, so that you can quickly find similar or contrasting features in the second extract when you read it. Of course, reading the second extract might well lead you to look for different features in the first extract from those you have already identified – so don't make the mistake of limiting yourself to your annotations when you revisit the pre-release extract. You need to be familiar with the whole piece.

Question 2

Question 2 will focus on a particular idea, but will be broken into several bullet points – probably two or three. This will cover Assessment Objective 1, but mainly Assessment Objectives 4 and 5. These might be targeted via a bullet for each Objective, but not necessarily – after all, you know by now that there is a strong relationship between the context of a text and how it is interpreted, by you and other readers. For the purpose of looking at the pre-release materials, though, it will be helpful to think about Assessment Objectives 4 and 5 separately.

Assessment Objective 4

Some of the writing presented in the pre-release materials will offer interpretations of the primary text given. You need to read through the materials identifying the interpretations offered in the items, and marking where they appear. This will help to focus your work in the examination. You then need to think about the interpretations you have identified – what they are saying, how they relate to the text, and how they relate to, and differ from, the other interpretations. Perhaps this is a point where making some notes for yourself might be useful; you can then, by comparing interpretations, take an overview of the merits of each of them.

Assessment Objective 5

As you work through the materials you need to identify the writing about contexts offered in the items, and to mark where they appear. This will help to focus your work in the examination. Remember to look for as wide a range of contexts as possible – your work in previous modules should help you to do this – and to indicate them by highlighting or underlining, perhaps with a brief marginal annotation. AO5ii asks you to 'evaluate the significance' of 'cultural, historical and other contextual influences on literary texts', so when you have identified the contexts you might gather them together in notes, and consider which might be significant, given the information that you have.

Working in this way through the materials will help to prepare you for the questions in the examination. It might even make you identify possible areas of questioning, but it is not a good idea to try to guess the questions and then to write a response – you don't know what the questions will be, and it's better to answer directly and honestly to those, not to the ones you've imagined.

A Sample Paper

On the following pages you will find the first sample paper for this module, followed by suggestions about how you could shape responses to the questions.

Sample Paper 1

Time allowed: 3 hours (including 30 minutes' reading time).

After reading time, you should spend about $1\frac{1}{4}$ hours on Question 1 and about $1\frac{1}{4}$ hours on Question 2.

The Assessment Objectives will be printed on the paper.

ITEM 1

Here are three extracts from *The Color Purple* by Alice Walker, published in 1982. The novel is in the form of a series of letters.

Extract A. This is very early in the novel. Celie's mother has died, and Pa, who has fathered Celie's child, is considering giving Nettie, Celie's sister, to Mr —, who wants to marry her. Celie wants to save her from this. She has seen what has happened to her 'new mammy' that Pa has married, and knows that Mr — loves Shug Avery, a beautiful singer.

Dear God,

I ast him to take me instead of Nettie while our new mammy sick. But he just ast me what I'm talking bout. I tell him I can fix myself up for him. I duck into my room and come out wearing horsehair, feathers, and a pair of our new mammy high heel shoes. He beat me for dressing trampy but he do it to me anyway.

Mr —— come that evening. I'm in the bed crying. Nettie she finally see the light of day, clear. Our new mammy she see it too. She in her room crying. Nettie tend to first one, then the other. She so scared she go out doors and vomit. But not out front where the two mens is.

Mr —— say, Well Sir, I sure hope you done change your mind.

He say, Naw, Can't say I is.

Mr —— say, Well, you know, my poor little ones sure could use a mother.

Well, he say, real slow, I can't let you have Nettie. She too young. Don't know nothing but what you tell her. Sides, I want her to git some more schooling. Make a schoolteacher out of her. But I can let you have Celie. She the oldest anyway. She ought to marry first. She ain't fresh tho, but I spect you know that. She spoiled. Twice. But you don't need a fresh woman no how. I got a fresh one in there myself and she sick all the time. He spit, over the railing. The children git on her nerve, she not much of a cook. And she big already.

Mr —— he don't say nothing. I stop crying I'm so surprise.

She ugly. He say. But she ain't no stranger to hard work. And she clean. And God done fixed her. You can do everything just like you want to and she ain't gonna make you feed it or clothe it.

Mr —— still don't say nothing. I take out the picture of Shug Avery. I look into her eyes. Her eyes say Yeah, it *bees* that way sometime.

Fact is, he say, I got to git rid of her. She too old to be living here at home. And she a bad influence on my other girls. She'd come with her own linen. She can take that cow she raise down there back of the crib. But Nettie you flat out can't have. Not now. Not never.

Mr —— finally speak. Clearing his throat. I ain't never really look at that one, he say.

Well, next time you come you can look at her. She ugly. Don't even look like she kin to

Nettie. But she'll make the better wife. She ain't smart either, and I'll just be fair, you have to watch her or she'll give away everything you own. But she can work like a man.

Mr ——— say How old she is?

He say, She near twenty. And another thing – She tell lies.

Extract B. In this extract, later in the novel, Shug Avery, who has become Celie's lover, is explaining her version of God, which is not the 'old white man' that Celie had always pictured.

Well, us talk and talk bout God, but I'm still adrift. Trying to chase that old white man out of my head. I been so busy thinking bout him I never truly notice nothing God make. Not a blade of corn (how it do that?) not the color purple (where it come from?). Not the little wildflowers. Nothing.

Now that my eyes opening, I feels like a fool. Next to any little scrub of a bush in my yard, Mr ———'s evil sort of shrink. But not altogether. Still, it is like Shug say, You have to git man off your eyeball, before you can see anything a'tall.

Man corrupt everything, say Shug. He on your box of grits, in your head, and all over the radio. He try to make you think he everywhere. Soon as you think he everywhere, you think he God. But he ain't. Whenever you trying to pray, and man plop himself on the other end of it, tell him to git lost, say Shug. Conjure up flowers, wind, water, a big rock.

But this hard work, let me tell you. He been there so long, he don't want to budge. He threaten lightening, floods and earthquakes. Us fight, I hardly pray at all. Every time I conjure up a rock, I throw it.

Amen

Extract C. In this letter from *The Color Purple*, Celie is describing the preparations for Sofia's mother's funeral. Sofia is married to Harpo.

Harpo say, Whoever heard of women pallbearers. That all I'm trying to say.

Well, say Sofia, you said it. Now you can hush.

I know she your mother, say Harpo. But still.

You gon help us or not? say Sofia.

What it gon look like? say Harpo. Three big stout women pallbearers look like they ought to be home frying chicken.

Three of our brothers be with us, on the other side, say Sofia. I guess they look like field hands.

But peoples use to men doing this sort of thing. Women weaker, he say. People think they weaker, say they weaker, anyhow. Women spose to take it easy. Cry if you want to. Not try to take over.

Try to take over, say Sofia. The woman dead. I can cry and take it easy and lift the coffin too. And whether you help us or not with the food and the chairs and the get-together afterward, that's exactly what I plan to do.

ITEM 2

This is an extract about Alice Walker from *Writing Women*.

Alice Walker: The Color is Purple

Alice Walker is one of the younger pathbreaking black women novelists to come to prominence in the 1980s. Already she has produced thirteen remarkable volumes of poetry and prose. She was born in 1944 in Georgia, 'halfway between misery and the sun'. The South has provided Walker with spiritual balance and an ideological base, *despite* racist domination through sharecropping (giving half the crops to the landlord) or by wage labour. A southern writer also inherits a 'trust in the community. We must give voice not only to centuries of bitterness and hate but also of neighbourly kindness and sustaining love.'

Sustaining care came from her mother, who had married for love, running away from home to marry at 17. By the time she was 20 she had two children and was pregnant with a third.

> Five children later, I was born. And this is how I came to know my mother: she seemed a large soft, loving-eyed woman who was rarely impatient in our home. Her quick, violent temper was on view only a few times a year, when she battled with the white landlord who had the misfortune to suggest that her children did not need to go to school.

Her mother laboured beside – not behind – her father in the fields. Their working day began early, before sunrise, and did not end till late at night. There was seldom a moment for either to rest: they were sharecroppers, working for harsh white landlords. Yet they both found time to talk to their children, and encourage their talents. Though her father cared a great deal for her, she talks of him as being 'two fathers' and for a long time felt so shut off from him that they were unable to speak to each other. Alice Walker pays particular tribute to her mother's creativity, to the garden she planted lovingly, and watered before going off to the fields. Her flowers and her quilts become a symbol of black women's creativity, which found expression even in the hard daily work:

> She planted ambitious gardens, brilliant with colors, so original in design, so magnificent with life … I notice it is only when my mother is working in her flowers that she is radiant … Ordering the universe in the image of her personal conception of Beauty.

Indeed Alice Walker claims that a black southern writer has not an impoverished but a rich inheritance given by 'compassion for the earth. The heat is so intense and one is so very thirsty, as one moves across the dusty cotton fields, that one learns forever that water is the essence of all life.'

When she was eight Alice Walker lost one eye in a traumatic accident. This led her to believe she was ugly and made her shy and timid for years.

It was from this period – from my solitary lonely position, the position of an outcast – that I began really to see people and things, really to notice relationships … I retreated into solitude, read stories and began to write.

ITEM 3

This is an extract from a critical commentary on *The Color Purple* for A Level students.

In order to understand how typical and/or atypical Celie's experience is, we need to consider a few facts about woman's status at the turn of the century. In much of the world, as well as in the United States, woman was seen as inferior to man. She did not have many of the rights we now take for granted. As recently as the nineteenth century, many American women could not be legal agents and thus could not own property or negotiate contracts, except through their fathers, husbands or brothers. American women could not act as political agents; they could not vote or be elected to political office. They were not expected to speak in public or operate in the public domain and were to remain primarily within the family. They were not regarded as economically independent. 'Respectable' women were not expected to work, particularly if they were married and had children. And women's goal in life was supposed to be marriage and motherhood.

In effect, women, 'the weaker sex', were under the control or 'protection' of their male relatives, and in many ways were conceived of as property. Husbands and fathers could not be prosecuted for physical or sexual abuse, and in many states, fathers, rather than mothers, had the right to children. Incest then, as now, existed although it was not often spoken about – young orphaned girls were considered particularly unfortunate since they had no access to power or even to protection. The Women's Rights Movement of the nineteenth century protested these conditions but it took some fifty years to achieve the vote for women.

Many people miss the fact that *The Color Purple* is not about a poverty-stricken black Southern family. Pa and Mister both are landowning blacks, of which there were many in Georgia at the turn of the century. In focusing on this class, Walker reminds us that many Southern blacks were economically successful during Reconstruction, though because of the Southern racist system, some were eventually dispossessed of their property.

In the case of *The Color Purple*, Walker does a critique of patrimony and how it is linked to the pursuit of power. Mister owns land that he has received from his father who, in turn, received land from his father, who was a white slaveowner. Mister's father objected to his relationship with Shug Avery, a woman who refuses to be owned. Mister doesn't marry Shug and complies with his father's wishes partly because his father determines whether or not he will inherit land. In a real sense, Celie's abuse is derived from that fact, for Mister gives up the woman he loves, and becomes a bully.

One aspect of woman's condition critical to Celie's story was the denial of education. Ironically, it was the creation of The Freedman's Bureau, which taught one and one-half million blacks to read and write between 1864 and 1970, that resulted in general public school education for poor Southern whites and women. But because of the passage of segregationist laws, blacks did not have equal access to education. Being able to read and write was considered as valuable a prize as it had been for slaves.

Black women, of course, had an even lower status than white women, who were often placed on a pedestal, even as they lacked independence. In *Their Eyes Were Watching God*, Hurston characterises the status of black women as that of a mule, an animal bred to work; creating an image that comes out of slavery. Walker makes great use of this image in the first part of *The Color Purple* as well as in the section set in Africa.

This is not to say that black women did not oppose these conditions in many different ways. Walker presents three different ways in which black women resisted their lot. Sofia represents the strong black woman who does not accept the definition of woman as weak and helpless and resists whites' attempts to diminish her. Often women like her have been denigrated both in black and white society as Amazons, or matriarchs, and punished for their resistance. Nettie represents women who did not marry but became missionaries, leaders, etc., and who used education as a means to transcend the low status of the black woman. As well, Walker uses Nettie to demonstrate the long history of relationships between Afro-Americans and Africa. Often these women had to separate themselves from their families and become 'exceptional' women. Shug represents another avenue, that of the blues tradition, an area in which black women could express their creativity and eroticism, and be economically independent. Though maligned as immoral by the middle class, female blues singers were often seen by other blacks as queens. They were openly sexual, often bisexual, and explored pleasure as a woman's right. They, too, risked the possibility of separation from their children and experienced volatile economic changes in the music business as well as intense racism from the white world. That few novels, until recently, have used female blues singers as central figures indicates the ambivalence with which particularly the black middle class has related to these women. Their economic independence, overt eroticism, and spiritedness subverted the society's definition of the good woman.

ITEM 4

This is an extract from notes about *The Color Purple* written for A Level students.

Black feminist critic Barbara Smith, in her review for *Callaloo*, a respected black literary journal, wondered if many of the reviewers had actually read the work … Smith focused on the womanist aspects of the novel. She called *The Color Purple* a classic because it does something new: 'what Walker has done for the first time is to create an extended literary work whose subject is the sexual politics of black life, as experienced by ordinary blacks.' Smith also pointed out that 'no black novelist until Alice Walker in *The Color Purple* has positively and fully depicted a lesbian relationship between two women, set in the familiar context of a traditional black community.' Smith ended her review with a provocative comment: '*The Color Purple* offers an inherent challenge to the Black community to consider fighting for the freedom of not just half but the entire race.'

Praise for *The Color Purple* as a womanist novel characterised reviews by other black women – Dorothy Randall-Tsuroto's review for *The Black Scholar* (published in Summer 1983, but apparently written before the novel received the Pulitzer), and Yvonne Porter's review for *Colorlines*, written just as Walker was awarded the Pulitzer. Porter began her review with the statement that '*The Color Purple* is a woman's womanist book …' She did warn her readers that some of them might be disturbed by Celie and Shug's sexual relationship, and reminded them that 'lesbianism is an aspect of the black woman that has seldom been dealt with in any depth.'

These positive reviews by black women were followed by others during 1982–84, not all of which were entirely complimentary. Maryemma Graham in the Summer 1983 issues of *Freedomways* called *The Color Purple* Walker's 'most compelling and thought-provoking work to date.' But Ms Graham thought that Walker identifies men as the sole source of female oppression, a view with which she disagrees. Graham also objected to the lesbian theme in the novel which she thought might 'muddy the waters' about female bonding. Her major objection to the novel was that it is bourgeois, that 'Walker has imbued her rural Georgia females with the strivings and potential for self-indulgence of the urban middle class.'

Another review by black woman critic Trudier Harris, in *Black American Literature Forum*, asked whether Walker hadn't reiterated white stereotypes of both black women and men. Ms. Harris who had previously written essays on Walker's earlier work, was clearly disturbed by the characters of *The Color Purple*.

ITEM 5

In this article Jennifer Nuernberg is responding to an essay by Jane Tompkins in *Me and My Shadow*, which is about feminist literary criticism.

I am shocked at what she says next:

'I wanted nothing to do with it. It was embarrassing to see women, with whom one was necessarily identified, insisting in print on the differences between men's and women's experience, focusing obsessively on women authors, women characters, women's issues. How pathetic, I thought, to have to call attention to yourself in that way. And in such bad taste. It was the worst kind of special pleading, an admission of weakness so blatant it made me feel ashamed. What I felt then, and what I think my unfriendly reader feels now, is a version of what women who are new to feminism often feel: that if we don't call attention to ourselves as women, but just shut up about it and do our work, no one will notice the difference and everything will be OK.'

Hearing it again, I am still shocked. Not shocked at what she says or that she says it, but stunned at how hard it hits home. When I first began to hear about 'feminism', when I used to see the slim 'Women and Gender Studies' class schedule while flipping through that thick course booklet, I wanted nothing to do with it either. How pathetic, I thought too, that women would feel the need to *study* themselves and talk *about* themselves, as women. I was a woman, yes, and had an affinity for women as well. As a matter of fact, I thought at great depths about women, wrote about women, and read women writers as often as I could. Still, something about 'feminism' rubbed me the wrong way, and Jane pegged it perfectly. I was afraid – afraid of being ridiculed, of being ostracized, of being left out of the important places and conversations. In short, I didn't want to call attention to myself *as* a woman because my experience had already proven that this is what happens to women who make big deals about being *women*.

The Color Purple

Answer **both** questions.

Read Item 6, printed after the questions.

30 minutes are allocated in the examination to the reading and consideration of this Item.

Question 1 will ask you to compare Item 6 with the passage from *The Color Purple* in your pre-release material, Item 1.

1. Compare and contrast the ways in which Alice Walker in Item I and Tony Roper in the extract from *The Steamie* present women.

   (40 marks)

2. All the items you have read on this paper – the extracts from *The Color Purple* and *The Steamie*, and Items 2–5 – are concerned with the position of women in society and in literature.

   In response to these items, write about:

   • the contexts identified in Items 2 and 3 which are reflected in the extracts from *The Color Purple*. Which contexts seemed important to you in reading the extracts?

   • the interpretations offered in Items 3 and 4. Which of these informed your reading of the extracts from *The Color Purple*, and how?

   • your response to the views expressed in Item 5. Thinking about your responses as a reader, do you 'want nothing to do with writing about women'? You can refer to the extracts in this paper if you wish, or to any of your own reading.

   (40 marks)

This is the unseen extract, printed on the examination paper and not seen before the examination itself.

ITEM 6

This is an extract from the play *The Steamie* by Tony Roper. 'Steamies' were communal laundries in Glasgow.

MAGRIT   ... Apart fae you dae mean?

ANDY   Cause. [*Glasgow drunk's hand-signals.*] Zat what ah'm here for ... now then ... Z'ivrything awright?

MAGRIT   [*this speech should be done with heavy irony to the audience, or she sings 'Isn't it wonderful to be a woman'*] Isn't it wonderful tae be a woman. Ye get up at the crack o' dawn and get the breakfast oan, get the weans ready and oot the hoose lookin' as tidy and as well dressed as ye can afford. Then ye see tae the lord high provider and get him oot, then wash up, finish the ironin', tidy the hoose and gie the flair a skite o'er. Then it's oot tae yer ain wee job, mebbe cleanin' offices, servin' in a shop or washin' stairs. Then it's dinner time. Well it is fur everybody else but no us 'cause we don't get dinner. By the time yer oot and run home, cooked something for the weans, yer lucky if you feel like something tae eat. I know I don't and even if I did ... the dinner hour's finished, so it's back tae yer work; that is efter ye've goat in whatever yer gonnae gie them for their tea, and efter yer finished yer work, ye'r back up ... cookin' again and they'll tell ye the mince is lumpy ... or the chips are too warm ... then they're away oot. The weans tae play ... the men tae have a drink, cause they need wan ... the souls ... efter pittin' in a hard day's graft, so ye've goat the hoose tae yersel' and what dae ye dae, ye tidy up again don't ye? Mer ironin, light the fire, wash the dishes and the pots etc. etc. and then ye sit doon. And what happens ... ye've just sat doon when the weans come up. 'Gonnae make us a cuppa tea and something tae eat' ... What dae ye's want tae eat? ... 'Och anything Ma' ... D'ye want some o' that soup? ... 'Naw' ... A tomato sandwich? ... 'Naw' ... A couple o' boiled eggs? ... 'Naw' ... A piece 'n spam? ... 'Naw' ... Well what d'ye's want? ... 'Och anything at all'. So ye make them something tae eat then ye sit doon and finally have a wee blaw ... a very wee blaw ... cause it's time tae go tae the steamie. Ye go tae the steamie, finish at nine o'clock and get the washin' hame. Ye sort it aw oot ... and get it put by and then sometimes mebbe take stock of yer life. What are we? ... skivvies ... unpaid skivvies ... in other words we are ... used ... but ye think tae yersel', well even if I am being used ... I don't mind ... cause I love my family and anyway it's New Year's Eve. I can relax and jist enjoy masel ... and any minute noo the weans'll be in an ma friends'll be comin' roon wi' black bun, shortbread, dumplin's, a wee refreshment and I can forget aw ma worries even if it's jist for a night and the weans arrive and ye gie them shortbread, sultana cake, ginger wine and there is just one thing missin', the head of the family. The door bell goes, ye

> open the door, and what is staunin there, ready to make the evening complete ... that's right ... your husband, your better half ... the man who was goin' to make you the happiest woman in the world and [*Gently.*] what does he look like ... *that* [*At Andy.*]
>
> DOLLY   Who were ye talkin' tae?
>
> MAGRIT   Masel.
>
> ANDY   So ... z'a ... wis sayin' girls ... everything aw right doon here... know ... cause ... that's what I'm here fur.

Question 1

Compare and contrast the ways in which Alice Walker in Item I and Tony Roper in the extract from *The Steamie* present women.

(40 marks)

Deconstructing the question

You need to look at the question carefully in order (a) to identify the Assessment Objectives you were expecting, and (b) to focus your reading and thinking on the terms of the task.

In Sample Paper 1, Question 1, 'Compare and contrast' is what you will have been expecting, as it focuses on the second part of AO2ii. 'The ways in which Alice Walker in Item I and Tony Roper in the extract from *The Steamie* present women' firmly targets AO3.

You have probably already made some notes and underlinings on Item 1, which will be useful, but read it again with this specific question in mind, making more notes if necessary. Then read the extract from *The Steamie* through once without making notes – remember you have not seen it before, so you need to get the whole thing clear in your mind – and then again, reading carefully and adding notes relevant to the task. You might even need to read it a third time. This may seem a lengthy process when you're anxious to start writing, but remember that the examination allows 30 minutes for reading.

There are a number of ways you might plan your response, but a key element is comparison – it's far better to keep comparing across texts than to write about one Item then the other. An obvious way is to work through the Assessment Objective dealing with form, structure and language in sequence, which is what the writer below has done.

Sample response

Both texts are clearly focused on revealing women's attitudes to men, and to their own situation, which in both texts is one of subjugation and oppression. The tones of the texts are quite different, though, and this is produced by differences in form, structure and language.

The differences in form arising from the genres of the texts are not quite as stark as the reader might expect. The impact of the letter form of *The Color Purple* is not really evident in these extracts, despite the 'Dear God' at the beginning of Extract A and 'Amen' at the end of Extract B. The extracts do contain much dialogue, however, so that they resemble drama in the way that attitudes and ideas are revealed, but with the addition of variations of 'he say'. Extract C is entirely dialogue, and reveals the tension between male and female, and the confrontation of attitudes – a function of drama. In Extracts A and B the letter form does allow for Celie's inner thoughts to be expressed, to 'God' or the reader – 'But this hard work, let me tell you'. Similarly, the extract from *The Steamie* is not quite what might be expected: nearly all of this extract is spoken by one character, so that in one sense it seems to resemble prose. The little dialogue that there is makes it clear that Magrit's speech is a soliloquy, despite the presence of other characters: it is to 'Masel', like Celie's inner thoughts to God – the audience, here.

The Steamie has other features of form, however. The stage directions play a key role in establishing the tone of the piece. The replacing of Magrit's speech with her singing 'Isn't it wonderful to be a woman', which is offered as an alternative, would clearly alter the tone drastically, as well as introducing another stage form entirely, that of the music hall, probably. The '*Glasgow drunk's hand signals*' help to establish the male's weakness and hopelessness in a stereotypical form, but with comic impact. The '*heavy irony*' as an instruction to the actress playing Magrit dictates atitude, but one laced with humour. Similarly, the word '*gently*' at the end of the speech, which could so easily be '*viciously*', softens the tone and impact of Magrit's remarks. Dramatic form is used at the end of the extract to reveal the hopeless, blind nature of the male: Magrit's 'that' focuses the audience's attention on the hapless figure of Andy, who is clearly ignorant and patronising, but apparently well intentioned, and again presented in a comic way.

Structurally, the three extracts from *The Color Purple* suggest that the novel moves towards a strengthening of women's attitudes, judging by the contrast between Celie's apparent acquiescence to Pa's attitudes in Extract A and 'every time I conjure up a rock, I throw it' in Extract B. The letters themselves seem to be individually shaped towards a final clear statement, as in the quotation above and 'That's exactly what I plan to do'. *The Steamie* has similarly clear statements of attitude carefully placed for effect in Magrit's speech, though not in the same way. 'Isn't it wonderful to be a woman' is almost a topic sentence for what follows, given the '*heavy irony*' which the stage direction demands. Unlike *The Color Purple* the direct statement of attitude, 'we are … used' comes not at the end, but after a long catalogue of drudgery and a rhetorical question, a structure which heightens its impact – although the writer chooses to soften this with 'I don't mind.'

On the surface, the language of the extracts seems quite different, as the dialects are so different, in vocabulary, grammar, and presumably pronunciation of common words. The language does reveal, however, some strong similarities in attitude. Both texts make considerable use of stereotypes, and the language of stereotypes, to reveal ideas and attitudes. Harpo's attitude to women, for instance, is that they 'ought to be home frying chicken' – a stereotype which Magrit clearly conforms to, as much of her day focuses on feeding the 'weans'. He also says that women are 'weaker', 'spose to take it easy', they 'cry', and should not 'try to take over'. The determined Sofia rejects this: she can do all the women's tasks and the men's too. In Extract A the desperate Celie, who lacks Sofia's strength at this point, conforms to her sexual stereotype in 'fixing herself up' for him in an unconscious parody of female seduction – and her reward is further physical abuse from Pa, who beats her and 'do it to me anyway'. Her role as a potential wife is to be sexually abused ('You can do everything just like you want to'), not to be smart in any sense, not to have possessions, but to work, ironically 'like a man' – Pa's highest praise for her. *The Steamie* does not seem to deal in the same physical and sexual abuse as *The Color Purple*, allowing a lighter tone, perhaps, but Magrit is clearly oppressed by her work. Her day from 'the crack o' dawn' to late at night revolves exclusively round her own job, and various types of housework. Like Celie, her efforts are not rewarded: the weans complain about her cooking (though this is presented comically, with a list of rejections followed by the comic punch line 'Och anything at all'), and her 'wee job' is menial – the choices open to her suggest a lack of economic power that amounts to oppression in the context of her society.

Men's position in relationship to women is also partially presented through stereotype. Magrit refers to the man as the 'lord high provider', the 'head of the family', the 'better half' – clichés which nevertheless reveal the man's economic power and societal status, but presented and undercut by Magrit's heavy irony, and 'that' – the pathetic Andy. Extract B from *The Color Purple* also looks at a dominant male figure (though without any comic sense here) through a stereotype – Celie's concept of God as 'an old white man'. This notion is being challenged, though, suggesting change and development for Celie – part of men's dominance, she suggests, is based on trying to 'make you think he everywhere' so that you 'think he God' – a 'lord high provider', in other words. But 'he ain't' – 'Man corrupt everything'.

Some of the other language indicators in the texts emphasise the contrast in tone. Extract A from *The Color Purple* stresses starkly the male perception of women and children as commodities. A woman who has had children is 'spoiled' – used goods, past the sell-by date – unlike one who is 'fresh'. 'She ain't gonna make you feed it or clothe it' reveals a child as an 'it' which costs money. Magrit's 'weans' are also generalised as mouths to be fed, the listing in the long first paragraph revealing the drudgery, but the tone is much softer here – 'I love my family' alters the view of the weans dramatically. There is some acceptance of situation in *The Color Purple*, but 'it bees that way sometime' is a weary acceptance of oppression because nothing can be done about it. By contrast, 'even if I am being used … I don't mind' is a mild feminism compared to the anger at the end of Extract B. After all, Magrit can 'forget aw ma worries' – a possibility not open to Celie.

Question 2

All the items you have read on this paper – the extracts from *The Color Purple* and *The Steamie*, and Items 2–5 – are concerned with the position of women in society and in literature.

In response to these items, write about:

- the contexts identified in Items 2 and 3 which are reflected in the extracts from *The Color Purple*. Which contexts seemed important to you in reading the extracts?

- the interpretations offered in Items 3 and 4. Which of these informed your reading of the extracts from *The Color Purple*, and how?

- your response to the views expressed in Item 5. Thinking about your responses as a reader, do you 'want nothing to do with writing about women'? You can refer to the extracts in this paper if you wish, or to any of your own reading.

(40 marks)

Thinking about the questions and organising the material

The first task in tackling the first two parts of the question is to identify and think about the relevant contexts and interpretations in the Items. You will probably have identified the contexts and interpretations as part of your work on the pre-release materials, and now you need to review them quickly for relevance. The last part of the question here asks a general question about your response to a particular type of literature. Simply think about it, and answer honestly – the examiner will have no preconceptions at all of what your answer might be, and certainly no view of what it should be. It is largely interpretations being targeted here, 'articulating independent opinions and judgement', but evidence is required too, from any reading.

You will be advised to spend half an hour reading (and thinking) in the examination, and then to divide your time equally between the two questions. This means there are only 75 minutes for Question 2 – so if there are three parts, as here, then only 25 minutes per part. This means that your responses do not need to be particularly long, but do need to be direct.

Sample response

- write about the contexts identified in Items 2 and 3 which are reflected in the extracts from *The Color Purple*. Which contexts seemed important to you in reading the extracts?

Several of the contexts mentioned in Items 2 and 3 are reflected in the extracts. Clearly Alice Walker's early life is a key influence, though not as a parallel – unlike Celie, she received the education which enabled her to become a writer, was encouraged rather than abused by her parents, and her role model was a mother who 'laboured beside – not behind – her mother in the fields'. It is interesting, though, that her relationship with her father appears to have been awkward – but he 'cared a great deal for her', a far cry from the sexual and physical abuse Celie receives from Pa.

Some of the contexts mentioned in Items 2 and 3 only impinge briefly on a reading of these extracts – the 'racist domination' in the South only appears here in the 'old white man' who represents Celie's concept of God, though it may be more significant in the novel as a whole, as may the 'black woman's creativity' symbolised by Alice Walker's mother's flowers and quilts – the only reference in these extracts is to God's creation of 'a blade of corn', 'the little wildflowers', and, of course, 'the color purple'.

Clearly, the most significant context for these extracts is the historical information offered in Item 3 about women's rights and situation. Celie's treatment at the hands of Pa is shocking to a twenty-first century reader. Her apparent pandering to Pa in Extract A suggests not only that she is inferior to men, but almost accepts it, and Pa's bartering with Mr —— about Nettie and Celie reveals that he sees them exactly as 'property' on the same level as the cow. Clearly, the women do not have 'many of the rights we now take for granted' – legal redress does not occur to Celie. Not only were women 'not expected to speak in public' or indeed show emotion – Nettie is so scared she vomits, but not 'where the two mens is'.

Part of the significance of this context in reading the text is in the way that women begin to take action against these conditions. Celie's realisation of man's manipulation of her thoughts, as well as her body, leads her to struggle against it, in her thoughts – 'Us fight' – and potentially physically: 'Every time I conjure up a rock, I throw it.' In Extract C, Sofia symbolises a black woman who did not accept these conditions – she does not accept the limitations Harpo tries to impose on her actions, or what 'peoples' are 'use to'. In a dramatic role reversal in the context of this society, she tells Harpo 'now you can hush'. Some women did rebel against their conditions; but it is tempting to see Alice Walker's late twentieth century views being put into the mouths of characters of a much earlier time.

- Write about the interpretations offered in Items 3 and 4. Which of these informed your reading of the extracts from *The Color Purple*, and how?

The interpretations offered by the writer of Item 3 make sense when revisiting the extracts. The critique of patrimony, and its link to the pursuit of power, is seen here in action: Pa exercises complete control over his daughters, apparently, physically, sexually, and in the determination of their lives, and both daughters are seen to suffer from it. In their treatment as commodities, they are presented as 'animals bred to work', clearly. The identification of Sofia as a 'strong black woman who does not accept the definition of women as weak and helpless' is very clear in the text, as is the 'spiritedness' of Shug Avery.

The concepts in Item 4 offer a little more food for thought. Barbara Smith's identification of Walker's subject as 'the sexual politics of black life' seems resoundingly true of these three extracts, which all focus on gender relationships, and the suffering and conflict that these entail; and her view of the novel as a call for black women to 'fight for freedom' is exemplified in the attitudes of Shug and Sofia. Celie begins to answer the call, too: 'Us fight'. Certainly in these extracts men do seem to be 'the sole source of female oppression', which is Maryemma Graham's criticism.

The last view quoted, that of Trudier Harris, does need some comment, though. She considers that Walker may have 'reiterated white stereotypes of both black women and men'. This can certainly be seen in these extracts, in Celie's parading of herself, in Pa's abuse, and so on. Harris' view seems to ignore, though, the use Walker makes of these stereotypes as she exposes 'patrimony' and shows women fighting against it. This is typified by Shug's view of God, which is hardly stereotypical, and by Sofia's specific rejection of the stereotyping which Harpo tries to force on her – her characterisation of the male pallbearers as 'field hands' is designed to show Harpo the shallow nature of a view of women as only fit to 'fry chicken'. Perhaps Ms Harris was so 'disturbed by the characters' that her critical faculties were suspended.

- Write about your response to the views expressed in Item 5. Thinking about your responses as a reader, do you 'want nothing to do with writing about women'? You can refer to the extracts in this paper if you wish, or to any of your own reading.

As a male reader, it would be easy to 'want nothing to do with writing about women', in the sense that the writer of Item 5 seems to mean: if the writing is 'making big deals about being women' that would seem to exclude the male reader, except as some kind of literary voyeur. There is another sense, too, in which the male reader may well feel alienated by 'women's' literature, in that the reader is often invited to deplore the various crimes of the male sex. Of course, history tells us that this is perfectly correct, on the whole, in that women have been ruthlessly oppressed, abused and exploited by men, and that literature merely reflects this – or rather modern literature does, as until the second half of the twentieth century literature too was unfairly dominated by the dastardly male gender. It is of course impossible to argue with this without been accused of being chauvinist, so that the individual male is made to bear the sins of all his sex in silence. Of course it is high time that women got their own back; but do they have to do it so personally?

It would also be easy for me personally to accord with the view expressed given my own experience at A Level. Though not 'focusing obsessively on women authors, women characters and women's issues', my female English teacher, perhaps thinking about her largely female class, did choose a female-centred set of texts, I think. Unit 1 was *The Color Purple*, which has surfaced again on this paper (are all English academics feminists?), where man is almost unremittingly 'corrupt', if not just stupid as a change, like Harpo. Even

Mr ——'s redemption as Albert is grudging; in the end he is matronised rather than achieving equality of esteem, I think. *Top Girls* as the drama text for Unit 2 was hardly a change of viewpoint, given that the first Act (by far the most interesting theatrically), dwelt solely on women's issues, and included a fair lacing of men, as usual. Shakespeare is often accused of writing largely about men, but there isn't much time to think about that when the teacher's chosen focus for the coursework task is interpretations of Gertrude or Ophelia. My teacher did accept my view of Ophelia as being a nasty combination of cunning and empty-headedness, though — why does she allow herself to be used as bait by Claudius and her father without a word of protest?

Naturally Aphra Behn's *The Rover* featured in Unit 5, and for Unit 4 we could choose from a list of texts to compare with *Oranges Are Not The Only Fruit*, which tended to set the agenda. We did a short course of modern poetry in preparation for this paper, centring on Dorothy Molloy and Carol Ann Duffy's *The World's Wife*. Again, the views of men are unflattering. Molloy pictures them as rapists and perverts, largely, and Duffy's wives usually see their men as vain or stupid: Mrs Darwin remarks that 'Something about that chimpanzee over there reminds me of you', while Mrs Icarus is not 'the first or last' to see her husband as 'a total, utter, absolute, Grade A pillock'.

These responses are too easy, though, and I guess I'm guilty of being as one-track as the feminists that the writer of Item 5 is concerned about. I actually really enjoyed all of these texts, and never once felt really 'got at', thanks to the attitudes of my teacher and fellow students. The development in *The Color Purple* was quite brilliant, and actually I felt that the resolution of structure in the last chapter, which had the feeling of magical realism about it, was enough to take the sternest male close to tears. I loved the poetry, actually: Molloy was breathtaking in her use of language, and Duffy always thought-provoking, and often — as above, of course — clever and funny. Maybe I've simply become indoctrinated. One of my favourite novelists is Margaret Atwood, even the apparently male-hating *Handmaid's Tale*. The best novel I have read this year is *Atonement* — by Ian McEwan, of course, but to me it didn't read like him at all. If you didn't know, you would think the writer was female.

> These responses to Sample Paper 1 are not intended to be exhaustive, and of course you might well find a number of other equally valid things to say in response to all the questions. They do indicate, however, what the focus of each response should be.

Sample Paper 2

Time allowed: 3 hours (including 30 minutes' reading time)

You should spend about $1\frac{1}{4}$ hours on Question 1 and $1\frac{1}{4}$ hours on Question 2.

The Assessment Objectives will be printed on the paper.

ITEM 1

This is an extract from *Hard Times* by Charles Dickens, which was published in 1843. 'Millers' in the third paragraph refers to the mill-owners – the employers in Coketown.

A sunny midsummer day. There was such a thing sometimes, even in Coketown.

Seen from a distance in such weather, Coketown lay shrouded in a haze of its own, which appeared impervious to the sun's rays. You only knew the town was there, because you knew there could have been no such sulky blotch upon the prospect without a town. A blur of soot and smoke, now confusedly tending this way, now that way, now aspiring to the vault of Heaven, now murkily creeping along the earth, as the wind rose and fell, or changed its quarter: a dense formless jumble, with sheets of cross light in it, that showed nothing but masses of darkness: – Coketown in the distance was suggestive of itself, though not a brick of it could be seen.

The wonder was, it was there at all. It had been ruined so often, that it was amazing how it had borne so many shocks. Surely there never was such fragile china-ware as that of which the millers of Coketown were made. Handle them never so lightly, and they fell to pieces with such ease that you might suspect them of having been flawed before. They were ruined, when they were required to send labouring children to school; they were ruined when inspectors were appointed to look into their works; they were ruined, when such inspectors considered it doubtful whether they were quite justified in chopping people up with their machinery; they were utterly undone, when it was hinted that perhaps they need not always make quite so much smoke. Besides Mr Bounderby's gold spoon which was generally received in Coketown, another prevalent fiction was very popular there. It took the form of a threat. Whenever a Coketowner felt he was ill-used – that is to say, whenever he was not left entirely alone, and it was proposed to hold him accountable for the consequences of any of his acts – he was sure to come out with the awful menace, that he would 'sooner pitch his property into the Atlantic.' This had terrified the Home Secretary within an inch of his life, on several occasions.

However, the Coketowners were so patriotic after all, that they never had pitched their property into the Atlantic yet, but, on the contrary, had been kind enough to take mighty good care of it. So there it was, in the haze yonder; and it increased and multiplied.

ITEM 2

This article about the context of *Hard Times* is from a set of notes for A Level students.

Charles Dickens was born on February 7, 1812, and spent the first nine years of his life in Kent, a marshy region by the sea in the west of England. Dickens's father, John, was a kind and likeable man, but he was incompetent with money and piled up tremendous debts throughout his life. When Dickens was nine, his family moved to London, and later, when he was twelve, his father was arrested and taken to debtors' prison. Dickens's mother moved his seven brothers and sisters into prison with their father but arranged for Charles to live alone outside the prison, working with other children at a nightmarish job in a blacking warehouse, pasting labels on bottles. The three months he spent apart from his family were highly traumatic for Dickens, and his job was miserable—he considered himself too good for it, earning the contempt of the other children.

Though the young blacking factory employee had considered himself too good for his job, the older novelist retained a deep interest in and concern for the plight of the poor, particularly poor children. The Victorian England in which Dickens lived was fraught with massive economic turmoil, as the Industrial Revolution sent shockwaves through the established order. The disparity between the rich and poor, or the middle and working classes, grew even greater as factory owners exploited their employees in order to increase their own profits. Workers, referred to as 'the Hands' in *Hard Times*, were forced to work long hours for low pay in cramped, sooty, loud, and dangerous factories. Because they lacked education and job skills, these workers had few options for improving their terrible living and working conditions. With the empathy he gained through his own experience of poverty, Dickens became involved with a number of organizations that worked to alleviate the horrible living conditions of the London poor. For instance, he was a speaker for the Metropolitan Sanitary Organization, and, with his wealthy friend Angela Burdett-Coutts, he organized projects to clear up the slums and build clean, safe, cheap housing for the poor.

Though he was far too great a novelist to become a propagandist, Dickens several times used his art as a lens to focus attention on the plight of the poor and to attempt to awaken the conscience of the reader. *Hard Times* is just such a novel: set amid the industrial smokestacks and factories of Coketown, England, the novel uses its characters and stories to expose the massive gulf between the nation's rich and poor and to criticize what Dickens perceived as the unfeeling self-interest of the middle and upper classes. Indeed, *Hard Times* suggests that nineteenth-century England itself is turning into a factory machine: the middle class is concerned only with making a profit in the most efficient and practical way possible. *Hard Times* is not a delicate book: Dickens hammers home his point with vicious, often hilarious satire and sentimental melodrama. It is also not a difficult book: Dickens wanted all his readers to catch his point exactly, and the moral theme of the novel is very explicitly articulated time and again. There are no hidden meanings in *Hard Times*, and the book is an interesting case of a great writer subordinating his art to a moral and social purpose. Even if it is not Dickens's most popular novel, it is still an important expression of the values he thought were fundamental to human existence.

ITEM 3

This is an extract from an internet students' resource on *Hard Times*.

Hard Times and Utilitarianism

Coketown, as described in 'Hard Times' is a construct of a typical industrial town, many of which were sited around the newly founded factories. It may be a fictional location of the industrial age, but it serves Dickens's purpose of presenting Utilitarianism at work. Many of the details of Coketown are based on truths about industrial towns, but Dickens slightly exaggerates them to focus the readers' attention on the points he would like to criticise.

It was believed that higher industrial output would increase the wealth of the country and therefore be desirable. Because of this Coketown exists solely for its industrial output and provides no comfort for its working class citizens. Everything inside it is extremely practical; no precious resources are wasted beautifying it, as they do not lead to an increase in industrial output. Dickens's contempt for Utilitarianism is conveyed through the opening description of the town.

The colours of the town are black and red – red brick covered in ash from the factories. Even on the surface, Dickens associates Coketown with 'the painted face of a savage' – the implication is that like a 'savage', industrialisation is cruel, barbaric and uncultured. On a deeper level, this image links to the colour symbolism that runs through the novel. Dickens associated richness of colour with the preservation of life and individuality; neither black, nor white are considered as colours, and hence, Coketown rejects the idea of individuality and identity. It is robbed of it by the Utilitarianism that is manifested in industrialisation. The lack of identity is further emphasised by all public inscriptions in the town being written in 'black and white'. The 'inscriptions' – the voice of the town are devoid of any identity. Everything in the town – a river, a canal – is of dark colour, firstly, because of pollution, secondly, at symbolic level, because the town lacks an identity. Dickens describes it as being 'severely workful' but significantly it is also in a 'state of melancholic madness', because everything in the town is dedicated to production.

Coketown's buildings are faceless. With bitter irony, Dickens describes the confusion between identifying the 'infirmary' and the 'jail' – Utilitarian practicality has deprived each of them of its own air and made the process of healing in an 'infirmary' of little difference from serving a sentence in a 'jail'. Even the Church is no different from a 'warehouse' – a building used to store the products of the industrial process. The Church was affected by industrialisation and Utilitarianism. Its decorations are compared by Dickens to the 'wooden legs' of a piano – items manufactured in great amounts, looking totally alike and hence lacking any identity. The destructive effect of Utilitarianism seemingly affected even the spiritual aspect of life.

The picture is made more complete by the addition of description of the streets – 'very like one another' and the final stroke of the brush is Dickens's epithet:

'Fact, fact, fact, everywhere in the material aspect of town; fact, fact, fact everywhere in the immaterial.'

This summarises the Utilitarianism that the town is drenched in – everything here serves a material purpose.

In his description of the Coketown community, Dickens highlights the fact that it is not a healthy society. The workers have no escape from their problems. People resort to alcohol and drugs; crime is rampant and there is no counselling for these people. The middle class only impose harsher restrictions on them and view them as utilitarian elements, not as people, thus only promoting social problems further.

It is important to note that all of the imagery associated with Utilitarianism has negative and often violent connotations. The town itself is associated with a 'face of a savage', a teacher is related to a 'cannon', the bells of a Utilitarian church drive the 'sick and nervous mad'... There is no comfort in Utilitarianism. Such is the Utilitarian society. Coketown resembles London or any other Northern industrialised town.

Dickens accuses Utilitarianism of being responsible for the social malaise; the destruction of personality; for robbing people of probably the only real valuable thing they have – their individuality; for oppressing the women and the working class; and finally of depriving the children of a special stage of their life – their childhood.

Dickens feels that Utilitarianism is wrong. At the end of the novel, all of the Utilitarian characters suffer a crisis. However, the unselfish ones are rescued by people who have preserved their humanity amidst all the destruction and violence. Sissy Jupe, a healer (which is symbolised by the bottle of 'nine oils' she carries with her) helps Louisa, the daughter of Mr Gradgrind, to live through her crisis. This is Dickens's way of showing that Utilitarianism tends to blow up and explode like a 'balloon' – another image associated with the boastful and self-important Bounderby, whose domination over the others bursts like a balloon when his true origins are revealed. Dickens shows his readers that Utilitarianism is based on unsound principles, which might get a person to the top, but will not keep him there. Perhaps, he is trying to predict a crisis of the Utilitarian society, but his book seems to work more on personal level. The fact that humanity rescues the 'lost' people shows, that there is 'Another Thing Needful' in this society. The society needs an understanding of human feelings. According to Dickens. The Victorian society needs to recognise the significance of human emotion. This philosophy is put simply through the words of Sleary, the master of the circus – 'people must be amuthed'. Materialism and practicality are impractical in the long run after all.

ITEM 4

This is an extract from *Hard Times: An introduction to the Variety of Criticism* by Allen Samuels.

The best starting point for any critical discussion of *Hard Times* is provided by the editors of the Norton Edition of the novel:

> Many of the most helpful critical discussions of Dickens's other novels have been interpretative, whereas most discussions of *Hard Times* have been primarily evaluative. About none of his novels has there been less agreement. (*Ford and Monod*, 1966, p. 330)

Not to put too fine a point on it, most of these judgements have been harshly antagonistic. George Saintsbury thought it the lowest amongst Dickens's novels; 'good things were buried in a mass of exaggeration and false drawing that one struggles with the book as with a bad dream.' (cited *Churchill*, 1975, p. 95) Stephen Leacock thought it 'half-story, half-sermon, – a large tract of the book is mere trash – the humour is forced … the pathos verges on the maudlin.' (*Churchill*, p. 95) George Gissing, a keen admirer of Dickens, regarded the novel so lightly, he ignored it. 'Of *Hard Times* I have said nothing; it is practically a forgotten book and little of it demands attention.' (*Ford and Monod*, p. 330)

One of the characteristics of *Hard Times* which all commentators have noticed is that:

> any account of Dickens's argument in the novel is bound to come to the conclusion that he attacks an unmanageably large and miscellaneous range of evils (utilitarianism in education and economics, industrial capitalism, abuse of unions, statistics, bad marriage, selfishness, etc.); that he mostly oversimplifies them … that he is unclear what evil causes what other evil. On the other side his proposed palliatives are feeble … (*Fowler*, 1983, p. 106)

Because Dickens is so unfocused (what is *Hard Times* principally about might be a good starting point) critics have often thought it a bad novel. But the argument can be seen in a double context. On the one hand, it is clearly satirical of contemporary society, for which Dickens received considerable criticism. But it is also about a particular way of seeing the world which is in contradistinction to the literary imagination, a way which is exemplified perfectly by Bitzer's rational arguments. In the conflict of the literary and sociological imagination what Dickens is showing is how a particular vision of life is becoming increasingly subject to abstract formalisation, into the narrow and the rigid. Like any writer he is concerned that his way of seeing will be granted tolerance and will endure, but he wrote knowing all too well that the sort of thinking that his novel opposes, Blue Books and 'ologies', was exercising a profound effect.

Hard Times can be seen as the defence of the novel, of literature as a valuable necessity and a valuable professional activity, and is consequently to be judged as such at the very time when a scientific and industrial society made any blithe confidence in such an undertaking impossible. What actually happens in the novel (as opposed to what one might like to think happens in it) is that the text reveals ironies and its indirections so that it becomes not a confident attack on the evils of systematisation, but exhibits instead a crisis in confidence. That doubt is dramatised in the language of the fiction at many points. Even the terms Fact and Fiction are themselves not at all clear.

I believe, therefore, that this novel still has a prescient relevance for us because the larger questions, or the more abstract ones it addresses, are still with us. But I also recognise that *Hard Times* will still not please many. This is a pity because apart from the pleasures which it undoubtedly contains, the reminder of what school can feel like, its delicate but penetrating exploration of the callousness of selfishness, the access to Victorian history, and its debates and ideas which it affords in a short and condensed way, it is also, as my epilogue will suggest, a novel which offers a comment on the decade of the 1980s. Some readers do, it is true, find it excessively gloomy. Some no longer wish to read of the heyday of British industrialism. Some find it unfunny (which it certainly isn't). Some, despite its deft economy, find it too long; for those whose only narratorial satisfactions come in the 1 hour 30 minutes of film or the 50 minute television play one can, alas, do nothing. However, one should not read Dickens with cloth ears. He can be, and he is particularly so in this novel, amazingly ironic. He was unafraid to be scornfully bitter about his opponents, usually systems or ideas rather than individual people, despite his reputed generous good nature. Orwell, one of his most sympathetic readers, said that, 'Dickens attacked English institutions with a ferocity that has never since been approached.' (*Orwell*, 1970, p. 455) This is marvellously true. Students are often reluctant to recognise openly what they may feel intuitively, that novelists and poets can be savagely and violently angry, and yet wholly serious, beneath their humour.

Hard Times

Answer **both** questions.

Read Item 5, printed after the questions.

30 minutes are allocated in the examination to the reading and consideration of this Item.

Question 1 will ask you to compare Item 5 with the passage from *Hard Times* in your pre-release material, Item 1.

1. Compare how the working classes are shown being exploited in the extracts from *Hard Times*, Item 1, and *An Inspector Calls*, Item 5.

    (40 marks)

2. Items 2, 3 and 4 are concerned with Dickens' purposes in *Hard Times*, and how critics view the text.

    In response to these items, write about:

    -   the contextual factors mentioned in Items 2 and 3. Considering these alongside the extract, which seem to you to be the most significant?

    -   what critics like about the novel, and what they dislike. Which attitudes do you find yourself sympathising with, and why?

    -   Allen Samuels's view in Item 4 that the Victorian novel still has relevance for modern readers. Do you find that older texts are still relevant to you? Refer in your response to any texts that you have read.

    (40 marks)

This is the unseen extract, printed on the examination paper and not seen before the examination itself.

ITEM 5

Below are two extracts from *An Inspector Calls* by J. B. Priestley, which was written in 1945, though it is set in 1912.

In *An Inspector Calls*, a police inspector is visiting the house of the Birling family after the death of a girl called Eva Smith. During the visit he shows how each member of the family was in some way responsible for the death. In Extract A, he is dealing with Mr Birling, the owner of the factory in which Eva was employed. In Extract B, he leaves the house after exposing the complicity of all the family.

Extract A

BIRLING	[...] and she'd been working in one of our machine shops for over a year. A good worker too. In fact, the foreman there told me he was ready to promote her into what we call a leading operator – head of a small group of girls. But after they came back from their holidays that August, they were all rather restless, and they suddenly decided to ask for more money. They were averaging about twenty-two and six, which was neither more nor less than the average in our industry. They wanted the rates raised so they could average about twenty-five shillings a week. I refused, of course.
INSPECTOR	Why?
BIRLING	[*surprised*] Did you say 'Why?'
INSPECTOR	Yes. Why did you refuse?
BIRLING	Well, Inspector, I don't see that it's any concern of yours how I choose to run my business. Is it now?
INSPECTOR	It might be, you know.
BIRLING	I don't like that tone.
INSPECTOR	I'm sorry. But you asked me a question.
BIRLING	And you asked me a question before that, a quite unnecessary question too.
INSPECTOR	It's my duty to ask questions.
BIRLING	Well, it's my duty to keep labour costs down, and if I'd agreed to this demand for a new rate we'd have added about twelve per cent to our labour costs. Does that satisfy you? So I refused. Said I couldn't consider it. We were paying the usual rates and if they didn't like those rates, they could go and work somewhere else. It's a free country, I told them.

ERIC	It isn't if you can't go and work somewhere else.
INSPECTOR	Quite so.
BIRLING	[to Eric] Look – just you keep out of this. You hadn't even started in the works when this happened. So they went on strike. That didn't last long, of course.
GERALD	Not if it was just after the holidays. They'd all be broke – if I know them.
BIRLING	Right, Gerald. They mostly were. And so was the strike, after a week or so. Pitiful affair. Well, we let them all come back – at the old rates – except the four or five ring-leaders, who'd started the trouble. I went down myself and told them to clear out. And this girl, Eva Smith, was one of them. She'd had a lot to say – far too much – so she had to go.
GERALD	You couldn't have done anything else.
ERIC	He could. He could have kept her on instead of throwing her out. I call it tough luck.
BIRLING	Rubbish! If you don't come down sharply on some of these people, they'd soon be asking for the earth.
GERALD	I should say so!
INSPECTOR	They might. But after all it's better to ask for the earth than to take it.

Extract B

INSPECTOR	[...] [Rather savagely, to Birling.] You started it. She wanted twenty-five shillings a week instead of twenty-two and sixpence. You made her pay a heavy price for that. And now she'll make you pay a heavier price still.
BIRLING	[unhappily] Look, Inspector – I'd give thousands – yes, thousands –
INSPECTOR	You're offering the money at the wrong time, Mr Birling.
	[He makes a move as if concluding the session, possibly shutting up notebook, etc. Then surveys them sardonically.]
	No, I don't think any of you will forget. Nor that young man, Croft, though he at least had some affection for her and made her happy for a time. Well, Eva Smith's gone. And you can't do her any good now, either. You can't even say 'I'm sorry, Eva Smith.'
SHEILA	[Who is crying quietly] That's the worst of it.
INSPECTOR	But just remember this. One Eva Smith has gone – but there are millions and millions and millions of Eva Smiths and John Smiths still left with us, with their lives, their hopes and fears, their suffering and chance of happiness, all intertwined with our lives, and what we think and say and

do. We don't live alone. We are members of one body. We are responsible for each other. And I tell you that the time will soon come when, if men will not learn that lesson, then they will be taught it in fire and blood and anguish. Good night.

He walks straight out, leaving them staring, subdued and wondering.

Achieving high marks

In order to achieve high marks, you need to satisfy the descriptors (or Assessment Criteria) for the mark schemes, which are drawn directly from the Assessment Objectives. Below are the descriptors for the top two bands, which encompass the Objectives tested on both questions. Your teachers will be able to show you the whole of the mark scheme.

Question 1

52–64 marks

AO1	critical terminology used accurately in detailed commentary
AO2ii	detailed knowledge and understanding in response to both texts and task
AO2ii	thorough and detailed comparison and contrast
AO3	explanation of a range of aspects of form/language/structure
AO3	detailed understanding of how choices of form/structure/language shape meanings
AO4	clear evidence of critical views
AO4	detailed and well evidenced personal response
AO5	analysis of a range of contextual factors

65–80 marks

AO1	accurate use of appropriate critical vocabulary/concepts
AO2ii	clear conceptual grasp of texts and task
AO2ii	perceptive comparison and contrast
AO3	sophisticated analysis of how choices of form/structure/language shape meanings
AO3	conceptually and analytically links meanings/purposes
AO4	conceptual grasp of critical views
AO4	perceptive and evidenced personal response
AO5ii	detailed exploration of contexts

This is the final module of the course, and this will be your final examination. As you will see through the work you do on these two sample papers, it draws together all the skills you have learned during the course. When you approach the examination itself, you need to have this firmly in your mind. Looking at the mark schemes above shows exactly what sort of thinking and writing you need to apply to each question.

The best final preparation for this module is to attempt sample papers unaided.

Alienation: an effect achieved by preventing the audience from believing in or trusting the actions occurring on stage, as happens, for example in Oliver Goldsmith's *She Stoops to Conquer*.

Amoral: a person who has no sense of morality, as is Beatrice Joanna in *The Changeling*.

Assonance: words where the vowel sounds (but not the consonants) are the same, for example *fate* and *save*, which share a long 'a'.

Ballad: a poem, often in short stanzas, narrating a story, for example Coleridge's *The Rime of the Ancient Mariner*.

Blood-letting: a practice used by surgeons in the 15th and 16th centuries. Blood was removed from a patient in the belief that infection was so freed from the body. Middleton refers to this in *The Changeling*.

Caesura: a break between words in a metrical measure which is used to create effects such as those in *The Rape of the Lock*.

Chevalier: a medieval knight on horseback, as in 'The Windhover', by Gerard Manley Hopkins.

Comedy of Manners: a witty comedy satirising the manners and social pretensions of sophisticated society. Examples include Congreve's *The Way of the World* and Goldsmith's *She Stoops to Conquer*. See: **Restoration Comedy**

Conceit: a far-fetched comparison in which you are made to admit likeness between two things, whilst always being aware of the oddness of the comparison. An example is George Herbert's poem 'The Pulley'.

Conformist: somebody who lives by complying with the rules of society, for example as Constance Neville does to some extent in Oliver Goldsmith's *She Stoops to Conquer*.

Context: in A2 Literary Study this is the fifth Assessment Objective. Contexts are the important facts, events or processes that have helped to shape literary works.

Dante: Dante Aligheri a late 13th century writer who called his beloved 'Beatrice'. His greatest work was *The Divine Comedy* in which hell was portrayed as a graduated conical funnel of decreasing spirals. There may be a reference to this in Middleton's and Rowley's *The Changeling*.

Divine right of kings: the belief that a king's right to rule comes from God.

Dramatic irony: an effect created when an audience is aware of a situation, in contrast to characters on stage who do not realise what is really happening. Examples are Marlow and Hastings in Oliver Goldsmith's *She Stoops to Conquer*.

Dramatic monologue: a poem in which a speaker seems to be addressing an imaginary listener.

Epic: a continuous narrative poem such as those by Homer and Virgil, imitated by Pope in *The Rape of the Lock* written to glorify the deeds of heroes.

Extreme Unction: the last sacrament of the Catholic Church, given to people when they are dying, as in Hopkins's poem, 'That Nature is a Heraclitean Fire and of the comfort of the Resurrection'.

Fall of Man: the Christian doctrine that Adam and Eve fell from grace and so were forced to leave the Garden of Eden.

Farce: a comedy in which situations and characters are taken to the point of absurdity, and which includes such devices as confusion of identity and of place. Oliver Goldsmith's *She Stoops to Conquer* is an example of this.

Feminist: a person (usually a woman) who holds beliefs that recognise and advocate the rights of women.

Fixed epithet: a traditional adjective or adjectival phrase used in epic poetry which conveys a standard or conventional aspect of a character or action, such as the word 'glittering' in Pope's *The Rape of the Lock*.

Generic: relating to genre.

Genre: specific type or style of literature or art.

Half-rhyme: in poetry, a rhyme in which the words contain similar sounds but do not rhyme completely. An example, from Wilfred Owen's poem 'Strange Meeting', is the rhyming of hall and hell.

Holy Ghost: in the Catholic Church, the third member of the Trinity of God, as in Hopkins' 'That Nature is a Heraclitean Fire ...'.

Immoral: having no sense of morality, like De Flores in *The Changeling*.

Inscape: the distinctive qualities of a person, place or object, as in Hopkins's poetry.

Instress: the force that holds 'inscape' together, q.v., and which comes directly from God, another of Hopkins's beliefs expressed in his poetry.

Interlaced: a medieval writing principle in which ideas are intricately woven together, as in the poetry of Chaucer.

Irony: an effect created when an action achieves the opposite effect from that intended. An example is the occasion in Oliver Goldsmith's *She Stoops to Conquer* when Marlow gives the jewellery to Mrs Hardcastle for safe keeping.

Legalism: a preference for a strict adherence to the law, rather than to the principles of the Bible and Christian virtue. The concept can be seen in Shakespeare's *Measure for Measure*.

Lyrical: having the quality of a short, song-like poem expressing the poet's thoughts and feelings.

Machiavelli: Niccolò Machiavelli (1469–1527) was an Italian writer and statesman who advocated the use of ruthless means to secure and retain power. The adjective Machiavellian is used to describe a person who practises duplicity and scheming in order to win political power.

Machinery: the trappings which form part of an epic poem and which are devices to help develop the meaning, such as Pope's sylphs in *The Rape of the Lock*.

Marxism: the social and political theories of the German philosopher Karl Marx (1818–1883). Marx believed that social change is driven by the conflict between the social classes, in essence between those who have money and power (who own the factories and businesses) and those who have no money or power (who have to work for others). He argued that this conflict was reflected in all aspects of society, even literature.

Medieval: relating to the Middle Ages.

Metaphysical: 1. literary term invented by the poet John Dryden (1631–1700) to describe a group of seventeenth-century poets, including George Herbert, who were characterised by the use of far-fetched imagery and witty conceits. See: **Conceit.**

Metaphysical: 2. in philosophy, relating to theories concerned with the fundamental concepts of thought, such as time, space, immortality, and the soul.

Milieu: the particular environment – social, academic, literary, etc. – in which a writer lives.

Mock-heroic: a poem which borrows conventions from epic poetry to create humorous effects, such as Pope's *The Rape of the Lock.*

Morality: an inner sense of what is right and wrong.

Morality Play: a form of medieval verse drama in which the characters are abstractions such as Vice, Faith, and so on; an example is the anonymous *Everyman*.

Motif: a recurring or important idea in a piece of literature, such as the role of women in society in Oliver Goldsmith's *She Stoops to Conquer.*

Mystery Play: medieval drama in verse in which biblical stories are retold.

Narrative poem: poem in which a story is told.

Negative capability: term used by the Romantic poet John Keats (1795–1821) to describe the ability to 'be in uncertainties, mysteries, doubts', in other words to think and experience without the need for proof or reason.

Opportunist: a person who takes advantage of situations and of people, such as De Flores in *The Changeling*.

Psychoanalytic: relating to the theories of the German psychologist Sigmund Freud (1856–1939). Freud believed that human behaviour is strongly influenced by forces so deeply hidden in the mind that we are not aware of them. These forces, he argued, evolve during an infant's early relationship with its parents.

Register: the words and expressions appropriate to specific circumstances, for example in writing about war; a religious register can be found in the poetry of Gerard Manley Hopkins.

Restoration Comedy: a form of comedy that developed in the period after the restoration of the monarchy in 1660. As a reaction against Puritan restraint, Restoration Comedy concerned itself with the witty, the frivolous, and the bawdy, the setting usually being that of fashionable society. The secular concerns of social satire now began to replace religious themes in drama. See: **Restoration Rake, Comedy of Manners**

Restoration Rake: an immoral but usually wealthy and fashionable man who is often a central character in Restoration Comedy. Often the Rake is reformed by a good woman, as is Marlow by Kate in Oliver Goldsmith's *She Stoops to Conquer.*

Resurrection: the Christian belief that Christ rose from the dead and ascended to His Father in Heaven, to redeem all mankind; as in Hopkins's poem, 'That Nature is a Heraclitean Fire …'.

Revenge Tragedy: a dramatic genre which developed in the Elizabethan and Jacobean periods; known also as 'the tragedy of blood', these plays, often bloody and violent, had plots based on the desire for revenge for a real or imagined wrong. Examples include Shakespeare's *Hamlet* and Middleton and Rowley's *The Changeling*.

Rhetoric: language designed to persuade or impress.

Sacramental: related to a religious ceremony, indicating inner grace or spirituality.

Satire: a literary work in which the aim is to amuse, criticise or correct by means of ridicule.

Scape: the surface qualities of a person, place or object, as in Hopkins's poem, 'That Nature is a Hericlitean Fire …'.

Sensual: related to the senses or sensations, usually with a sexual rather than spiritual or intellectual connotation.

Sensuous: appealing to the senses, but with no restriction to fleshly or sexual pleasure.

Shrieve (or shrive): to hear someone's confession.

Socialist: relating to the political and economic theory of socialism, which advocates state ownership and control of the means of producing wealth.

Specification: the syllabus for a subject issued by an examination board.

Sprung rhythm: a system of stresses in free verse which is meant to echo the sound of the speaking voice, as in some of Hopkins' poetry.

Stock: standard or typical (often used of a character in a play).

Structuralism: a literary theory that sees the meaning of a work as deriving from the subtle interrelationship of its parts, and not from its capacity to reflect 'real life'.

Sub-genre: a subdivision of a genre. An example is Oliver Goldsmith's *She Stoops to Conquer,* which as a **farce** is a type of comedy.

Sub-plot: a minor plot in a play which runs parallel to the main plot, such as the madhouse plot in *The Changeling.*

Suspend disbelief: to dispense with the need to look at a work of literature realistically; this way, as in the case of *Measure for Measure*, and *She Stoops to Conquer*, we can accept situations, characterised by events which are in themselves unbelievable, but which create the effects intended by the writer. See **Alienation**.

Underthought: Hopkins created this term to suggest the themes of his poetry.

Wandering Jew: a legendary figure who was condemned to wander the world without rest. He gradually acquired great wisdom and encouraged others to avoid sin and turn to God. The story influenced Coleridge's *The Rime of the Ancient Mariner.*

Wit: intelligence, understanding and ingenuity in dealing with a situation; a feature characteristic of Restoration Comedy.

Zeugma: a yoking together of ideas which at first sight seem incongruous or ill-matched, as in Pope's *The Rape of the Lock.*